The Alex P. Keats
Trilogy
On Wisdom, Love & Happiness

Born To Be Happy
How to Uncover Your Natural State of Happiness

When Wisdom Blooms
Awaken The Sage Within

The Dance Of Imperfection
Living In Perfect Harmony With Life

Alex P. Keats

Right Now
Publishing

Right Now Publishing

ISBN-13: 978-0615960104
ISBN-10: 0615960103

Copyright © 2014 Alex P. Keats

All Rights Reserved. No part of this publication may be reproduced in any form or by any means, including scanning, photocopying, or otherwise without prior written permission of the copyright holder.

First Printing, 2014

Printed in the United States of America

For Jamie

Introduction

The Alex Keats Trilogy On Wisdom, Love and Happiness is an invitation to step into the fire of the unknown with openness and curiosity, and to question everything you presently think is true. Make no mistake about it, true liberation is found in the midst of the fire, not in the absence of the fire. Right now, as you are, you have absolutely everything within you to live a life full of peace and joy. You need not learn a thing; you simply need to remember what you've forgotten. Learning implies you don't already know – and I tell you, you *do* know.

Authentic happiness arises naturally, wisdom blooms effortlessly, and self-love spontaneously stabilizes (seemingly out of nowhere) only when we're willing to let go of absolutely everything. Only then can we be free. *The Alex Keats Trilogy* consists of three separate books that can be read in succession and digested as one, or if you desire, you can skip around and read in no particular order. In the end, if you have the willingness to slow down and digest what you read, you may awaken to a view of life that's more whole and unified.

~ Alex P. Keats, February 2014

born to be happy

How to Uncover Your Natural State of Happiness

Alex P. Keats

Born To Be Happy

How to Uncover Your Natural State of Happiness

Alex P. Keats

Right Now
Publishing

Right Now Publishing

ISBN-13:978-0615929132
ISBN-10:0615929133

Copyright © 2012 Alex P. Keats

All Rights Reserved. No part of this publication may be reproduced in any form or by any means, including scanning, photocopying, or otherwise without prior written permission of the copyright holder.

First Printing, 2012

Printed in the United States of America

Dedication

This book is dedicated to my wonderful and loving parents, Joe and Kay, who possessed an extraordinary amount of patience and compassion when it came to dealing with all the years of unhappiness I couldn't help but spread around.

Happiness arises spontaneously for the one who sees how experience unfolds.

Contents

Introduction	i
Note To The Reader	xvi
1 - You've Been Conditioned To Be Unhappy	1
2 - The Hole That Can Never Be Filled	11
3 - Investigate What You Hold As True	21
4 - Argue With Reality And Suffer	35
5 - What You Run From Can Only Chase You	46
6 - What You Do To Others You Do To Yourself	57
7 - You're Most Present When You're Most Absent	65
8 - What You Pay Attention To	72
9 - Wanting What You Have	80
10 - For The Highest Good Of All	88
11 - Be Responsible For Your Entire Experience	95
12 - Gratitude Is Your Doorway To Happiness	106
One Final Note	119

Introduction

Sadly, most people live their lives – all the way to the grave – not being truly happy. What's even more unfortunate is that it doesn't have to be this way.

What's unfortunate is that we don't have to go through our lives experiencing so little joy, while clinging to the fleeting moments of feeling happy.

It's a natural human impulse to want to experience true and lasting happiness. It's only natural to want to experience as much happiness as we can, isn't it?

Don't you sense that?

When you're happy, don't you have a tendency to want to share it with others? Of course you do. Happiness is a vibration – like everything else – and it's contagious!

You may have heard countless times that "happiness is a choice" and that you can choose it in any moment.

IF being happy is simply a matter of choice, then why would you ever choose to be unhappy?

Why would you ever choose unhappiness when you can choose happiness?

If happiness is indeed a choice, isn't it very strange then, that so many people wake up each day choosing to be unhappy? It doesn't make a whole lot of sense, does it?

While there is some bit of truth in the statement that happiness is a choice, there's so much more to the formula of being happy.

Most books on happiness claim that in order to be happy, you must engage in certain types of behaviors and refrain from others. In other words, "choose" the behaviors that bring happiness and refrain from those that don't.

While there is also some bit of truth in this, there's so much more to the formula of being happy.

Have you noticed that your actual and direct experience of this popular approach is usually very short-lived, having a beginning, middle and an end ... like all experience?

In other words, the happiness you feel (as a result of this approach) is a fleeting experience and not something that is organically present most of the time.

It's a manufactured happiness that comes and goes – and not the happiness that sticks around for the long haul. Techniques and methods for happiness by nature can't last.

That said, I don't mean to imply that it's a useless approach, nor am I criticizing all those well-intended authors. After all, there IS a direct relationship between happiness and how we behave, right?

What I am saying is that there's a fundamental flaw in this type of approach. Since most of it isn't based in timeless truths, it must fail to deliver the lasting happiness we desire.

So here's the invitation: Instead of using an "either or" approach to happiness, let's use a "both and" orientation and notice the difference in our long-term experience.

If being happy was a game, like any other game, there must be rules. Without rules, the game wouldn't make much sense. And like any game, who plays to lose?

This book is about discovering what those rules ARE and then abiding by those rules.

This book is about working with – and not against those rules – in order to win the game.

Can I assume you want to win? I mean, really win?

There are no "secrets" to happiness and there never was. All those authors out there telling you that there are "hidden secrets" to anything (including happiness) are flat out lying to you.

In fact, they are manipulating you, manipulating your desires and emotions in order to fatten their wallets because they are acutely aware that one of the greatest human motivators is the fear of loss.

They know that if they can convince you that there are secrets that you don't presently know about, secrets that would give you what you desperately want, that you'll purchase what they are selling – or you'll lose out!

If you do a search on how many self-help books (or DVDs or other materials) have the word "secrets" in their titles, you'll see what I mean.

It's natural to be drawn to these sorts of titles because they seem to imply there's something you don't know, something that's been withheld from you.

It's a common marketing trick, to be honest, and it irks me to no end.

Think about the last time you bought a product of some sort that promised a transformation of sorts based on some type of "secret."

Didn't you feel an energetic longing and a natural curiosity that led you to pull out your credit card, sometimes so fast that you hadn't even finished reading the product description?

I fell for this so many times and was always disappointed when the so-called "secrets" didn't work ... or at the very least, were not the magical solution they were presented to be.

Do that enough times, as I did, and it can really take the wind out of your sails.

Here's what I know: Your own inner wisdom doesn't need manipulation. There is no magic. There are no secrets.

But (and this is hugely critical) if you don't know how to uncover the "happiness wisdom" that already resides within you, then they might as well be secrets because the truth is, the wisdom lies untapped within you, like a forgotten treasure buried underneath the very foundation of your house.

As you read this book, you'll discover how to find that treasure already within you. More importantly, you'll discover how to open that treasure. You'll see that it's been sitting there all along and you'll jump for joy when you uncover it.

It's actually simple – and since our minds love to complicate things – we sometimes make it harder on ourselves than we really have to.

Wouldn't you agree that the most profound truths in life are often the simplest ones?

Don't fall into the trap of thinking you need to undertake a complicated journey to "seek" happiness.

In fact, because we are essentially no different, I am convinced that this book is all you'll need to uncover the happiness that is your natural state.

No, I'm not exaggerating.

In chapter 3, you'll discover the one thing that you absolutely must do in order to be genuinely happy almost all the time. I say "almost all the time" because in life, pain is inevitable.

It's what we do with the pain that makes all the difference.

It's my sincerest hope that you'll experience many "A-HA!" moments while reading these pages, moments that can ultimately deliver the real happiness you seek – IF you play by the rules.

It's time to tell you one very crucial thing: Throughout the course of this book you'll come across the phrase, "don't believe me, find out for yourself."

The reason I repeat this so often is because I am acutely aware that it is human nature to rely on belief instead of checking in with our own direct experience and see what our bodies are telling us.

There IS a way to find out what's true and what isn't. Sometimes we don't know, can't know – but the key is NOT to draw a conclusion that creates a belief.

Be willing to not know; it's another rule in this game of happiness.

This "don't believe me, find out for yourself" phrase isn't meant to annoy you or insult your intelligence.

It's simply a friendly reminder to point you back to your own experience – without relying on belief, without creating belief.

We often ignore what are bodies are telling us. There's so much wisdom in the body and it speaks to us moment to moment.

The question is, do we listen? Do we listen when our bodies are contracting and not at ease – and see why? Do we listen when our bodies are relaxed and at peace – and trace it back and see why?

You may wonder why I am qualified to even write a book on the subject – or even if I am. I don't blame you one bit. I'd wonder the same thing.

Who wants to read a book by an author who doesn't walk their talk? I sure wouldn't want to.

Happiness was something that escaped me for a good chunk of my adult life.

Granted, I was pretty happy as a kid and my parents truly loved me, but at the age of about sixteen or seventeen, things started to really change.

Without going into my full story here (you'll read more of it in chapters 10 through 12), I was the type of person who would openly share with you just how unhappy I was.

It was as if I was walking around and pointing to my open wounds and saying, "See, look here, it really hurts."

I can only imagine what a joy I was to be around and I wonder how many people would duck around the corner when they saw me coming.

I can honestly tell you that these days, I travel light. It is my sincere intention to show YOU how to do the same, that is, if you want it enough.

And since it's contagious, naturally I want to share it with you.

But enough of my story, this is about YOU.

I don't like to throw guarantees around, mostly because they're basically for the mind that needs to know in order to feel safe and secure in this world.

Besides, the truth is, tomorrow isn't guaranteed. The truth is, your next breath isn't even guaranteed, either.

Since it's very likely you will be gifted with a next breath and you will be gifted with another tomorrow, I will give you a very solid and absolute guarantee:

Uncovering your natural state of happiness won't happen a moment sooner than it's meant to happen.

Knowing this truth, you can relax.

Truth and relaxation go hand in hand.

When we see and realize what's true, something lets go.

What's MOST important is that you are earnest and rigorously honest with yourself – and willing to see for yourself what's true and what isn't true in your actual experience.

The above statement is so critically significant that I really must ask you to read it one more time. Will you? Good.

This "game of happiness" really isn't that difficult a game to play IF you're willing to really LOOK and SEE what its rules are and how it's played in order to win.

I can tell you that unconsciously relying on belief and assumptions isn't one of the rules!

Here's another rule: Always be mindful that the word is never the thing. The concept is never the actual.

Can you drink the word "water?"

Can you be burned by the word "fire?"

No, of course you can't.

Any word (concept) or group of words you ever read anywhere is never the thing. It's never the actual. They are "pointers" to the actual, not the actual itself.

Consequently, we see that language and descriptions aren't the reality, either ... and can only point to the actual.

This book is no different. However, this book is full of pointers to the real – pointers that (IF investigated and tested out in your own experience) can uncover what you already know to be true.

If you're presently aware of a belief that tells you that you don't deserve to be happy – or that it's only reserved for others, bring that along with you.

All is welcome here.

In fact, absolutely nothing will be left out and you'll soon see that you are all of it and that there is no escape from anything you feel or perceive.

See the truth in the wisdom of no escape.

To resist any part of it is to bring more of what you don't want. Once you really SEE this, you're playing in a whole different ballpark.

In Chapter 5, you'll recognize (and remember) something that is absolutely critical as you look to uncover your natural state of happiness.

Once you see this and prove it true for yourself, not only are you playing in a different ballpark, now you're playing in a ballpark with the clearest and brightest, illuminating lights.

Once you discover how it all works and consciously live in alignment with your natural state of happiness, it begins to take on a life of its own.

You'll find, much to your delight, that living in harmony with your natural state of happiness unfolds automatically and spontaneously by itself – but ONLY AFTER you see what's really true.

I can't tell you how cool this is.

I can tell you this without a shred of doubt: you already possess the blueprint within you right now – and that you need nothing other than a sincere and nonjudgmental willingness to look and see for yourself.

This book is the blueprint that will show you where to look so that you can confirm it experientially for yourself and validate what you already know.

Don't ever believe a word you read here and don't believe what others say.

That's a rule.

Find out for yourself.

This book will show you how to read (and apply) that blueprint in your own life so that you can uncover and uncover your natural state of happiness.

Here's a disclaimer: You won't "learn" a thing here because that implies you don't already know.

You will, however, recognize and uncover what you've always known but have simply forgotten.

And then you'll pass it on (because that's what we do) and your presence will bring comfort and ease to those around you. In fact, you may even be a joy to those around you.

Please know that I'm NOT assuming that you're presently miserable and unhappy. How can I know this?

I'd be pretty foolish to believe just because you're reading this that you're absolutely miserable and unhappy, wouldn't I?

Perhaps you want more happiness or maybe you want to find out why you aren't as happy as you'd like to be?

You may be curious to see if this book might tell you anything different than others you've read before on the subject.

You may even be curious to see if there might be one golden nugget here that opens you up in a way that you've never experienced before.

You may even be as happy as you want to be and just want to read how this author points to the happiness that already is your natural state.

Either way, it doesn't matter. There are no coincidences and besides, your reasons aren't critical.

IF you actually experiment and really see for yourself and IF you approach the words you are about to read as if it's the first time you've ever read a book on happiness, then something very beautiful can happen for you – yes, you.

IF you literally drop all your concepts, beliefs and conclusions about what you think it takes to be truly happy – and commit to not believing a word you read here – you're playing by the rules.

IF you follow along and experiment with these simple yet powerful pointers, your natural state of happiness will reveal itself in ways you never imagined – and in circumstances and situations you never imagined.

Once you discover how you've been blocking it, happiness will naturally arise in situations that will surprise and delight you.

So, for the time and energy you invest in reading this book, I humbly ask two things of you. First, consider the possibility that I really am pointing you in the right direction, okay?

Secondly, I ask that you absorb this book slowly and find out for yourself what's really true in your experience without relying on belief, okay?

Can you do this? Can you come from this place? If you can, you're much more likely to uncover your natural state of happiness.

Obviously, you're free to read this book in any way you like, but if you want the most benefit, I do highly recommend this way.

So discard anything that you think you know to be true about happiness, no matter what. Leave all that stuff at the door because it won't be needed here.

Because you ARE worth it, you may even want to take your shoes off before you enter – and bring a spirit of reverence and innocence to this undertaking.

All that's needed here is your willingness to follow through and go beyond conceptual belief and see if the following statement is ultimately true in your experience:

You need nothing to be happy; you need something to be sad.

Together, let us prove this by exploring experientially and not conceptually for it is only when we experience a thing in our being that true knowing occurs.

In the beginning of the sixteenth century, Michelangelo was asked how he was able to create the masterpiece Statue of David in such remarkably, fine detail. He said this:

"In every block of marble I see a statue as plain as though it stood before me, shaped and perfect in attitude and action. I have only to hew away the rough walls that imprison the lovely apparition to reveal it to the other eyes as mine see it."

Uncovering your natural state of happiness requires a very similar vision and attitude as the one Michelangelo possessed.

So get out your tools of focus, attention and awareness. Don't forget to bring willingness, wonder, great curiosity and courage, too.

Like Michelangelo, prepare yourself to chip away all that covers up your natural state of happiness – and watch what eventually must reveal itself.

Don't be surprised when you see that (all along) it was all so very simple – and that it was your mind that insisted it was complex.

Don't be surprised when you see that there never was such a thing as a true belief.

And you believed it.

It gives me great joy to share this direct "no secrets, nothing held back" book with you.

I'd be honored if you decide to investigate this seemingly elusive thing called happiness with me.

It may very well end up being the most fulfilling and rewarding thing you've ever done.

A Note To The Reader

I welcome you to these pages you're about to read – or perhaps I should I say, that you're about to immerse yourself in.

Have you ever read a book in which you felt it was just you and the author, perhaps alone in a room, intimately engaged in a timely conversation about the things most significant to you, things that normally wouldn't come up in your everyday life with those you associate with?

It is my wish for *that* sense to arise within you – where it's just you and me, alone together in a completely safe environment, intent on looking at what may prevent happiness from spontaneously arising in your experience – and just as important, to rediscover the various ways in which true happiness *does* arise.

Haven't you always suspected that real and lasting happiness is for you, too … and not just reserved for the lucky or the fortunate?

And haven't you also suspected the distinct possibility that there might be *something* in your consciousness that's keeping you from enjoying life to the fullest?

Either way, I have complete and absolute trust that your inner wisdom (that we all possess) knows what's real and true, despite what your mind thinks. By looking and identifying what your mind *believes* to be true and real, you take the first crucial step in uncovering your natural state of happiness.

Please be advised that you'll get so much more out of this book if you read it from below the neck – where your heart wisdom resides – and not with an analytical, comparative mind that likes to evaluate and judge what it reads with what it *thinks or believes it knows* from past experience.

Read this book and drink deeply from the experience that exists BEHIND and BEYOND the mere words. And find that experience within yourself as you go about your day after you put this book down.

This is something to be lived from your innermost self rather than from an act of simple reading comprehension – or as an act of just reading "about" concepts.

I hope that makes sense because it's so vitally important. There will be times throughout this book where you'll read a sentence and want to put the book down because it struck such a personal and profound chord within you.

I encourage you to listen to that pause and to live within that pause ... and to keep looking in the direction where you're being pointed ... because the word or concept is never the actual.

It's just not possible to stress how important this is. If you truly DO desire lasting happiness (that *isn't* dependent on circumstance or condition) it takes a sincere willingness to explore and test these concepts.

By "explore" I mean *experientially* and not just *thinking* about them.

If indeed it is our perspective that really does determine our experience, it stands to reason that *this* kind of orientation can only greatly increase the possibility where stable, permanent and transformational shifts happen – shifts that bring about what you've sensed and desired all along.

There's one last very significant thing worth mentioning. You'll come across the word "see" many times throughout this book. The way it's intended is not to "see" with your physical eyes, but rather, with your nonphysical, conscious awareness.

For example: *See* what's true. When we *see* what's true, we *realize* what's true – not in our heads but in our hearts, in our gut.

So go right ahead, my friend, dive in. I eagerly await your full and present participation in our uncommon dialogue.

If after reading this book you want to explore further, upcoming books called *When Wisdom Blooms: Awaken the Sage Within* and *The Dance of Imperfection: Living in Perfect Harmony with Life* will be coming out in the middle of August 2012. Until then, enjoy yourself and keep it real.

~ Alex P. Keats, March 2012

Chapter 1
You've Been Conditioned To Be Unhappy

People have been unhappy since time began, losing their jobs, their homes, their spouse, their children and even their lives but that's life, is it not?

We do our best to deal with it, don't we? Much of this capacity to cope is predicated on what we're presently aware of in that moment in time, based on our perspective and our past experiences.

Born To Be Happy

We possess remarkable instincts and unmatched intellectual capacity – and the ingenuity to transform innovative ideas into reality.

When it comes to negotiating our emotional lives, however, we have a tendency to contract and go into an unconscious, trance-like state – a state that typically ends up not being real effective, at least not towards experiencing what we truly want.

We have a tendency to want to crawl in bed, pull up the covers and disappear, until it dawns on us that life must go on.

Instead of asking why these things happen or wondering what kind of God would allow these things to happen, we rarely see that there must be something we have to discover here – that there must be something to see here.

Instead of offering ourselves to the glory and beauty that is life, we lose ourselves in thinking. We lose ourselves in thinking about what should or could be happening instead of dealing with reality – or what is actually happening.

And since we also have a tendency to believe what our minds are telling us, we suffer.

We engage in the fantasy of the past and the fantasy of the future, while neither have any reality. We keep the past alive with memory and anticipate the future with our imagination.

But then a very interesting thing happens. When we're threatened with our very existence, when we're told that we only have two or three weeks to live, suddenly we realize that life is so precious.

All of a sudden, we become aware of our next breath, the sound of the wind blowing in the trees, the birds singing and all the wondrous diversity on display all around us.

Deep gratitude, a sense of wonder and awe – and a burning desire to live become our experience and we take nothing for granted anymore. Oh, how much we want to live!

Very few of us speak of now or attend to now – yet everyone craves to be now – whether we are conscious of this or not.

This is what we're all endeavoring to do, to bring our minds to rest by consciously living in this present moment only, where problems don't exist, where happiness does exist, whether we know it or not.

To live in the reality where there's no past or future is to live in the kingdom of heaven. When we realize that the kingdom of heaven is within us, then it must happen outside of us.

This is a law of life.

When we experientially realize that the kingdom of heaven is within us – when we see that the present moment is THE reality – then our natural state of happiness shines through, radiating in all directions.

When we don't, we identify with the thinking mind. We believe what our minds tell us. In fact, we believe most of what our minds tell us – even if it makes us miserable.

We seldom ever look at the cause of all of our stress and strain – and we cling to our beliefs, opinions and preferences (like sticky Velcro) as if our lives depended on them – as well as our religions, dogmas and theories.

We don't always see that all of this causes inner division that not only must be felt and experienced by us, but by those around us, too.

And ironically, none of what we cling to brings us what we want, yet we continue on, usually in the same fashion, not realizing that the happiness we seek is right here and right now … waiting patiently for us to see it needs nothing to shine.

In fact, it's already shining, like the sun above the nastiest stormy weather you could imagine. Your natural state of happiness is like the sun, self-shining in all directions, untouched and unharmed.

So why is this all so difficult and foreign to most of us? Why isn't happiness our actual experience most of the time, especially since mankind is so much more advanced now?

For starters, we were rarely ever shown this – and we rarely ever witnessed this "happiness for no special reason" in those around us.

Uncover Your Natural State Of Happiness

Like a pot of clay molded by a potter at his wheel, we've been conditioned to be happy (only when specific circumstances and conditions are met) and we've been conditioned to believe happiness is a result of when "good things" happen to us.

On the face of things, I agree that this seems ludicrous, but sadly it is true. Let's explore this notion that we've been condition-ed to be unhappy further, shall we?

Granted, in the first 6-12 months, babies are happy just as long as their basic needs are met, but then something else starts to happen.

They gradually learn to be unhappy because they're taught to be unhappy.

And it's unintentional. I mean, who decides to have a baby with the intent of raising an unhappy child?

Weren't you rewarded early on for the behaviors your parents (or guardian) approved of and punished for the behaviors they disapproved of?

How many times did you hear the words, "bad boy" or "bad girl" when you behaved in ways they didn't like?

Consequently, you (unconsciously) linked up your behaviors with your self worth and this in turn affected your degree of happiness ... because it had to.

You were a small child, how could you know any better?

Born To Be Happy

How many of us were actually taught that we weren't our behaviors? How many of us were taught that our inherent self worth is untouched and unharmed by our actions and behaviors – that is has absolutely nothing to do with our actions and behaviors?

I'd say less than one percent of us.

Every time you were scolded and heard "no, don't do that!" another layer was added onto your natural state of happiness.

You've most likely been taught (since you were a toddler) that happiness is reserved for those who do what's expected of them.

You were taught (more often with subtle messages) that those who attained the things in life that others deemed most worthwhile were the happiest – and those who earned the respect and admiration of others were the happiest.

Even if you didn't receive a lot of this conditioning at home, wouldn't it be accurate to say that most of us were raised in a culture where we learned that in order to be truly happy, we must have the right education and a good paying job?

How about a nice car and wardrobe ... a nice home and plenty of money in the bank, too?

Today it's much more overt. Just turn on the television, open the newspaper, check your smart phone and read the magazines. It's certainly all over the Internet, isn't it?

Uncover Your Natural State Of Happiness

Today's generation is constantly bombarded with this message.

Since profit is such a driving force in this world, much of it is marketing and the attempt to get you to purchase something, but haven't we come to believe that what they're pitching equals happiness? Isn't that what the sly marketers want?

Hasn't this message actually become a living, organic thing within us? Hasn't it become so ingrained in our collective consciousness – or should I say collective unconsciousness – that we believe it and act on it?

No wonder that real and lasting happiness is the exception and not the rule for so many of us! None of this was or is true, but we believed it … and so our lives went, so our life goes.

While it can seem to make a whole lot of sense to go to battle with our conditioning, pointing the finger and playing the blame game only makes it worse and locks it into our experience.

For many years, I beat myself up over so many things. No wonder I was depressed and living a life of quiet desperation. Nonetheless, I always knew there was a way out.

Beating yourself up can only give your conditioning more power over you. More important, beating yourself up is a result of ignorance – and happens when we think we are to "blame" for our unhappiness. This attitude, this perspective, allows your conditioning to remain in the driver's seat, with its hands gripped firmly on the steering wheel, taking YOU for a ride.

While we aren't to blame for our unhappiness, we are responsible for our happiness.

Again, nobody (including ourselves) intentionally wanted us to be unhappy, at least not those who truly loved and cared for us.

You've forgotten that happiness is your natural state because everyone else around you – including your parents, siblings, friends and teachers has forgotten it. Even your mentors and therapists have forgotten it. They too, must live out what they believe.

It's been forgotten (or buried over if you prefer) due to a lifetime of countless untruths piled on top of each other, one belief, one assumption and one opinion at a time.

This is neither wrong or right, it just is. Generations of this conditioning occurred – and will continue to occur, until it doesn't anymore, until our consciousness is raised.

Consciousness is a funny thing. It's easily influenced and it easily succumbs to hypnotic, trance-like states, states where we walk around numb wondering why the heck we aren't that happy.

Unless you make happiness a top priority in your life – and act in accord with this priority – and unless you really look at what's suppressing your natural state of happiness, not much will change.

As the saying goes, if nothing changes, nothing changes.

Take five minutes right now and write down some examples that you recall from your own childhood. What sorts of things were you told that might have taught you that your worth was based on how you behaved or what you achieved?

How did that shape the person you are today? What would it feel like to not have anything to "live up to"?

Will you break the chain? Will you stand up and say enough is enough?

Will you commit to discovering why it is that happiness is such an elusive thing for so many, perhaps even for you?

I sincerely hope so because if you do, you can be a shining example for so many – and you can have such an impact on this world that needs you.

Happiness is truly a contagion that this world needs to catch!

This world is suffering from a severe lack of happiness and it all starts with you uncovering this "open secret" to being happy.

The fact that you are here reading these words is a very good sign, don't you agree?

The best way not to experience happiness is to go searching for it.

How's that for a paradox?

Instead, seek not happiness ... instead seek (look at) what suppresses happiness and watch happiness reveal itself.

Like Michelangelo, chip away all that is untrue and watch happiness reveal itself in ways you never could imagine.

Chapter 2
The Hole That Can Never Be Filled

Unless you decide to go live in a cave in the Himalayas, a Zen monastery or a shack in the woods with no television or Internet, it's unlikely you'll escape this constant message that in order to be truly happy, certain conditions must be met.

If one believes that something more is needed for happiness – and that something better or different is needed for happiness – more money, more sex, more power or more recognition, then that individual will inevitably experience lack and limitation.

So what to do? Is there an escape or way out here? How do we fill the hole inside, that hole that tells us that we are incomplete unless we achieve that certain thing, be in a certain type of relationship or gain the respect and admiration of those we deem important?

Can there ever be a point where we've accumulated enough stuff to make us happy?

Have you concluded that real happiness is for others and not you?

Or might it be possible that we're asking the wrong questions? Is it possible that we're looking in the wrong direction when it comes to our own happiness?

If we want to enjoy a spectacular sunset, will we have that ability if we're facing east? No, of course not.

We must turn completely around (180 degrees) and face the right direction if we want to experience that sunset.

Have you ever considered that maybe the better questions are, "In what ways am I suppressing my natural state of happiness?

Another great question we might ask is, "Is the conditioning I received even true – and based in reality?"

Uncover Your Natural State Of Happiness

Do you see how these kinds of questions determine your orientation and therefore, your experience?

Do you have a belief that you really need the approval of others to be happy and content?

If so, what tells you so?

How might your experience be different if you knew without any doubt at all – because you are totally secure with yourself – that what others think of you is none of your business?

Probably very liberating, wouldn't you say?

Is it really about achieving the goals we set for ourselves that is the key to this thing called happiness? Is it really about satisfying every desire we have that brings lasting happiness?

Face the proper direction and contemplate the truth (whether you realize it or not right now) that you literally don't need anything to be happy!

How do we rid ourselves of this void inside that never seems to go away? Is this void even real, despite it feeling real?

For starters, stop believing the voice that says "you need so and so" in order to be happy.

Just because these thoughts arise in your mind, does it mean they're true?

Does it?

Ask yourself, "How do I know this is really true?" Ask yourself, "How can I know this is true?"

Please don't skip over these questions because the answers you arrive at just may radically change your life.

Would you agree that you don't know what you don't know?

That you're unaware of what you aren't aware of? I just sensed that you just nodded your head yes ... so let's continue with this theme.

Admittedly, this seems very obvious but don't we generally stop at this powerful realization without exploring what it is that we don't know ... that insight or realization that just may hold the key to whatever it is we're struggling with?

If this is so, can we see that since we're generally unconscious of this powerful realization (that we don't know what we don't know) that reminding ourselves of this critical insight may prove difficult unless we devise a plan to remember it?

Well, one way to remind ourselves is to use any undesired situation we find ourselves in as a trigger to remind us that there must be something we aren't presently seeing, that if we did see it, it would make all the difference.

Isn't logic and reason a beautiful thing?

Furthermore, how can we consciously live out the rest of our lives in such a way so that we no longer work against ourselves and against the laws of life that govern every single one of us?

Uncover Your Natural State Of Happiness

Isn't that what we all want? Don't we all want the least amount of inner division and discord? Don't we want to enjoy this life and enjoy the company of those we care for most?

Of course we do. We are wired to want to be happy.

Are you ready and willing to inquire into every belief you have and every assumption you have in order to uncover your natural state of happiness?

What would that be worth to you?

Is there anything you aren't willing to look at that may be covering over what's naturally, already shining?

To be truly happy you must become more conscious than you are right now. Try as you may, there is no way around this.

Of course you have every right to achieve all your goals and dreams and find out if it brings you the happiness you desire. No one is saying don't go for what you want in life.

By all means, go for what you truly desire in this life! I'm certainly not suggesting that accumulating all that you desire is a bad thing.

There's nothing inherently wrong with accumulating material possessions. It's when we believe that that particular object will make us happy.

If you set it up this way (if this is your view) then prepare for the emotional rollercoaster ride that is your life.

There can be no real and lasting happiness in that which is impermanent. It's literally not possible.

I don't care how much money you have in the bank or how many possessions you surround yourself with or how luxurious you live – you're kidding yourself if you don't think it could all be washed away like a sand castle at high tide.

History shows this again and again. And while it makes for "difficult" times, it's actually good news for your happiness because you can choose to consciously SEE this illusion for what it is – and free yourself from the agony of chasing a thing that must inevitably die out.

Seeing that everything is impermanent, we see that we set ourselves up for failure when we seek permanent and lasting happi-ness when we acquire things and experiences that are impermanent.

It is totally appropriate to enjoy things and experiences – just be aware that it will have a certain life span and can't ever give you lasting happiness independent of circumstance and condition.

You can choose to consciously see this NOW and free yourself from the agony of chasing this illusion once and for all.

But first, you must want to see it in order to be free of it.

Henry David Thoreau was an American author, poet and philosopher. He hit the nail on the head when he said:

Uncover Your Natural State Of Happiness

"Happiness is like a butterfly: the more you chase it, the more it will elude you, but if you turn your attention to other things, it will come and sit softly on your shoulder."

Once the novelty of that new and shiny thing wears out (and it will because it must) what will you do then? Typically, you set your sights on another new and shiny thing, right?

It's a never-ending cycle. Do you really want to live your life this way, like a dog chasing its tail?

Is it just materials things we seek to fill the void inside? Don't we also seek to fill the void inside with other things like sex, drugs, alcohol, food, sleep, television, video games, going to the movies and even cigarettes?

How about seeking approval from others? Can you ever be truly happy seeking approval from others?

Heck, we could come up with a much bigger list, but you get the point.

There's nothing inherently wrong with any of those activities. Aside from cigarettes, alcohol and drugs, I enjoy every one of them.

It's when we use those activities as a means to temporarily escape the unhappiness we feel inside that it becomes problematic.

We seek to forget ourselves and to take the focus off of ourselves, don't we? Don't we want to forget about our struggles, even for a short while?

Getting a reprieve from our life is our goal. Sometimes, we even become addicted to these activities, only making matters worse and strengthening its hold on us.

This book wouldn't be complete if I didn't mention this:

If you're presently using drugs and/or alcohol and you KNOW that it impacts your well being, just be aware that you're literally trading these temporary behaviors that must lead to unhappiness ... for the chance of real and permanent happiness.

This trade off seems so obvious yet it took me years to see this very simple truth!

Additionally, if you use stimulants of any kind to excess, like caffeine or whatever, consider that your body must be at rest before the mind can be at rest – for they are one and the same.

It's also worth mentioning that absolutely NONE of this is cause for beating yourself up, especially if you want to uncover your natural state of happiness.

If you beat yourself up over what you're actually doing (reality) you will keep in place the VERY behaviors you want to remove.

Instead, just notice it without resistance or judgment and intend for something else, something more desirable. This is SO essential.

Okay, let's move on from drugs, alcohol and any other stimulants that must lead to unhappiness.

Uncover Your Natural State Of Happiness

Since you can only understand what you are first aware of, you see that there must be something you aren't noticing that's causing any pain or dis-ease you may be experiencing.

Drawing conclusions (when you don't know what's true) limits and confines you because the truth often is something other than what you think it is.

Actually, since the truth is prior to thoughts or words – and what is being pointed to, it can never be what you think it is.

Become aware that your mind will attempt to tell you that there must be some thing (or group of things) that you can possess or activities you engage in that can make you happy for the rest of your life. If you only had that thing, you'd be happy. If you only could engage in those activities, you'd be happy.

You may even conclude that most wealthy people seem to be happy so money and a more comfortable lifestyle must be what you need to be happy.

Despite how strongly you may believe this, it just isn't true. There are many unhappy, wealthy people in this world – they just have bigger holes to fill because they, too, spend their attention and energy towards trying to fill the hole that can never be filled.

Now they may have the ability to put bigger and more expensive things in the hole they feel inside

– and engage in any and all the activities money can buy, but the same law applies to them.

Their hole cannot be filled, either. It too, is a bottomless pit, just like my brother-in-law, Chuck's stomach!

When you set it up in your experience that lasting happiness is found in loving things and using people, you're looking in the wrong direction. You'll never experience the happiness you seek. Never.

Happiness doesn't need any "thing" to be happy.

Again, it's when we think that a particular object will make us happy is where we go wrong, where we delude ourselves.

Happiness just is, right here and right now, patiently waiting for you to realize it literally needs nothing.

Happiness stands alone, all by itself, naked and free.

You certainly have every right to be rich and happy – and enjoy any experience you want on this beautiful planet, but in order to be happy you don't need to be rich.

Since everything changes (including your experiences) see the insanity of trying to permanently fill the apparent hole felt with things and experiences that must change.

Until then, happiness must elude you.

Chapter 3
Investigate What You Hold As True

Investing the time and energy to look at what you hold true is one of the single most powerful and transformative things you can ever do.

In fact, there aren't many things that can have a greater impact on your life and the lives of those around you than consistently doing this one thing.

This isn't always a quick and easy thing and can take a good bit of attention and persistent looking, but the rewards are well worth the time and energy invested.

Like many things in life, it's a process, a journey, but one well worth it.

It's rather simple actually, but not necessarily easy. If it was that easy, we'd be living in a much happier and kinder world, don't you agree?

You must be willing to look in places you may not want to look, despite any fear or reluctance that may arise.

This is what stops most people from making the breakthroughs they desire. Fear. Most people erroneously conclude that since they feel a thing (like fear) that it must be real, otherwise it wouldn't be present in their experience.

They also conclude – without knowing whether it's true or not – that the fear will be too much for them to handle. Putting your feelings aside for the moment, is that really true?

Courage has been defined as "acting in spite of the fear you may feel," so if you feel you must summon courage, then by all means, summon courage.

One of my favorite lines in a movie happened to be in my favorite movie, "Brave Heart."

When young William Wallace's father lay dead after battle, William dreamed that his father opened his eyes saying to him, "Your heart is free, have the courage to follow it."

Uncover Your Natural State Of Happiness

It sent chills down my spine and touched me deeply because it resonated within that we're here on earth to follow the heart, no matter what our minds believe. We are here to express and enjoy ourselves and give ourselves to each other.

We are here to live out (and live from) what we have determined is our purpose in life.

Your mind thinks it knows the way when all along, your heart knows the way.

You can trust it, you really can.

Here's a useful suggestion: Since we make everything up anyway, consider setting it up within yourself that your desire to uncover your natural state of happiness is significantly more important than believing in the reality of the fear you may experience.

Secondly, don't assume that any fear that may arise is more than you can handle. It isn't if you (say and declare) that it isn't.

It's like when you have the perspective that the person you're arguing with is significantly more important than the topic you're arguing about.

With this perspective, what are the odds of the argument getting full blown and nasty? Not real high, right? Wouldn't it be more of a "spirited debate" than a testy argument?

Knowledge is found above the neck and wisdom resides below the neck.

If this is true (it most certainly is) then why do we keep looking for truth and happiness in our minds? It's not there, nor does happiness arise from there.

Happiness and wisdom both arise from below the neck, but don't take my word for it.

If wisdom resides below the neck in our hearts (being) then why do we keep looking to our minds for wisdom? Why do we constantly go to our minds to look for the answers when all along we know in our hearts what that "answer" is?

Almost all the time, FEAR can be an acronym for false evidence appearing real.

Just because you feel fear doesn't mean it's real, does it?

Since when have your feelings been a barometer for what's true and real? Isn't it almost always worse in our minds than the actual reality? It sure is.

Like everything else in this world, fear is just energy. Everything, including you, is just energy.

The earth is energy, the sun and the stars are just energy.

Thoughts, beliefs and feelings are energy. Your car and home is made of energy and the food you eat is energy.

If you are intrigued by this check out quantum physics. It will have you question everything you hold as true.

Uncover Your Natural State Of Happiness

Quantum physicists have proven that absolutely everything is energy, vibrating at different frequencies, blinking in and out of existence all the time.

Also, the very fact of our observation and how we observe a thing changes that thing and changes how it behaves.

Here's something you may not have considered before yet we touched on it in chapter one: Almost every belief and assumption you have was never created by you.

You have (unintentionally) assimilated all your beliefs and assumptions from your upbringing and society in general.

Can you imagine the implications of this one insight?

If you don't believe this (or are unaware of this) be willing to take a real hard look at the vast majority of beliefs, assumptions and opinions that are guiding your life right now and trace them back as far as you can go.

You'll discover one of two things: that you are not the author and you never were. You literally picked them up along the way, from someone or somewhere, like a cross-country truck driver that habitually picks up hitch- hikers.

And the other discovery – if you're totally honest with yourself – is you just don't know where they came from.

Once you've confirmed this in your own experience, you can drop the beliefs that don't serve you. Because you brought them out of the darkness and into the light of your conscious awareness, they will dissolve spontaneously – or at worst, gradually.

Now you're able to consciously choose the perspective that serves you and those you most love and care about. You DO NOT have to be at the mercy of your beliefs anymore.

Until then, I'm afraid the only option is to live out your life based upon the conditioning you've unconsciously taken on … and on what you believe to be true.

Consider the ramifications of discovering what you truly value and what your expectations of life and those around you are.

Do you actually expect to be happy and do you expect good things to come your way?

If you don't, how might your life be different if you woke up each day expecting to be happy and expecting to make valuable contributions to the lives of others?

Since we get what we expect in life, expect to be happy and expect others to enjoy your company.

Expect to be healthy, happy and successful and watch what unfolds in your experience.

Again, do you see that it's what you aren't aware of right now that must be the key to uncovering your natural state of happiness?

Uncover Your Natural State Of Happiness

If you find yourself desiring more happiness, then doesn't it make sense that you must be unaware of something very significant that isn't presently in your field of conscious awareness?

Becoming more conscious of your habit patterns and tendencies is the first step to understanding them. Until then, you are destined to live out your days much like Bill Murray in Groundhog Day.

If you haven't seen the movie, I highly recommend you do so. It's funny, insightful and very inspiring.

It's been said that you can find out what you actually value by noticing where you invest your time and energy –and not what you say you value.

Often, what we say and what we do are two very different things.

For example, if you say you really value doing volunteer work or being kind to others, do your values match what actually manifests in your life?

Do you do volunteer work and are you actually kind to others?

You can say you value a certain thing but if it's not a reality in your life, then you probably don't really value it.

Most likely, you value the idea of it and not the actual experience of it.

Most people would be very shocked at many of the beliefs they have that they don't even know they have – and just how these beliefs show up in their lives.

For instance, do you believe you're incomplete? Do you really need that some thing or some one to make you feel fulfilled and complete?

If so, what tells you this? Is it a belief that tells you this?

What would you say if I told you that you're already complete and that it's just a thought that tells you otherwise?

Stop believing the thoughts in your head because despite feeling true, they aren't true! They aren't even close to the truth and they aren't even yours to begin with.

Have you ever wondered what a belief is anyway? Can we further dissect this thing called belief?

In a nutshell, beliefs are mental constructs created in the mind as a substitute for when we don't know what's true.

The majority of beliefs are spontaneously created (by the mind) in order for the mind to feel safe and in control – and to help you navigate and negotiate in this world.

Have you noticed yet that most beliefs you hold weren't consciously chosen by you? This is very cathartic to see.

Can you remember the day you decided to create the beliefs that you presently operate from? Of

Uncover Your Natural State Of Happiness

course you don't remember because aside from a few here and there, you never did it.

Don't believe me when I tell you that it is in fact your beliefs, assumptions and opinions that suppress the happiness you desire.

Don't believe me when I tell you that what others think of you is none of your business. Rather, find out for yourself, in your own direct experience if this is true.

Allow me to remind you not to use (and approach) this book like all the others you've read in the past. The beauty is, is that this is a fresh, new moment to see if what you believe is actually true.

This is a fresh, new moment to notice how often your natural tendency is to create beliefs in your mind versus actually finding out what's true in your experience.

And if we don't know what's true, are we willing to admit that we just don't know? Can we admit that often times, we can't know?

It is in THIS space that pure potential and limitless possibility loves to play! It is in THIS place where our freedom lies.

Again, the truth is, beliefs, assumptions and opinions are substitutes for when you don't know what's true.

Your mind doesn't like the unknown. It likes what it thinks or believes it already knows and then compares, contrasts and evaluates everything in relation to that.

Beliefs lock us into a certain way of perceiving that filters reality... like a veil that conditions our actual experience of life.

Humans invest way too much stock in their beliefs and opinions, beliefs and opinions that typically lead to what we don't want.

Have you noticed that belief often likes company – even seeks out company? Don't we feel comfortable and safe when we're in the company of those who believe as we do?

Truth stands alone and needs no company. And unlike most belief, it doesn't need any defending.

There's an inner knowing – where absolutely no doubt is present, that allows truth to securely stand all by itself, that needs no confirmation or validation.

Find that place and the ballgame is over.

Don't we actually believe that our opinions and judgments have so much significance, especially to ourselves?

Isn't it my belief versus yours?

And naturally yours is right and mine isn't.

Don't we often want another to see that we're "right" and don't we often want another to "come to our side" and agree with our perspective, the "right" perspective?

Uncover Your Natural State Of Happiness

How many millions of people have been killed in the last 2000 years over differences in belief? How many wars have been fought, how much blood has been shed over my belief vs. your belief?

If one believes that this world is full of dishonest, selfish people, one will experience mistrust and have their guard up at almost every instance.

If one believes oneself to be on the receiving end of repeated mistreatment, then one will undoubtedly feel like a victim and expect to be mistreated at every turn.

Now I'm not saying that all beliefs are bad or wrong, nor am I implying that you should attempt to do away with them altogether, so please don't infer this.

Some beliefs are very useful and even serve as a way to protect you from harm. Some beliefs can act as a bridge, bringing you from where you are to where you really want to be.

For example, if you feel you're doomed to a life of unhappiness – even believe you won't ever be happy – you'd do well to turn that around and come to believe that you do deserve to be happy – and to believe that no human is more or less than you.

I don't know for sure (I can't know for sure unless I did it) if I were to drive a racecar around a track at 175mph whether I'd crash into the wall or not.

Since I don't have any experience (frame of reference) driving a fast racecar, I would lean on the side of caution and believe that I probably would lose control and crash.

Call me a wimp, but I'd probably pass on the opportunity.

If you really desire to improve your lifestyle and you want to become a self-employed entrepreneur instead of working for others – and you want to double or triple your income, believing that you can achieve this goal is very empowering.

In fact, you could say it's critical in order for you to put into action your plan of achieving that specific goal.

So let's not throw the baby out with the bathwater...

Not all beliefs are a disservice to you. Not all beliefs lead to undesired outcomes. The key is to be vigilant and aware of those that serve you and those that don't.

However, when it comes to being authentically happy, unexamined beliefs and assumptions rarely, if ever, serve you – especially if you aren't the happiest camper around to begin with.

If you want to experience the happiness you deserve, then strap on that spotlight of conscious awareness around your head (it's already there, just use it) and look to see the beliefs and assumptions you're currently operating from.

Uncover Your Natural State Of Happiness

Don't be misled into believing that it's a painful, arduous and fearful thing to do. Yes, fear may come up, but so what? Don't let that stop you. It's just energy and nothing more – I promise, you won't die.

If you need to create a belief that says, "God won't ever give me something I can't handle"… then by all means, latch onto that belief and use it as means to get you through that challenge.

And always remember, you almost always get what you expect.

In the absence of belief, there is clear seeing and openness, infinite potential and possibility.

The late Zen Master Suzuki Roshi said it best: "In the beginner's mind, there are many possibilities. In the expert's mind, there are few."

See that the seeming hole inside is created by a belief in lack and incompleteness.

You have free will to believe anything you want and you also have free will to investigate and see what's really true, too. It depends on the kinds of experiences you really want to have.

The key aspect here is to be honest with yourself and admit that if you believe it, it means that you don't really know if it's true or not – and then proceed accordingly.

Lastly, the willingness and courage to NOT KNOW is essential if we want to uncover the

Born To Be Happy

happiness that is already shining, right here and right now.

Chapter 4
Argue With Reality And Suffer

Reality can be described as that which is actually occurring in any moment. Reality is what is.

In other words, what is means what's actually happening before your mind labels it as good or bad, positive or negative.

No doubt you've heard the popular saying these days, "It is what it is?" The true meaning of this phrase is that a thing, situation or event "is what it is" before the mind labels it as good or bad, positive or negative.

One of the most effective ways to suppress your natural state of happiness is to go to battle with what is – or what is actually occurring.

Do you want to be right ... or do you want to be happy? I can report from my past experience (and you can, too) that often times when I was "right" I was also unhappy!

The only problem you ever really have is to want something to be different than it is – or to want someone to be different than they are. Period.

Your mind will argue that it can't be that simple! Your mind will tell you that things can be different than they are and things should be different than they are, but is this really true?

Can anything ever be different that it is in that moment?

Can it?

If you really see this (that the mind's main function IS to argue with reality) I can tell you that you're way ahead of more than 99% of the world's population.

REALLY.

Argue with reality and suffer – only every time.

Argue you with reality and you bang your head against a brick wall.

Yes, things are very often different than they were but are they ever different than they are?

Seeing the truth and simplicity of this can radically change your life. And the really cool part is that once you really SEE this, you can never go back to the old way of seeing.

Sure, this (resisting what is) will still come up in your experience but you don't believe it anymore. Since you don't believe it, it doesn't hang around in your experience for long. As a result, you won't suffer, either.

I chuckle inside every time I hear someone say that their favorite sports team "should have" won that game!

Depending on the degree and intensity, resisting what is can only bring discomfort, dis-ease, pain and/or suffering.

Notice what happens when you would like to have a different experience from the one you're actually having.

Have you ever considered IF it's even possible to have a different experience than the one you are having?

No really, have you?

If the thought that it's possible to have a different experience than what you are having is entertained, then it looks as if you can change it into something more desirable.

And this is where the train leaves the track, often traveling right over the gorge, falling hundreds of feet to the thick, dense jungle below.

As soon as you don't want the experience you are having, the not wanting is also an experience (with another layer) added onto your experience.

This layer of resistance leads to a contraction you feel in relation to what is actually happening.

You cannot escape this contraction if you resist what is – it must manifest because to put it simply, this is the way it works.

We seldom ever consciously examine (or notice) this contraction we feel in the body – and consequently, unconsciously believe that if we resist a thing that we don't want, it will actually help us in some way.

We tell ourselves that we can't just passively let (what we don't want to happen) to just happen without a fight.

We believe that to struggle against something will somehow protect us from what we don't want to experience, shielding and protecting us in some way.

The reality is, that when we resist what is, we reinforce it and lock it into our experience.

We actually reinforce that which we don't want to experience.

It's like we're banging our head into a brick wall thinking it will help us feel better.

Uncover Your Natural State Of Happiness

The VERY interesting part is that we rarely ever verify this strategy to see if it's actually true in our experience.

Again, please don't believe me, but please do check it out in your own direct experience. It's very easy to do.

Most people haven't a clue as to what causes suffering.

Resistance to pain causes suffering. You may have heard that pain is inevitable, but suffering is optional?

As human beings, from time to time we will inevitably experience pain. It comes with the package of being human.

Pain is an inherent aspect of the finite, physical experience.

If pain wasn't a potential experience, could you experience happiness and joy?

Nope.

If we understand and live in harmony with the laws that govern us (that we cannot escape), pain can be minimal and short lived.

If we see that pain and happiness are two sides of the same coin and that we cannot experience one without the other (like life and death and hot and cold) we can allow whatever is happening to happen.

You already know this because you experience this all the time.

You can't have one without the other.

Notice how often your mind tells you that whatever is presently happening shouldn't be happening or that it could be happening differently. Has this ever been true in your life?

Or how about when your mind tells you that you "should have known" better and consequently done better? Based on your awareness at that moment in time, can that ever be true?

Can it?

If you're greatly impaired with a health challenge (or disease) that's progressively worsening ... and can't do most of the things you could before, what must be your experience if you resist what is?

Granted, you won't be happy about the situation, but you can certainly be at peace about it.

Why not enjoy the rest of your life in peace and let go to the fact of your condition instead of wishing things were different than they are?

If you say, "It's not that easy Alex, you try being in my shoes." I'd have to agree with you and perhaps say, " I hear you, I really do...and I have great compassion for you, but what's your alternative?

How do you want to spend the rest of your days?"

It's a fork in the road (we're at again, literally in each moment) where we can either reject or accept what is. Our perspective makes all the difference.

Uncover Your Natural State Of Happiness

So feel what you feel, process it on your timetable and then let's get on to accepting the reality of the situation if we want peace.

Granted, this perspective of accepting what is doesn't always happen right away, so please understand that appropriately, there's a great deal of compassion for you if you face this particular situation.

Many things in life involve a process of coming to terms with the reality of what is – and this situation certainly applies. Upon receiving news we'd rather never get, who among us responds with, "Oh great, this is just what I hoped for!"

If your current job or career really sucks, fully accept that you have it now (want what you have) ... especially IF you aren't actively looking for another one.

Or, fully accept that it's your job or career now, without resisting it now, as you happily look for another one. Imagine the energy you bring when you are interviewing for another position.

Do one or the other, but only if you want to be happy.

Do one or the other, but only if you care about how you impact those around you that you love.

Besides, carrying around this type of energy will open way more doors than if you hate what is. Don't you already sense this?

I can't tell you how "guilty" I was of doing the above, the majority of which occurred in my twenties. I say "guilty" (not in terms of blame or shame) because I wasn't aware that my perspective of resisting reality was creating the suffering I didn't want.

Today, I can look back in amusement at the fact that it seemed to take forever to see how this law of life worked, especially since I got such immediate and direct feedback.

Apparently, I was very asleep and not ready to see what was true, until I was – and not a moment before.

If you've experienced a fair amount of pain and unhappiness in your life up to this point, you can choose to experience its opposite – happiness – for the remainder of your days.

Fully accept that you've experienced your life this way (and that it couldn't have been any different) and then choose to experience the other side of the coin, that is, the happy side.

But first, you must become aware and conscious of how you've created your experience up to now ... and then intend for a more desirable experience by living in harmony with the law of your experience.

Just by being curious, open and nonjudgmental, we can be scientists in a lab experimenting with our direct experience and discover exactly how our experience is literally created.

We finally SEE that it's ALL an inside job, always and in all ways.

Can you think of a more worthy undertaking than learning how these laws that govern life work in your life – and then to actually cooperate with them?

Our lives become so much more enjoyable when we willingly abide by the laws of life.

Remember, you're playing to win, right?

The good news is that each moment gives us the opportunity to see this. Each moment gives us a fresh opportunity to see what's really true for us.

History does not have to repeat itself. You do have the power – and it's with your conscious awareness.

We can verify (in our experience) that when we don't want that pain, if we push that pain away, we feed it and keep it in place … and ultimately suffer.

Where your attention goes, energy flows.

Trust in life's intelligence and trust in your own being for they are one in the same. Even though your being and life's intelligence may appear separate, they aren't. You are Life itself.

The appearance is not the reality. It never is.

If we recognize and accept that pain is a fact of our existence, we can allow for pain to be our experience. We know that if we resist it, we give it continued life.

We see that by resisting anything, we are owned by it.

Pain is not the enemy and it never was! Your resistance to the pain was the problem. Pain itself is never the problem.

Allow what is natural do its thing. Pain is a natural energy of emotion and if we just let it run its course, it will not hang around and torture us.

We can see that all emotions are like the weather – they come and go. Stop feeding your painful emotions with resistance, accept that it arises and see what happens.

Watch that storm pass quickly.

When it was finally seen how this law was operating in my own life for almost twenty years, I knew I could intend for a much different experience.

I realized that I was literally a hamster on a wheel, unaware that not wanting the pain kept the wheel of suffering in motion! I was unaware that I was feeding (and giving life to) that which I did not want to experience – and my experience told me so.

I was working against myself when all along my body was telling me what was true, prodding me to work with life and not against it.

Trust the innate wisdom of the body – it knows and never operates from belief.

I truly cannot remember the last time I suffered. Why would I suffer anymore when I know what causes suffering?

Uncover Your Natural State Of Happiness

Allow the pain to wash through you, allow it to run its course in its time (not yours) and watch how quickly it dissolves.

It's all energy. It will amaze you, I promise. The truth is simple, so simple in fact that your mind cannot comprehend it.

Stop believing it has to be complex in order to be true. See that the mind deals in complexity – and rarely simplicity.

Stop arguing with reality and strip away this particular unneeded layer that covers over your natural state of happiness.

No more sabotaging yourself – you deserve to be happy. It is your birthright.

Even if you notice a preference arise for something else, offer that no resistance … and notice your experience.

Would you like a real simple formula for being at peace … peace that leads to happiness?

Allow what is to be exactly as it is.

Chapter 5
What You Run From Can Only Chase You

Have you noticed that running away from a particular problem in your life typically makes it worse?

Don't we have a tendency to think that by *not* dealing with something (that causes us pain) it will hopefully go away?

Intuitively, we know that the exact opposite is true so *why* do we continue to do it? Why don't we *do* what we *know* to be true?

Uncover Your Natural State Of Happiness

It was the apostle Paul who once said, "I do not understand what I do, for what I want to do I do not do, but what I hate I do."

For starters, don't we fail to take it one step further by examining what happens if we allow our experience to be as it is?

There's so much waiting for you if you do this one simple thing.

Also, isn't it in our make-up to avoid pain? Won't we usually go to any lengths to avoid pain and gain pleasure?

This isn't wrong or bad – it just doesn't ultimately serve you. You could say it's in our DNA to swim against the current of life at times, so don't go blaming yourself.

We're often like salmon swimming upstream to spawn when it's so much easier for *us* (and less draining) to go with the flow of the current of life.

Instead, why don't we row, row, row our boat, gently down the stream … merrily, merrily, merrily … life is but a dream.

To flow with life means to accept what's actually occurring in any moment.

We go against the flow until we don't anymore, until we see (in our experience) that swimming upstream doesn't actually serve us, until we see that going against life *brings us* suffering.

Call it cause and effect if you like.

We're wired to avoid pain and gain pleasure. Knowing this, why beat yourself up about it? Beating yourself up is another form of running and will keep the energy (that you don't want) in place.

Running IS resistance. Running *from* anything creates a negative energy that has nowhere to go and therefore, *must* stay with you.

What might happen if you take an approach of curiosity, without any judgment at all? What would that energy look and feel like?

Is it closed, limited and imprisoning – or open, spacious and free?

Which energy (approach) do you think will actually serve you? Which further imprisons you?

Do you sense that the path of least resistance comes from your own inner wisdom that is sensed below the neck?

Or do you sense the "smart way" of trying hard with lots of strain and effort that comes from a thought in your head, above the neck?

Do you sense that the truth is simple and not difficult?

Naturally, curiosity and wonder doesn't conclude and therefore, pigeonhole, limit and confine, does it?

Wouldn't you agree that cultivating a non-judgmental attitude allows what is to be *as* it is?

Uncover Your Natural State Of Happiness

Someone once said, "You don't define others with your judgment; you define yourself as a person needing to judge."

Instead of continuing this unconscious pattern that invariably leads to unhappiness and suffering – and because you want happiness – why not intend to cultivate the habit of facing and embracing that which causes you pain – and see what happens?

Have you ever really done this? If so, what was your experience?

That which we face and embrace must dissolve and leave our experience. This is law - this is the law of your being in any moment.

Hey, don't believe me, okay?

You're a scientist in a lab experimenting with this insight, seeking to prove it true in our experience, right? Don't believe anything until you prove it true in your own experience.

If you *can't* prove it at first, be okay with *not* knowing. Admit that you don't know in that moment.

It really is okay not to know! What does it feel like not to know? Isn't there an open, spacious feeling present?

If there isn't, then you must be listening and believing in the concepts and opinions of what your mind is telling you.

We've been conditioned to believe, like Pavlov's dogs, that *not* knowing isn't a good thing. Like we're stupid or something…

And it's a big crock of you know what.

The unknown is nothing to be afraid of and certainly nothing to be ashamed of.

The unknown is more beautiful and peaceful than you can imagine.

You already know what the known gets you – so relax into the unknown – this is where your freedom is found. This is where your freedom is waiting.

The truth is, you're already free.

Here's the crucial thing you must see if you no longer want to be jerked around by the all those UN-useful, UN-serving beliefs in your head.

Some beliefs serve you, many don't. The trick is to find out first what you believe in – and then see if it serves you or not. If they don't, then discard them like you would a winter coat on a warm, summer day.

Also, know that it's okay to have a belief as long as you admit to yourself that you really don't know – or you wouldn't believe.

If you find yourself running from the unknown, what can only happen? You guessed right. The unknown will freak you out *and chase you at the same time.*

Uncover Your Natural State Of Happiness

What's the antidote? Stop running from the unknown. Turn around and face what you don't presently know.

In fact, if you really inquire within, you'll discover that you don't know much at all. It is in *this* state of discovery… in *this* fresh, new moment where true joy is revealed.

Anything else is just conceptual knowing and conceptual knowing has no real power.

It's all an inside job and it always was. See that you're *already* part of the whole and that nothing is separate from you, despite any appearance to the contrary.

Sure, we are different and distinct from each other but the essence of what we are is exactly the same. Physical bodies are separate but what's animating them isn't separate.

Did your mind just have something to say about that? Do you believe it?

You'll be pleasantly surprised and even relieved, at what happens when you cultivate this new habit in your life.

At first, you'll need to be conscious of your present habit patterns in order for them to be old habit patterns.

You see *how* they were sustained and reinforced for so long and it became a way of being. Running away from things we'd rather not face is human nature after all – but does it *ever* really give us the experience we really want?

No, it doesn't.

Does it strengthen what we don't want?

Yes, it sure does – so see what's true and be free.

Eventually it will become automatic and it will become a habit pattern that happens all by itself. You aren't really "doing" anything here so don't fall into the trap of believing that this takes a lot of effort and strain.

It *does* take a willingness to look and inquire into what's really true. It does take a good bit of awareness and intent, but it doesn't take much effort – and it certainly doesn't require straining.

If happiness is indeed your natural state (it is) does it make much sense that we must effort and strive for what's natural, spontaneous and effortless?

It's not that your natural state of happiness wasn't present – it's just that it has been covered over with so many layers of untruth that you can't feel it, sense it.

Avoid nothing if you want real happiness. Avoidance is another form of running that can only chase you.

Do you agree that it's very possible we have dreams of being chased *because* we do so much running away in our lives?

When you know that everything must die, including the worm that's eaten by the bird in order to survive, you realize, "My God, I can cling to nothing. But I can enjoy what I have and when it goes, I'm no longer surprised because I know that I can't hold on to anything, including my own life and those I love dearly."

What is born must die. The body is born so the body must die.

Are you the body or do you *have* a body? Can you see the difference? It's extremely important.

At the risk of sounding strange or creepy, I must be honest with you. As far back as I can remember, I've always been drawn to cemeteries.

Aside from the peace that's felt there, cemeteries are such an "in your face reminder" of how fleeting this human life really is.

When you know that death only happens to the body and not you, funerals and cemeteries aren't creepy at all. Sure, funerals are naturally very sad and we feel much grief, but we see that without death, there can be no life, either.

As I write this section, I'm in a cemetery watching a funeral procession of cars pass through on their way to the gravesite of a loved one.

I can't help but wonder whether or not the newly deceased ever discovered the key to genuine and lasting happiness, hopefully long before *this inevitable day*.

My family will tell you just how much I like these kinds of reminders. They may even tell you just how much they don't always appreciate these reminders quite the way I do!

I guess I can be more respectful of that, huh?

Aside from the wonder I'm feeling as I watch the hearse go by, I can't help but *also* feel the sincere gratitude for the wonderful experience of being human, no matter how short it may be.

When I see what's really true and offer it no resistance, I am free.

Relatively speaking, it will *soon* be your last day that must come.

Do you know *when* your day will come? *Can you know when* your day will come?

How might your life be different if you absolutely and without condition, welcomed the fact that your day soon must come?

You'd be mostly free from the fear of the fact (that along with everyone else) your body must die, wouldn't you? Would you be chased by this fear anymore?

Despite an occasional fearful thought that might arise, you wouldn't.

So why do so many of us run from what must inevitably happen by nature, by design? Why do many of us fear that which billions have already experienced before us – and what billions must experience after us?

Well, wouldn't you agree that it's mostly because we fear the unknown? If we can't comprehend or grasp something, we usually fear it, don't we?

Isn't it interesting, even fascinating, that human beings run from what's literally inescapable, like the fact that our body must die?

If we delve deeper, don't we really fear the idea of no longer existing and not that our body must die?

Can you verify that you will no longer exist after your body dies? No, you can't.

When we run from the idea of our own physical death and the death of those we love ... and when we run from conversations about death, we make our fears of what's natural seem even more real.

And then we fear not only death, but really living as well.

When we see that absolutely nothing lasts forever and that nothing is safe from physical death, we can allow what must happen to take its natural course – because it will anyway, whether we want it to or not.

When we see and accept that the grand design isn't accidental or haphazard, we are no longer chased and haunted by our own thoughts "about" it.

Here again (as it always presents itself) we are wise to see the wisdom of no escape, aren't we? I mean, especially if we want to be truly happy in this relatively short human life we get to live?

Once we can truly accept and trust this Grand Design, don't you think we are much better able to enjoy our lives – even be happy with our lives because we know it won't last forever?

When we see (that for the most part) we really don't have control over any of it, don't we give ourselves that ability?

Wouldn't this truth realized in our hearts set us free?

Face life as it is, not as you want it to be.

Life IS integral; it's ONE life. You can't separate bits and say, "Oh, that's unacceptable and this is okay." You've got to encompass all of it or you'll always suffer.

No avoidance. Stay right where you are.

Running away from anything covers over (and puts to sleep) your natural state of happiness, every time.

Strip those layers away and face what's facing you

Chapter 6
What You Do To Others You Do To Yourself

This is one of my favorite laws of happiness, probably because it's so obvious. It talks to you all the time, sometimes very loudly.

And it's very difficult not to hear it. It's very difficult not to feel it, too.

It even gives you immediate feedback in every moment and never leaves you.

Some laws of life are subtle and more difficult to sense than others.

This one isn't subtle at all. This one is right out in the open – inviting us to see just how simple and consistent it really is.

If everyone on the planet lived in harmony with this one obvious and consistent law, we'd surely have a much different planet.

We'd have a planet full of happy people with a vibration easily felt by those who weren't happy.

This law was revealed to me in my early twenties one day while I was being unkind to a girl-friend.

For some reason, it hit home (like a sledgehammer) that it was impossible to feel good about myself as I was mistreating her.

I can still remember the voice inside that said verbatim, "What you do to others you do to yourself."

This wasn't exactly an earth shattering revelation as I had always suspected this, but something deeper happened.

Something energetic traveled from the thought (in my head) to the realization in my heart (being) that in order to be truly happy, I could not mistreat others.

You could say that real knowing finally happened (because it went from the head to the heart) and I knew that things would be very different than before.

In other words, I finally saw something hugely significant and something so profound yet simple, that I just knew that my life would never be the same.

I realized in that moment, that true knowing wasn't conceptual – that it could never be just conceptual.

I saw that "conceptual knowing" was basically a contradiction in terms. It was when you knew "about" something – much like philosophy, dogma or ideology.

The philosophy of happiness or the philosophy of spirituality is essentially "ideas about" happiness and "ideas about" spirituality and never, ever the actual.

Just as the word or concept is never the actual (can you drink the word "water" or be burned by the word "fire") philosophy is never the actual, either.

Philosophy can, however, act as a stimulus (or catalyst) that can spark a recognition or remembrance within of what was always and already known.

Then it moves from the conceptual to the experiential, becoming alive and organic in our experience.

It was from that day on that I realized to truly know something it had to be "known" below the neck and not above the neck. In other words, in order for anything to be truly known, it had to be understood and validated in my gut.

And that anything else (excuse the metaphor) was basically mental masturbation!

Gratitude washed through me as I knew this was truly a gift of grace and not something I did or deserved of my own accord.

The good news is that this law or principle is very easy to prove true. In fact, you can do it right now if you desire.

Imagine that you insult another person. How do you feel as you insult that person? Not too great, right?

Instead of imagining, go back in your memory to a time you mistreated someone. How did you feel as you mistreated them?

You'll find that it's literally impossible to feel good as you mistreat another, right?

It's pretty straightforward, don't you agree?

Have you ever fully realized that what you do to others, you do to yourself, too?

We go around forgetting this one simple thing, this one simple thing that makes such a huge difference in our experience – and the other's experience, too.

Similarly, when you hug someone in a genuine way, look another in the eyes and say something heartfelt ... or simply do a good deed without any expectation of receiving anything in return ...

How do YOU feel?

Pretty darn good, right?

This is different than the golden rule that says, "Do unto others as you would have them do unto you."

The golden rule is more of a commandment that tells rather than a law that demonstrates (shows) what you are, I am – and that I cannot escape or wipe my hands clean of how I treat another.

Pretty amazing isn't it? And it was right here all along, never hidden.

With this newfound insight, go out and truly be for others, do for others and see what happens.

Much of what causes our unhappiness is our belief in separation, our belief that there is a limited amount of resources to go around (scarcity mentality) and our belief that we must struggle to get what we want in life.

Therefore, instead of cooperating (heart) with others knowing abundance is the true reality, we compete (ego) with others because we believe that there isn't enough to go around, so we must get ours.

In short, we compete when we are ignorant of what's true.

How many of us actually test the assumptions that literally dictate our daily experience?

Seems like a worthwhile thing to investigate, don't you agree?

Do these assumptions and beliefs actually have significance or is it just a thought that tells you they're significant?

If we can only ever operate from our perspective of life, wouldn't it make sense to find out if our perspective is even true in the first place?

Wouldn't that be one of the most worthwhile things one could ever do, especially if one seeks to enjoy lasting happiness?

Wouldn't it?

If our perspective is based on separation, scarcity and the inevitable struggle – is it even possible not to project that onto those around us?

Here's the point: You cannot escape what you are and what you cling to as true. You cannot escape the effects of what you vibrate and since everything is energy, what you vibrate you must attract.

Therefore, embrace the wisdom of no escape and see that what you do to others, you do to yourself.

Now check this out. On the flipside, what you do to yourself you also do to others. It's a closed loop with nowhere to go but right where you are.

If you aren't happy with yourself and if you truly don't love yourself, it's virtually impossible not to consistently mistreat others.

I know someone personally who epitomizes this (don't we all) and unfortunately, she simply refuses to be willing to be honest with herself.

She refuses to take a good, hard look and see how she creates her own experience – and to see the inevitable and destructive impact she has on others.

Uncover Your Natural State Of Happiness

In her mind, it's always someone else's fault. The finger is always pointing outward and like a boomerang, it all must come back, right to where it originated – from her perspective based on her beliefs.

And her experience of herself rarely ever changes. She'll forever be stuck on that wheel of suffering (unless and until) she has the desire and courage to look and see for herself.

What happens when you squeeze an orange? OJ must come out, right? Not apple juice, but OJ.

If you have bitterness and resentment in your heart and mind, what must come out? Conversely, if you have happiness and gratitude in your heart and mind, what must come out?

What you're vibrating at any moment is what must come out, only all the time.

Despite what you may believe, you cannot love another more than you love yourself.

If you want happiness, first find out why you aren't happy. It's so simple that your mind overlooks it.

Do not be deceived by the illusion of apparent separation. As no man is an island, absolutely nothing exists isolated from the wholeness of Reality.

If you believe you're an island unto yourself, then is it any wonder that you experience dissatisfaction and lack?

The good news is that ALL OF THIS is in the past and doesn't have to be your experience in this fresh, new moment.

The question is, will you keep a dead thing (the past) alive? Will you repeat the same patterns over and over?

What about right now?

It's up to you and no one else.

Chapter 7
You're Most Present When You're Most Absent

Have you ever noticed that when your focus is off of yourself and your problems that you are most present and alive? How does this *feel* and what is your experience when you aren't thinking about yourself?

Aren't you at peace when all this "stuff" is absent?

Aren't you very present in the moment, often without a care in the world?

Well, naturally!

How cool is that?

Isn't it also peculiar that we often think of ourselves first (and what we want) *before* thinking of others? Channel WIFM – what's in it for me?

Don't we also often wonder why we aren't nearly as happy as we would like to be?

Don't we sometimes wonder *how it is* that our friend or co-worker seems to be so happy when we aren't?

This is because me, me, me is a recipe for misery....

How do you think your life would be different if you didn't reference everything back to you?

How might things be different in your life if you realized that all your struggles were directly related to your habitual focus on yourself – and how absolutely everything impacted *you*?

See that the majority of your struggle in life stem from being self-absorbed and trying to fill the void inside with things external to you.

For the next week, consider trying a little experiment and commit to being in service to others. Commit to making others happy, whether it's with a kind word or a good deed.

Take careful note of the results. I bet it will be one of the most fulfilling weeks of your life. I bet you'll feel more present than you have in a long time – because you weren't absorbed with yourself.

Uncover Your Natural State Of Happiness

If our main focus, energy and attention is about satisfying our own needs at all costs (and even sometimes at the expense of others) happiness must escape us.

I can tell you with the utmost assurance that those who are truly happy don't possess this me-first orientation.

It's literally impossible to have this "me-first" orientation AND be genuinely happy.

Truly happy people know without any doubt that there is no secret to happiness.

In fact, they know it's rather simple, open and available to all. They know that in order to be truly happy and free, they must live in accord with the natural laws of happiness that govern all of us.

Happy people aren't smarter (and know more) than unhappy people.

Most happy people are, however, consciously aware of (in tune with) what suppresses happiness, so in this sense you could say that they "know more" because they see something unhappy people don't yet see.

Whether this awareness was through years of being unhappy or not matters not.

They know it because they live *from* the laws (or principles) of happiness, now.

Why do you suppose so many people are drawn to meditation?

If done correctly, meditation can be a very effective tool in facilitating a reprieve from the dissatisfaction we experience on a daily basis – and even bring us temporary peace and happiness.

Don't misunderstand the point here. I'm not suggesting meditation isn't useful because it can be very useful.

Meditation (or sitting in silence as I like to call it) serves many purposes, one of which is to calm an overactive mind that can wreak havoc.

I have meditated quite a bit in the past and have discovered so much from this practice. However, what inevitably happens when you're no longer meditating?

After the usual short period of calm subsides, where your mind is pretty quiet and not telling you what's wrong and what's missing in your life, don't your "issues" typically come roaring back in?

Any practice (including meditation) has a certain life span. There is a beginning, middle and an end.

Likewise, any experience you have also has a beginning, middle and an end, too, does it not? In other words, it's temporary.

When your mind is focused primarily on itself – and all the things it deems unsatisfactory, *how can satisfaction ever be felt*?

How can we be happy if we believe we are incomplete?

Uncover Your Natural State Of Happiness

Conversely, a mind that is still, a mind that *isn't* focused on itself and its problems leaves one feeling almost absent and as if they aren't there.

What is actually absent is all their life struggles – the struggles that dominate much of their existence.

The wonderful thing is that this is when "you" are most present. When you are no longer self-absorbed and referencing everything back to yourself, you feel absent but very much alive and present at the same time. And dare I say happy?

Yes, this is also when happiness arises, when you are most absent.

Discover this and be free from yourself, free from your mind that tells you that you must have this or that in order to be happy.

In this way, you free others as well.

You free them from *your* projections, *your* expectations and *your* judgments.

Allowing another to *be as they are* is truly a gift of giving and one that is always received with gratitude and appreciation.

Let us see what might happen in our experience if we change the order of the wording in this chapter title.

What if this chapter was called, "You Are Most Absent When You Are Most Present?"

I am not talking about disassociation here. That is an altogether different state, a state you may want to seek a therapist for.

Born To Be Happy

What do you suppose would be *your actual and direct experience* if all your "problems" were absent in the present moment – or any moment for that matter?

And that in no way were you referencing anything back to yourself?

What if there was no resistance to what was actually occurring in any moment? In other words, you were cooperating (consciously or not) with Reality – or what is?

As you have probably have seen by now, you'd be very content, even happy.

You'd be happy because you know happiness won't arise, *can't* arise, when you're paying attention to what's missing in your life or what's missing in your experience.

It's just not possible.

When you become fully present in the only point of power, this now moment, your natural state of happiness must arise for this is law of presence, the law of your experience.

At the risk of having you roll your eyes, I have to repeat it. Don't believe a word you read here, but please do check it out in your direct experience and validate for yourself whether this is true or not.

The power of your presence trumps absolutely everything, even unhappiness. Your presence is most powerful and radiant when the focus is off of yourself.

Uncover Your Natural State Of Happiness

When you bring your full attention to this moment and take your focus off anything you may be discontent with, notice what arises.

This is where happiness is felt.

The past is memory and the future is imagined. Both are created in the mind. Despite what your minds says, the truth is, there's only now.

The more you consciously "do" this, the sooner it happens naturally and spontaneously – all on its own.

Talk about cool.

Knowing how it all works is the key but if you avoid the actual looking and willingness to experiment, nothing will change.

You can take this to the bank – it will pay out in dividends like you've never seen before, I CAN guarantee this one

Chapter 8
What You Pay Attention To

"I'm nothing, and yet, I'm all I can think about."

You've probably heard the saying, "what you focus on expands and grows stronger."

And that *what* you pay attention to *must* manifest itself in your experience.

If you pay attention to how sad you are, is it likely you'll feel happy? Is it likely you'll feel less sad?

If you pay attention to *all* the things you are grateful for, is it likely that you'll feel sad?

HECK NO.

Uncover Your Natural State Of Happiness

If you focus on why you aren't happy and if you look at all the things that make you unhappy in your life, you become unhappier, don't you?

If you focus on what you don't have or what you feel is missing, you feel lacking and you feel incomplete, don't you?

If we pay attention to (and believe) a perspective that says we aren't complete, we'll naturally *feel* incomplete, right?

And since you can feel it, don't you almost always conclude that it must be true *because* you feel it?

What happens when we pay attention to a belief that says we aren't enough? Can we feel anything other than insecure and less than?

No, we can't.

What happens when you focus on the silence and stillness in between each thought you think and each word you speak?

Try this now please.

You become more still, don't you?

Did you confirm this for yourself or are you just reading concepts here?

If our attention gets caught up in thinking that we need to have a certain lifestyle to be happy, don't we feel a dissatisfied longing *until* that lifestyle is met?

Since what we focus on usually expands, don't we often get increasingly dissatisfied when we focus on what's missing?

Is it even true that something is missing? Or is it a thought or belief that tells you something is missing?

We get what we pay attention to, every time.

While much of this goes on unconsciously and without your intention, it doesn't have to continue to be this way.

We don't wake up each morning with the intent of feeling crappy that day, do we? It just happens this way, until it doesn't anymore.

It happens this way until we become aware that it's even happening – and then we can be aware of a new intent.

And then we can pay attention to acting in harmony with our new intent.

That is the beauty in all of this. The moment that just passed does not have to match the next moment. History does not have to repeat itself unless you remain at the same level of consciousness.

It was Albert Einstein who said, "Problems cannot be solved at the same level of thinking that created them." And he also said, "A man should look for what is, and not for what he thinks should be."

Here's what I know from my actual experience: when I notice something I'd rather not have in my life and offer no resistance to its presence, I see that it has a very short life span.

Since I'm already very aware (via my actual experience) that wanting something *other than what I've got* only feeds what I don't want, resistance rarely comes up.

If resistance does come up, it's seen almost immediately and let go of. Consequently, I am no longer in bondage to that thing.

Most of this happens automatically now but in the rare times that it doesn't, I know that there *must* be some resistance present or it would not be in my experience.

It's very simple actually, mostly because it's easily validated. It is felt energetically in the body and *this is its way of telling you* that you are in resistance to that thing.

If you listen and trust what your body is telling you – and allow what is happening to simply happen, it lets go. It must because you just took away its energy and life force.

Notice where your attention goes in each moment, because where your attention goes, energy flows.

Imagine that in *each* moment there is a fork in the road.

Going in one direction your attention is placed on what is actually happening – and being absolutely okay with what's happening.

In the other direction your attention and energy is placed on what you think *should* or *could* be happening.

If you were to come to this fork in the road – this fork that resides in each new moment – which direction will you travel if you want your desires met?

You got it, the side where there's no opposition to what is actually happening.

Don't believe me....

If you've read this far (and been in a state of open discovery and have been looking for yourself) I imagine that you are beginning to see – and feel – that there is no way to be genuinely happy if you argue with what is.

Please don't misunderstand what I am saying. This doesn't mean you must passively 'lie down' and be okay with anything and everything that comes your way.

Part of the wonder and joy of being human is that we will always have our unique likes, dislikes and preferences. That's part of being uniquely you.

Manifesting your likes, dislikes and preferences is your natural right.

This does mean, however, that if you want something to be different than it is, allow it to be exactly as it is *as you intend* for something more desirable.

It's not rocket science, is it?

Uncover Your Natural State Of Happiness

How many of us were raised with this awareness?

Why energize and bring life to what you don't want?

In other words, thank whatever arises for appearing and then tell it you're grateful for it's appearance because it reminded you of what you REALLY want.

Use what you don't want as a trigger and accept its presence.

Use that newfound awareness as the springboard for what you really desire and watch what you desire come to you quicker than you ever imagined.

I also hope at this point that you *see* why I keep saying, "don't believe me check it out in your own direct experience."

I cannot stress enough the importance of actually *doing* these simple experiments and REALLY SEE FOR YOURSELF how you create your experience.

Otherwise, this will sadly just be another book you've read "about" the subject of happiness!

Don't let this book be just another set of concepts that you read "about" how to be happy.

I hope you don't use this book as just a temporary escape from your life, either. If you do, you can be sure that it's patiently waiting for you once you're done this book.

Use this book for which it is intended – to show you how to understand and abide by the rules (or principles) of happiness.

If you take on the experiments in this book and commit to following them through AS IF your life depended on them, you will uncover your natural state of happiness.

If you try to fix or change what is already occurring, what presently arises in your experience, happiness eludes you.

It must.

If our orientation is one of wanting more, better or different (while going to battle with what is) we are uneasy and not at peace.

When we put our attention towards allowing what is (to be just as it is) our experience is no longer one of contraction and limitation.

It is in this open spaciousness where no conclusions or judgments are made where happiness comes out to play, where happiness *only* likes to play.

Granted, much of the unhappiness we bring about happens automatically and unconsciously.

However, if we become aware of what we pay attention to in any moment, we're much less susceptible to falling into the trance-like states that flow from being unconscious.

Happiness doesn't like to come out and play when this happens.

Uncover Your Natural State Of Happiness

If your orientation is one of a deep contentment with what is actually occurring in any moment – and where nothing needs to be added or subtracted – you *will* experience a whole different reality.

You will because you must. This is the law of life.

So we do well to be mindful of the fact that wherever we place our attention and energy is what we literally ask for.

Only when we pay attention to what we pay attention to, do we give ourselves the opportunity to uncover our natural state of happiness.

Only when we pay attention to how we suppress our natural state of happiness can lasting happiness begin to be felt.

Chapter 9
Wanting What You Have

I remember back in college when I would go to the gym and work out. I was six foot two and about 175lbs – on the leaner side for sure. I wanted more muscle, especially in my legs! I'd look at the guys in the gym with the body parts I wished I had. No matter how much wishing or hoping, it never happened.

No matter how many exercises I did or amount of weight I pushed or pulled, I just couldn't duplicate what they had.

It bothered me and consequently, I felt insecure.

I failed to recognize that I would never have what they had, that I would always be uniquely me, with the body I was given.

The mind comes up with some of the most ridiculous notions that have nothing to do with reality! That isn't the problem though – *the problem is when we believe in and identify with those notions.*

I mean, if you told me back then that I'd never have what *that* guy had, I'd agree and even see how silly my wishing was. We'd probably even have a laugh together.

Even still…the hoping and wishing would arise from time to time and I'd inevitably feel more insecure.

It wasn't until I really consciously saw how ridiculous it was for me to entertain (and identify with) the wishful comparisons that my mind came up with that it stopped happening.

When I saw what was *really* true – and when I was ready to fully accept that truth and its implications, liberation happened. I no longer 'wished I had' what others had.

Today, I'm content and happy with the body I have, mostly because I know just how ridiculous comparing to others is – and where it must lead.

Besides, the human body is so amazing, with the ability to heal itself and do so many remarkable things. The human brain is far more advanced than any supercomputer ever made.

Admittedly, from time to time I'll make fun of my calves and compare them to my brother in law's calves (yes, the one with the bottomless pit for a stomach) but it's all in fun nowadays.

There's one exactly like me in this world and there's no one exactly like YOU in this world. Celebrate this wonderful fact of existence and revel in the beauty of it!

Do you compare yourself with others? Have you ever looked to see if you do this?

Maybe you do it financially?

Maybe you find yourself trying to keep up with the Jones' and wish you had what they have?

Do you feel insecure about the car you drive or the home you live in?

How about the profession you're presently in, you know, the one where you spend about forty plus hours a week?

Do you wish you had the career someone you know has? Do you resist and bemoan the career you actually have? What's that experience like?

Do you compare your appearance with others? Do you wish you were more attractive than you are?

Do you believe you'd be happier if your significant other was more attractive than he or she is? Do you wish he/she was as attractive as your friend's partner?

I'm sure you see where I'm going here and the common denominator: you are resisting what is –

you're wishing for things to be different than they are – when you know it can never be different than it is.

Do you see just how crazy and silly your mind can be? Do you see how you mind really likes to mess with you?

Do you SEE that the mind doesn't give a HOOT about reality (what is) and that it often wants something other than reality?

And then you believe what your mind tells you?

Naturally, by law, this causes varying degrees of unhappiness. If you really take a look at it, it's literally insane.

Imagine someone coming up to you and complaining about how the sky is always blue. "It should be green!" they say. "Wouldn't that be better?!" And they spend their whole life wishing the sky was green instead of accepting the reality that it was blue all along.

You'd say that person was literally insane, wouldn't you? Or at the very least you'd say that person was totally delusional, right? Well, that's how most of us spend our lives, until we don't anymore.

Anytime we compare or demand that things be different than they are, we essentially tell ourselves that something isn't quite right and that something is indeed missing in our experience.

Can you ever be happy with this perspective?

Nope.

So why do we do this to ourselves?

Actually, you don't consciously (and intentionally) do this, unless of course you're a masochist.

Can I ask you a strange question? Are you a masochist?

Do you want to know *how* this is true – that you *don't* consciously intend for this to happen? Okay, I'll tell you.

Do you *decide* to oppose what's actually happening in any moment and then wish for it to be different than it is?

Or does it happen spontaneously and without your intention?

If you're honest with yourself, you'll see that it happens all on it's own. You'll see that it arises by itself without you deciding for it to.

This is what your mind does and it's up to you to notice it *and* its impact on your experience … BUT ONLY IF you want to be happy.

Resisting what is, is a form of insanity. Believing that anything *can* be any different than it *is* right now is insanity. Do you see this? I mean, really *see* this?

See the humor at how your mind just loves to compare and contrast, evaluate and judge… even to the point of making you miserable.

Even though most of us have been taught that others can "make us unhappy" the truth is, no one can make us miserable (including our own mind) *unless we give our permission.*

It's all an inside game. See this and be free.

Welcome all of it and laugh your butt off. Laughter is NOT resistance. Laughter doesn't feed what you *don't* want.

Laughter disperses and laughter dissolves what you *don't* want.

Have you ever seen a picture, figurine or statue of the laughing Buddha? He's laughing at the realization of the insanity of the mind – and its tendency to resist what's actually happening.

Curiosity, non-judgment and laughter are three medicines that will go a long way in uncovering your natural state of happiness.

But don't believe me.

You'll always be uniquely you and *never* will you be remotely close to another.

Consequently, you'll always have what you have, and never what another has.

Just as there are no two snowflakes or fingerprints that are identical, there will never be another just like you, ever.

Now isn't that beautiful?

Do you think this is by accident?

Can you imagine a world where we all looked very similar, had very similar capabilities, attained similar levels of success and had very similar challenges, likes and dislikes?

BLAH!

Diversity *is* beautiful, don't you agree? If you don't see the beauty and splendor *in* diversity, you *will* once you watch the 6-minute video at the end of this book.

If you don't, I suggest (like Kramer on Seinfeld) that you consider electric shock therapy, okay? Just kidding.

Do you believe that this (wide array of diversity) is just a random thing – or something part of a grand, order and infinite intelligence that's so far beyond what your finite mind can comprehend?

I invite you to look at the arrogance that says *you should be different than you are!* And to even entertain the notion that The Source or God (or whatever name you choose) got it wrong.

You are meant to be you, *just* the way you are. Geez, I just heard Billy Joel singing *Just The Way You Are* in my head.

You are designed specifically to have the certain set of skills and abilities, tendencies and personality traits that *only you* have.

Am I saying you can't cultivate other traits and abilities you would like to have? No, I am not. You *can* achieve almost anything you set your mind to.

What the mind can conceive the mind can achieve, right?

Uncover Your Natural State Of Happiness

The key here is <u>want what you have</u> AS you seek to manifest something more desirable in your experience.

Wanting what you already have emits an energetic vibration of gratitude that can only attract more in like kind.

The other big key is to focus on what you want, *not* on what you don't want. I invite you to look at how often we focus on what we don't want.

Allow what is, be a lover of what is (as you happily intend for something more desirable) and you will effortlessly draw to you that which you truly desire, happily.

Temporary happiness arises when we get what we want. Lasting happiness arises when we want what we have.

And unless you're happy with who you are, you will never be happy with what you have.

Chapter 10
For The Highest Good Of All

Do you know people who are so transparent that it's easy to tell that they just don't want the best for others?

I am in my later forties now and I have yet to meet a person that is happy (that doesn't want) the best for others.

Conversely, I have met many unhappy people (who don't want) what's best for others. Some will even tell you!

It actually irks them when they see others, including "friends" or family succeed or benefit in any kind of way.

One reason for this is that unhappy people generally don't like to see others happy because it only increases their insecurity and dissatisfaction – and often validates their belief in their own perceived incompleteness.

Are you beginning to recognize how fragile and self-fulfilling minds can be?

There are those who even become increasingly somber when others are happy and content. Sadly, they fail to see that their VERY attitude is *the thing* that keeps their lives the same.

I worked as a house painter in college with a guy who had an established contracting business. He's basically a decent guy and definitely fun to be around when money isn't involved, but you just got the sense that he didn't want you to be more successful than him.

It's as if it threatened him and reminded him that he wasn't doing as well as he'd like to – and that as long as he was doing "better" than you, everything was good in his world.

He'd deny it to this day and even swear on his grandmother's grave. He still has the "I need to be more successful than you" attitude today – and unless he's willing to really see how this belief manifests in his experience, he'll likely take it to *his* grave.

There's nothing wrong with this. After all, it's his life and he can live it out as he wishes. It's just that it doesn't have to be this way.

However, it's a shame in a way because there truly *is* enough for all. The reality is that abundance is all around us and that we are literally bathing in it. Scarcity and lack is the illusion.

It is the mind that believes in scarcity and lack.

There's a huge difference in our experience when we come from a spirit of cooperation versus when we come from a spirit of competition.

Which do you live from?

If we aren't as happy as we would like to be, one way to be happier is to want the best for others.

Allow me to bring this point home further. No doubt you have heard of the law of attraction? It basically says that whatever we think about, we bring about.

Wherever we place our attention, we get more of that, whether we want it or not.

In other words, you are literally a magnet, drawing to you all that you entertain in your mind and emotions.

In fact, the more emotion and expectancy you have around a certain thing, the quicker you draw it in your experience, whether you want it or not.

This law or principle doesn't give a hoot whether you believe in it or not because it surely believes in you.

Uncover Your Natural State Of Happiness

While there is much more to this law than I will go into in this book, I will say that understanding some of the basics can be very useful to you as you seek to reveal your natural state of happiness.

The reason I said in the prior chapter to focus on what you want and not on what you don't want is this:

If what you resist persists and if everything is indeed energy – including thoughts, beliefs and emotions, what do you suppose your experience *will inevitably be if you don't want what's best for others?*

You got it, more misery and scarcity for you.

Not wanting the best for others literally sends out a vibration of lack and limitation and you virtually tell the universe, "Give me more lack and limitation, please!"

If you want to be happy, be genuinely happy for others. If you think you can fool the laws of happiness, think again. Unless you truly want what's best for others, happiness will be as present as a deadbeat dad, as present as snow on a hot summer day.

On a more personal note, I was a pretty decent athlete growing up. While I enjoyed most sports, basketball was the main sport I excelled in.

I remember deriving much of my confidence (and self esteem) from the fact I was a good basketball player. Little did I know that I linked my esteem up to something that *had to* come to end one day.

Born To Be Happy

Anyway, a few years after we moved into our new home in the early 1970's, my father had concrete poured over fifty percent of our backyard and my grandfather, a pipe fitter by trade, erected a ten-foot basket with three long pipes (a tripod) with plywood as the backboard. Finally, the basket and net was secured.

It was THE BEST basketball court in the entire town (it was huge) and so many kids came to play at my house, year after year! There was even a very bright halogen spotlight attached to the house so we could even play at night.

If you build it, they WILL come!

Sorry, I digress. I was reliving so many fun times as a kid for a few minutes there.

Anyway ... since much of my identity was wrapped up in being a "good basketball player" there was naturally an underlying insecurity that went with it.

In fact, *there had to be* because being a good basketball player isn't a permanent and lasting thing. When I stopped playing, you can imagine the sadness and confusion I felt.

I still remember sensing that when I stopped playing, this experience would happen.

When we identify our self worth with that which is fleeting, that which comes and goes.... insecurity and discontent must arise.

I remember noticing that in my mid-later teen years it became very apparent that I had real difficulty complimenting others, whether on the basketball court or just in general.

Instead of just chalking it up to being super competitive, something else arose. I got real curious and wondered why it was so hard for me to praise people.

Was it just because I was so competitive and had to win at all costs? I soon discovered, after some digging, that I had a belief that told me I would be "less than" if I praised others.

This was my belief and I believed it hook, line and sinker. Do you think I was insecure? You bet I was.

Was my belief that I'd be "less than" (if I praised others) actually true? Heck no! Did it feel true?

YES, it sure did.

I would have gone on believing this untrue thought for years and years if I hadn't seen what was really true that one day.

It wasn't until much later that I discovered what had happened. When you shine the light of your own conscious awareness on anything (and bring it out of the shadows) it can't survive much longer.

In other words, when you meet anything with a welcoming awareness, it won't continue to hang around.

How cool is that?

I saw that if I wanted anything to dissolve or leave my experience, I was best served with a neutral and impartial looking – without emotion, resistance or judgment.

Anyway, from the age of about seventeen to my early thirties, I wasn't the happiest guy to be around. I couldn't help but spread that vibration, as it's truly a package deal.

In retrospect, I know that it could *not* have unfolded any differently than it did, despite how silly it seems now.

If you want to play by the rules and win, want the highest good for everyone you encounter.

If it's NOT authentic, then there's something you haven't seen yet. Keep looking inward.

You can't fool the laws, the universe, Nature, God, Jesus, Buddha, Your Higher Self or *whatever* you wish to call it.

Heck, call it "Fred" if you wish because you know the word isn't the actual.

Only the phonies don't get to uncover their natural state of happiness.

It's not possible to uncover your natural state of happiness if you don't want the best for others.

In fact, it's a very good way to keep it covered over.

Chapter 11
Be Responsible For Your Entire Experience

By Frits Ahlefeldt

For many years I went through life believing I was a victim, even convinced I was a victim. I was like Curly in The Three Stooges believing I was a "victim of coicumstance!"

I couldn't see that it was not the circumstances that got me down but rather my response to them that determined my experience.

I believed I was a victim of the circumstances as a result of my upbringing and my chemical makeup. My belief system even told me what I could and couldn't do.

I was pretty good at arguing for my limitations, too.

I even gave a fifteen-minute oral presentation in college on Epictetus, a Greek sage and philosopher who said, "It's not what happens to you, but how you react to it that matters."

I had a strong sense back then that I really was responsible for my entire experience, but I wasn't ready to really investigate and see if it was ultimately true or not.

Apparently I needed another twelve more years of unhappiness to be ready.

Interestingly enough, there wasn't much denial present about my experience in life; I'd tell you *exactly* what was wrong with my life.

I was that over-share, TMI guy (too much information) and shared my misery with almost everyone around me. I can only imagine how draining I was to be around – and how often others must have cringed inside when I wore my heart on my sleeve.

What I *wasn't* aware of, though, was the fact that I kept speaking into existence how unhappy I was, *inevitably bringing more of what I didn't want.*

I was totally ignorant that by not taking full and complete responsibility for my own happiness (or

Uncover Your Natural State Of Happiness

lack of it) that I was essentially blocking it, covering it over.

Despite listening to my Father often reminding me of this truth, for some reason, I just couldn't *hear* it. Apparently, I wasn't ready to hear it.

I failed to see that when I pointed the finger outward, I was playing the victim. I couldn't see that when I played the victim I also kept happiness away.

I lacked the real humility needed to be honest with myself and even turned to alcohol for a period of time to temporarily escape the pain that just wouldn't go away, no matter what I did.

I really identified with Pink Floyd's song, "Comfortably Numb" but I was anything *but* comfortable.

If we believe that anyone can "make us feel" anything, we aren't seeing the truth – and we're essentially giving up responsibility for our feelings.

No one can make you feel anything without your consent. In fact, if you look and see, it's almost always what we say to ourselves that determines our experience – and not what the other says.

If you disagree with this then by all means you can be right, but you won't be ultimately happy.

As the fifth youngest of six kids in a pretty close knit family, I always felt that I had to prove myself by trying to one-up you, only to find ways to sabotage myself later, because deep down I felt unworthy.

I was also great at quitting things, including relationships. I'd start something new with great enthusiasm, and then once I got really close to achieving something – that breakthrough moment – I would turn my attention to something else.

I always attributed these things to "well, that's just the way life works." Yeah, it *does* work that way when you're chronically unhappy all the time.

What made it worse was that I'd often hear a voice inside saying, "You're looking in the wrong direction." It wasn't really helpful because I didn't know where to look.

And I certainly didn't know that seeking happiness was an effective way *not* to experience it.

It's like when you're thirsty and you want to cup water in your hands in order to take a drink. What naturally happens if you grasp it tightly?

You won't experience quenching your thirst, will you?

Similarly, if we truly desire something, grasping at it causes it to move further away. On the other hand, when we allow and welcome something, it moves closer.

I've come to love metaphors and paradoxes like this one (life is so full of them) but I love truth even more because its impact is so much more powerful and lasting.

While I see it all so clearly now, I was stuck in a thick and self-induced fog, suffering the consequences of being unaware that I literally created my own experience, moment to moment.

It took many years to see that *all* the unhappiness and suffering that I experienced was meant to unfold exactly as it did ... and in fact, could *not* have unfolded in any other way.

Even if a genie granted me the wish to erase those twenty plus years of pain and suffering and replace them with happiness, I'd certainly decline the offer.

The happiness experienced today really *is* sweeter as a result of all those painful years. The happiness experienced today really *is* more delightful because I experienced the opposite of it for so long.

In this world of duality we live in, it's literally impossible to experience true joy and happiness if pain and misery isn't a potential experience, too.

SEE this truth and welcome all of it.

I had a new understanding and appreciation for the true adage that says, "the truth sets you free" ... and I wanted more of it.

Once I was willing to really look inside and question everything I believed to be true, things began to improve – slowly but surely.

I saw that for me personally, nothing good ever came from alcohol. I saw clearly that alcohol actually sustained and reinforced that which I *didn't* want.

It was a vicious cycle to say the least.

Thinking that I had intentionally abused alcohol, I naturally felt guilt and shame.

When I finally realized that alcoholism is a disease that induced a physical and mental craving for alcohol, all the guilt and shame that I carried around for so long was lifted.

Seeing the truth, I was set free and yet, I was still responsible.

So when I really saw the role alcohol had in my life and that I'd never be truly happy if I continued to drink – and when I *really* saw that I couldn't be a social drinker (and that I had a disease that made me crave alcohol) a burden so heavy was lifted from me.

I stopped that day (rather it was removed from me that day) and haven't had a drink – or desire to drink in over 12 years.

It was only then that I was able to see the direct relationship between taking full responsibility for absolutely everything in my life (uncaused disease or not) *and* being truly happy.

I soon began to validate this in my experience when I saw that it wasn't possible to be depressed or sad for very long *when I was willing to be responsible for my feelings and emotions.*

Then an interesting thing happened. When I refused to accept responsibility, unhappiness would arise again! As an experiment, I even tried to take partial responsibility to see if THAT worked.

As I suspected, it did not. I was onto something and it gave me a new sense of purpose.

I was committed to discovering the truth of this thing called "responsibility" and how it worked in my life.

I wanted to find out how my life might be different if I actually took responsibility for everything that showed up in my experience, regardless of whether I believed I was the source or not.

So little by little by little, my life began to improve and happiness wasn't so elusive anymore. I started noticing happiness arise for just being alive, for just being able to see, touch, feel, taste and hear.

I saw that I wasn't entitled to enjoy these physical tools of perception that allowed me to intimately experience the beauty and diversity that life continually bestowed – including all the pains, struggles and challenges, too.

I saw that these sensory tools were truly gifts I received in order for me to experience and express myself in this life – and not something I earned or had rights to.

I no longer took for granted that I could walk, talk, laugh and cry. Birds singing, squirrels running up and down trees, dogs playing, my adorable ragdoll cat napping and children playing touched me in ways I never felt before.

Every now and then tears would well up in situations where I saw so much beauty in something that would have seemed so mundane before.

And it was all because I saw the truth of responsibility. It was because I saw that being happy *and* taking responsibility went hand it hand.

I realized (in my actual experience) that happiness would always be elusive if I wasn't willing to be entirely responsible for every-thing that arose in my experience.

Whenever I pointed the finger and blamed others for anything in my life, I felt crappy. Conversely, whenever I felt crappy, I wasn't taking responsibility. I couldn't escape!!

Being ignorant to what was really true was the real culprit. I began to see that when I didn't know what was really true, some degree of angst *had* to arise.

I began to realize that when I saw what was true – and what wasn't, that something very different began to happen in my experience.

I saw (and more importantly, experienced) that when the truth was seen, something let go its hold on me – usually for good.

I finally understood that when I really saw the truth of *anything*, that I was no longer owned by that thing.

Wow! I came to see that when I lived in alignment with the law of responsibility, I felt happier. It was if I was rewarded for it and to be honest, I know this to be true.

I don't mean to suggest reward in the sense of reward versus punishment, but rather in the sense that you reap what you sow.

There was an accompanying energetic feeling (and experience of myself) when I took responsibility that was much different than when I didn't.

It's very liberating to *see* this. The feedback is almost immediate and very clear.

The very fact of how we observe, evaluate and judge anything literally determines our experience.

If this is true then, isn't it plain to see that when we perceive everything as outside and separate from us, we invite suffering and dis-ease, actually call it forth in our experience?

When we run from anything, when we argue with reality, when we don't want what we already have, are we taking responsibility?

No, we are not.

What must our experience *inevitably* be? We get more of it.

Where must this energy go? Where *can* it go? You got it, nowhere but right where *you* are.

We can't fool the law of our experience. It's so consistent, neutral and predictable.

Are you really starting to see (and feel) how you already know all of this?

I sure hope so.

When this truth is seen (by looking and experimenting without judgment or resistance) we can begin to work with ourselves and not against ourselves. We see that we really do create our experience with our beliefs and our perspective in life.

We become aware that to resist *any* part of it is unintelligent and senseless, for we know we are the sole cause of our experience, every time.

In fact, it's never about what the other does; it's always about how we interpret, how we respond that matters in our experience of ourselves.

We finally see that it REALLY IS an inside game and it always was. We just weren't aware before!

We see that life mirrors us. We understand that there are no causes in the observable world; the observable world is the world of effects, without exception.

As a result of this seeing what's true, we render ourselves power-ful and response-able.

We literally gift ourselves with (response-ability) in the only point of power, this present moment.

Is it ever *not* right now?

Take initiative, be the example and step up and be counted in this world. The truth is, you are no less valuable or worthy than anyone else in this world.

If you believe otherwise, it simply means you believe in your conditioning and the BS of what society attempts to tell you. Remember, society is conditioned just as much as you are and quite possibly, more than you are.

Your family and friends (and your circle of influence) can really benefit from the happiness you'll begin to vibrate.

I refuse to be on my deathbed looking back on my life with regret, "wishing" I took more responsibility for my own happiness, especially since I always suspected that it was no one else's responsibility but mine.

I decided many years ago that I would not be in a position where one day I'd look back on my life regretting that I didn't fully show up by taking responsibility for all of it.

How about you?

How do *you* want to feel as you look back on *your* life?

Chapter 12
Gratitude Is The Doorway To Happiness

If a sense of entitlement and an unwillingness to be responsible closes the door to happiness – and believing the thoughts in our head *without* investigating whether they're true or not *locks* that door – then *what* unlocks and opens that door?

Gratitude that's based in reality – and not fantasy – unlocks and opens that door. What's actually happening in *any* moment IS reality.

Uncover Your Natural State Of Happiness

It's not possible to experience the lasting happiness we desire without being truly grateful for *everything* in our lives.

We've been taught to believe that the best way to feel grateful (*and happy, by the way*) is by *cultivating gratitude* or by creating a gratitude notebook or journal, writing down everything we can think of – that when we *really* think about it – we're grateful for.

If you've tried this method (like I have) you may have seen that the purpose of consciously doing these exercises on a regular basis is to remind yourself of all the things you're grateful for, *should be* grateful for and *could be* grateful for – and heck, let's add – are willing to be grateful for.

While there's definitely some use and benefit to this approach, there's *so much more* to the formula of being truly grateful.

Have you noticed that your actual and direct experience of this popular approach is usually very short-lived, having a beginning, middle and an end … like all experience?

In other words, the gratitude you feel (as a result of this approach) is a fleeting experience and not something that is organically present most of the time, right?

Like all methods and techniques, it must have a certain life span with a beginning, middle and end. Since this approach is manufactured and created in the mind, it can't last because it's based in that which comes and goes.

Gratitude that's based on conditions and preferences *must be short-lived* because conditions are always changing, always in flux, agreed?

Aren't we usually left wondering why gratitude comes and goes, unlike the way in which the author intended?

And while we have a strong sense that gratitude indeed is the key to happiness, don't we often fail to see *why* it's so challenging to *actually be consistently grateful*?

We may conclude that it's too difficult to be grateful when there's so much "wrong" in our lives. We often believe that if we're grateful for what's wrong in our lives, those wrongs *won't* ever go away, when the exact opposite is the case.

Don't we find it much easier to be grateful AFTER we remove all the problems and suffering from our life?

Isn't our gratitude usually reserved for the people, places and things that we most value and enjoy and not for those we don't value and enjoy?

Because we're wired to avoid pain and gain pleasure, isn't our tendency to be grateful usually conditional? Isn't it easy to meet what we prefer to experience with gratitude – and meet what we don't want to experience with resistance or avoidance?

Isn't this the way most of us have it set up?

Uncover Your Natural State Of Happiness

As you might imagine, how we meet anything determines our experience.

As in every moment of our lives, we're always at that fork in the road, where we can either resist what is or accept what is – or even be grateful for what is.

It's easy to be grateful when life is flowing in the way we like, isn't it? However, *meeting whatever arises with unconditional gratitude* swings the door wide open to happiness, but don't take my word for it.

So let's take a different approach, shall we? Let's experiment by taking an approach where we work with ourselves and not against ourselves – because we really do want to be happy.

Can we toss aside (at least for now) the approach of trying to manufacture feelings of gratitude by reminding ourselves of *all that we could, should and might be grateful for,* especially since our intent is for real and long-term happiness?

Gratitude that's not based on circumstance and condition isn't short-lived and fleeting. Because it's based in reality or what is, it hangs around, without our intent for it to hang around.

In my opinion, there's no greater feeling and no greater experience than being genuinely *and* unconditionally grateful for literally everything in my life.

Born To Be Happy

Since I'm aware that in the world of duality we live in, I can't have what I like without the potential of having what I don't like, I'm grateful for both experiences – especially since I desire lasting happiness.

For instance, I'm actually grateful for the fact that I had a problem with alcohol from the ages of 18-34 years old – and for the fact that no matter how much willpower I summoned and no matter what strategy I came up with, I just couldn't consistently drink socially.

I found I could "control it" sometimes, but ultimately I discovered that it was only a matter of time before I was out of control. My experience (and not my mind) told me so.

When I finally admitted to myself that I was in fact powerless, I rendered myself powerful – and something was lifted, namely the obsession and desire to drink.

I came to see that I had a disease that was stronger than my intellect, willpower and intention. I saw that I wasn't in the driver's seat anymore and like a rudderless ship, I was unable to successfully navigate where I wanted to go.

Seeing this truth, shame and guilt vanished almost instantly – and yet I knew that I was still responsible for staying away from that next drink, that is, if I wanted to be happy. I realized that I couldn't have both anymore, so I had to make a choice.

Uncover Your Natural State Of Happiness

I knew I was not only *responsible for* myself but also *responsible to* those I loved and cared for.

I'm grateful for this disease because it eventually forced me to really look at the role alcohol played in my life – and it led me to doing the inner work that's made all the difference.

There's no closer relative to true happiness than real and unmanufactured gratitude that comes from the heart and not the head.

If you're unhappy in life, you aren't very grateful, either. That's not a judgment, by the way. Just look and see what's real in your experience.

I can't tell you how many times I heard my Dad try to remind me about the importance of "an attitude of gratitude."

He'd often follow that up with telling me how people with a *sense of entitlement* are those who aren't very happy because they feel as if they are owed something.

I'd look at him and nod my head, trying to give the impression that I knew what he meant. Either he thought I was a total moron or he sensed I hadn't truly heard what he was saying because he kept on planting the seeds of this truth for several more years, hoping one day they'd sprout.

My Dad *knew* that it wasn't possible to have a sense of entitlement (towards anything) AND simultaneously have an attitude of gratitude! It's like trying to mix oil and water. It just won't work.

He knew that the two were mutually exclusive. He also knew that to the degree that I had a sense of entitlement towards anything in my life, to THAT degree would I be ungrateful.

Seeing the big picture (and how it all fit together like a puzzle) he knew that to the degree that I was ungrateful, to *that* degree must I experience unhappiness, too.

He'd tell me that an ingrate's frequent focus is on his or her perceived lack and social standing in the community. This insecurity would inevitably lead to a yearning to appear as someone *other* than they were – to "put on airs," as he put it.

This person would invariably love things and use people, leaving them feeling empty and isolated from the world around them.

An ingrate, he'd say, was much more of a whiner than a winner. An ingrate frequently made excuses and blamed others for their lot in life and was generally unwilling to be responsible.

A grateful person on the other hand, is sensitive to themselves and others – and has an abundance of humble, self-confidence that easily praised and supported others.

The grateful person has an orientation of being in service to others and therefore, responsive to the needs of others. And despite any setbacks and challenges in life, the grateful person always has an eye on self-improvement and a better version of himself.

The grateful person isn't necessarily religious but tends to be spiritual.

But most of all, he'd remind me that a truly grateful person possessed integrity (self honesty) and real character built on rock and not sand – and a willingness to do what the unsuccessful people *weren't* willing to do.

I hope he knows – I hope he now sees – that these seeds finally took root and sprouted, with the ability to weather any and all storms that may come my way. I guess the apple really doesn't fall far from the tree.

Thank you for your persistence and non-judgment, Joe. I love you dearly. And Mom, the absolute truth is, is that I can *never* repay *you* for all you've done for me. Never. Raising six kids was the hardest job that required the most love. I love you dearly, Kay.

Gratitude arises spontaneously and is a natural and organic byproduct of seeing what's true. Resentment, on the other hand, arises when we are ignorant of what's true.

For me, perhaps what's most beautiful today is that the gratitude FELT for my parents today isn't created or manufactured out of some sense of obligation or attempt to appear "appropriately respectful or grateful." It's based in truth and therefore, real and lasting.

It's worth mentioning that for many years I had unresolved issues with my parents. I blamed them for a good bit of MY unhappiness when it wasn't their fault. It only kept me stuck in my unhappiness.

I didn't want to see that I was solely responsible for all of it, my perceptions, beliefs, grudges and life experiences.

When I didn't see what was true, I suffered. When I saw what was true, something let go and I was free. My mind didn't tell me this. My actual experience did.

I wasn't ready to see that it was ALL an inside job, always and in all ways. The liberation and freedom I feel today is beyond what my mind could ever imagine. This seeing of what was true freed them, too.

And I know they feel it. Talk about a win-win situation.

It just comes up of its own accord, like the annual flower that sprouts each year because you planted the proper seed, because you saw what was required.

True vision (that leads to true perception) is the catalyst for gratitude to arise on its own, without your intent.

See what's true and the rest takes care of itself, all by itself.

Uncover Your Natural State Of Happiness

On the flip side, if you don't feel grateful for all that you have or if you've somehow convinced yourself that you're entitled to certain things in life (or anything for that matter) gratitude won't arise much at all.

If this is the case in your experience, then it's a sure sign that there's something you haven't yet seen.

So we see that a sense of entitlement is the *antithesis* of gratitude and that they don't arise together. If one is hanging out at a party, the other won't come. In fact, the other isn't invited.

We clearly see that it's literally NOT POSSIBLE to feel entitled *and* grateful at the same time.

We realize that the best way to feel ungrateful is to feel a sense of entitlement. Feeling *entitled to anything* covers over our natural state of happiness.

Are we actually entitled to anything or is everything TRULY a gift?

If we think we're entitled to anything, we're simply deluding ourselves into believing we deserve that thing because we "earned it" ... or because we're "family" or because we're your "friend"... and that's what friends are for.

If our very life is a gift of grace, then isn't everything we get to express and enjoy in life also a gift – and not something we're entitled to?

Did you decide to be born? Can you take credit for the fact of your very existence? The truth is, it's all grace and it's all a gift, including your life, isn't it?

How would your experience be different if you paid attention to this one truth?

Have you recognized that we frequently feel entitled to those things that we take for granted, particularly those things that are always present?

For example, don't we usually take for granted our next breath, our next heartbeat, the next sight seen or the next sound we hear?

Are we *actually* entitled to our next breath? Are we entitled to our next heartbeat, sight we see or next sound we hear? Are they not gifts also?

Do you suspect that if you were suddenly faced with death that (you'd also suddenly) very much appreciate and be grateful for your next breath? And how about your next heartbeat?

Are we really entitled to experience the wonder and joy and love that this life offers us?

Helen Keller was an American author, political activist and lecturer. She was the first deaf and blind person to earn a Bachelor of Arts degree. This is what she had to say:

"So much has been given to me; I have no time to ponder over that which has been denied."

Do you think Helen Keller, someone who never had the privilege to experience hearing all the various genres of beautiful, soothing music, birds singing, the ocean roaring and babies laughing was unhappy in life?

Do you think Helen Keller, someone who never had the privilege to experience seeing the incredible and vast array of beautiful sights most of us get to see and enjoy, was unhappy in life?

Not a chance.

Not surprisingly, Helen Keller also wrote this:

"When one door of happiness closes, another opens: but often we look so long at the closed door that we do not see the one which has been opened for us."

If there's a direct relationship between taking things for granted and being ungrateful, aren't we wise to see the benefits of being truly grateful for all the gifts freely and unconditionally given to us?

And if what we pay attention to dictates our experience of ourselves, then doesn't it make perfect sense to pay attention to the things we most take for granted, especially since it's happiness we seek?

A thankful heart is a heart that sings a song of joy and peace. A thankful heart can't be an unhappy heart. A thankful heart can't help but look for the good in all situations and all people – and certainly doesn't take anything for granted.

And a thankful heart really does attract the highest good for all concerned because it's inclusive and cooperative.

Meister Eckhart, a German philosopher and mystic of the 13th century said:

"If the only prayer you said in your whole life was, 'thank you,' that would suffice."

Open your heart and be grateful for the countless blessings bestowed on you – blessings and gifts you never earned and were never entitled to … but only if you want to be happy.

After all, you can never know when your last breath is.

Well, I really hope that you enjoyed this book and I wish you nothing but the best as you continue to uncover your natural state of happiness.

After all, you were born to be happy.

One Final Thought

Remember when you first learned how to drive a car? Remember how you had to consciously think about what to do next, especially if you learned on a stick shift like I did?

After you had a few months under your belt, remember when driving became automatic, where something just "took over" and drove the car without you thinking about it?

This is what can happen for you if you continue to look and see what's really true in your experience. Please don't let fear or any other obstacle (like belief or circumstance) deter you.

Uncovering your natural state of happiness *will happen* if you really want it to happen – and wholeheartedly intend for it to happen. Besides, it's right here and right now, right where you are.

Your own happiness is the greatest service you can render to the world.

Peace and happiness,
Alex P. Keats

When Wisdom Blooms
Awaken The Sage Within

Alex P. Keats

Right Now
Publishing

Right Now Publishing
ISBN - 13: 978-0615940373
ISBN - 10: 0615940374

© 2012 Alex P. Keats

All Rights Reserved. No part of this publication may be reproduced in any form or by any means, including scanning, photocopying, or otherwise without prior written permission of the copyright holder.

First Printing, 2012
Printed in the United States of America

Dedication

This book is dedicated to the objects of my affection: the 210 acres of The Ellis Preserve in Newtown Square, Pennsylvania. Even though you don't have to try, the perfection and majesty of your presence truly inspired this author. And to Momma groundhog and your three babies: Thank you for grazing less than ten feet from me, week in and week out, trusting I would bring you no harm. Your trust was well placed; what you are, I am. To harm you and your babies would be to harm myself. My deepest appreciation goes out to you and your kin.

"The foolish reject what they see, not what they think; the wise reject what they think, not what they see."

~ Huang Po

Contents

Introduction	i
1 - Freedom Beyond Belief	1
2 - Dead On Arrival	28
3 - Return To Sender	50
4 - No Story, No Suffering	68
5 - When Wisdom Blooms	88
6 - You Are What You Want	113
7 - The Greatest Gift You Can Give	135

Introduction

This isn't a book about how to make you feel better, wiser or more spiritual. And it's certainly not a book meant to add to your current level of knowledge. It's a book that is intimately practical and engaging in the sense that it's more about how to live our lives more openly and directly, without relying on belief or past experience. It's about looking at the ways in which we unconsciously cover over our natural state of wisdom, and discover the ways in which wisdom naturally blooms.

Indeed, it is about awakening the sage within, while being fully human and down to earth. It's an invitation to look within, unabashedly – and see what tendencies are hurtful and divisive, and once and for all, transcend those tendencies without going to battle with them. It's an invitation to recognize the value of words and concepts as a means for going *beyond* words and concepts, entirely to the direct realization of reality or truth. Reality is so much more immense than any conceptual framework we can come up with, so it's best not to cling to the words in the traditional ways we've been taught.

Rather, look beyond the words to where the words point – for wisdom, truth and freedom are beyond the words. In speaking about wisdom, it implies that its opposite quality, ignorance, needs to be examined as well. Taking a closer look into the ways we unconsciously erect barriers that block our natural state of wisdom is one of the chief aims of this book.

As there's no up without down, there's no wisdom without ignorance. Ignorance *ignores* truth or reality. Identifying the barriers *to* wisdom gives us the ability to tear them down. In actuality, we can't decide to tear them down, like we decide to tear down a wall in our living room blocking our view of the backyard garden. When we *see* what's really true, and when we recognize what's really been running our lives, those barriers come down by themselves. Being conscious drives out the false; being un-conscious lets in the false. Make no mistake about it; once these barriers are identified and deconstructed, our natural state of wisdom reveals itself.

Like the intelligent farmer who knows the proper conditions must be met in order to realize a plentiful harvest, we need to realize the kind of soil in which wisdom blooms. How can we live our lives in harmony with life, and not from the mind's longings, aversions and biases that invariably lead to struggle and strife? How can we meet the moment as it actually unfolds, rather than how we wish or hope it unfolds? If *seeing* what's true, rather than believing what's true makes all the difference in our experience, in which direction do we look? How do we know we're even looking in the direction where wisdom resides, and where wisdom ultimately blossoms?

If wisdom really is fully present and available within each one of us, why does it seem so elusive and difficult to be in tune with? What might happen if we suspend all that we know for a time – and set aside everything we've accumulated in the past, for the very real possibility of experiencing a different reality, right now?

What might happen when we approach concepts we may have already been exposed to, in a very different manner – a manner without any conclusions, expectations or reference to the mind to tell us what's real and true? Whether it's from a direct question or by looking in a particular direction, when we simply allow the answers to arise, honestly and truthfully, a light is shined on the underlying beliefs and assumptions that maintain personal suffering.

The common thread throughout is one of *seeing* and *realizing*, not thinking, believing and evaluating. To *see* is to realize what's true. Unless we *see* (not with our physical eyes, but with our nonphysical awareness) and *realize*, we're just deluding ourselves. Wisdom is found below the neck; conceptual knowledge in the form of thinking, judging, comparing and calculating, is done above the neck. If it's wisdom we're after, by default, truth automatically stands at the front of the line. Without hydrogen, there's no water. Without truth, there's no wisdom. Sometimes we discover that posing a question, or looking in a particular direction, isn't meant to elicit a conceptual response from the mind.

Rather, questions can serve as a catalyst to experience, in our being, what it's like to rest in the question itself. The purpose is to facilitate an opening so that you can explore deeply within yourself the beliefs, concepts and opinions you have assumed to be real and true – and which until now might have gone unquestioned. Looking in the direction suggested by the question gives us the opportunity to see what arises from beyond the mind – for both wisdom and truth aren't realized *in* the mind. It is in this looking and resting (without any intent to answer the question conceptually) that allows us the opportunity to see clearly what hasn't been seen before.

Delving deeper into the book, you'll discover how to discern truth from falsehood, why your mind creates and maintains its stories – and ultimately, how to break free from the train of thought and let wisdom bloom. Living from your inner sage is your birthright, and your natural inheritance; claim what's already yours. Since the mind can't see or discover this, YOU'LL be reminded how to look in such a way that wisdom blooms – and you'll know when the mind is trying to usurp this looking. Don't be surprised if you find yourself void of any knowledge or conceptual understanding. It is in this aware empty space, devoid of any conceptual knowledge, that "your answer" may be realized. Only when we allow ourselves not to know, does Truth reveal itself as that which is eternally present.

Only when we empty our cup can it be filled. Only when we're willing to unlearn can we really begin to know. I invite you to read the words to follow unlike any other time, with an open heart and mind, allowing them to penetrate you in ways never experienced before. It is my sincere hope that you take full advantage of this opportunity and let your answers flow, unedited from your mind. You may want to put the book down at certain points throughout – and write them down. There's something powerful in putting words to paper.

When Wisdom Blooms – Awaken the Sage Within consists of seven chapters, with each chapter building on the previous, challenging and re-examining habitual patterns of thinking and unconscious ways of being. Instead of blindly following tradition, hearsay, religious text – or any other "authoritative" outside source, this is a book that encourages you to look and *see* for yourself what is true. The conditioned beliefs we unconsciously cling to, and the habitual tendency to seek outsides of ourselves for happiness are examined in depth.

The opportunity available within these pages is to examine the inherent pain and suffering in the mind's endless pursuit of pleasure and avoidance of pain. The point isn't to fix or change anything, but instead, to recognize what's really driving the bus. When we finally recognize that the known has never revealed what we're after, we allow ourselves to look in a different direction – and relax into the unknown. If it takes courage, then it takes courage.

When we step outside our habitual and conditioned ways of being, by *seeing* without the mind's preference or partiality, we allow for ignorance to be dispelled. This seeing *is* the light of awareness that coaxes untruth out of the darkness, allowing us to see it for what it is – simply concepts believed to be true that determined our activities. It's important to notice that we can't *decide* or *make* wisdom bloom; we can only let wisdom bloom. We let it bloom by uncovering the false.

All that's asked of you is to look in the directions you're being pointed – and not just one time. Look until you *see*, knowing the false cannot stand up to close examination. So many have already examined and discovered – and they didn't die. Granted, many have experienced varying degrees of reluctance, fear and trepidation, but so what. If that's what must be experienced, then so be it. It's all just energy anyway – and illusory, so it can't harm or touch what you really are. Nothing can – so don't let what's unreal stop you.

Lastly, you'll find certain words and phrases repeated throughout the book. I ask that you excuse and look beyond any redundancies. In the Zen tradition, this repetitive method is sometimes used in an attempt to wear down the mind in order to go beyond the mind – and realize you're already beyond the mind. This is not the intent here.

Nonetheless, there's a fresh and brand new opportunity to find out what's really true – even in any apparent redundancy you may encounter. Since Truth is singular – and if it's Truth we're really after, pointing to the same changeless essence is requisite. Since there's no wisdom without truth, both are intertwined, forever arising in unison.

Chapter 1
Freedom Beyond Belief

"The word 'belief' is a difficult thing for me. I don't believe. I must have a reason for a certain hypothesis. Either I know a thing, and then I know it – I don't need to believe it."

~ *Carl Jung*

Any book on wisdom wouldn't be complete if belief wasn't discussed. In fact, if you ever come across a book about wisdom and the topic of belief isn't included, put it down – or just know it's incomplete. It's like ordering cherry pie only to find it didn't come with cherries when you went to eat it. Almost everything we say, think, feel and do is based on belief – or more accurately, our belief system. Strangely enough, we rarely ever look at this mental construct, this thing that governs and dictates so much of our existence. If we're really and truly interested in truth, it is essential that we look at what belief really is, and how it stacks up to truth.

Webster defines belief as *"A state or habit of mind in which trust or confidence is placed in some person or thing. Belief is the mental act, condition or habit of placing trust or confidence in a person or thing, a mental acceptance or conviction in the truth or actuality of something; to believe is to accept with veracity."* I prefer to define belief as "unquestioned acceptance of something in the absence of reason; unquestioned acceptance of an alleged fact without positive knowledge or proof." We say, "I believe in God; I believe that people should be kind to animals and the elderly; I believe that blue is a more soothing color than green, and I believe that the Republicans have a better plan to revitalize the economy than the Democrats."

And? None of it really means anything, intrinsically anyway. But it does dictate our experience. The fact is, on this planet right now of almost seven billion people, there are literally millions upon millions of differing beliefs swirling around in people's heads. There's nothing inherently wrong with belief, but how easy do you think it is to find agreement among beliefs? How easy do you think it is to engender the kind of mutual respect for another, even when beliefs are diametrically opposed? When someone says to you, "We have polar opposite worldviews," what are they really saying to you? *Hey, I really like the way you think; let's get together real soon!* I highly doubt it. They're not trying to bond or connect with you, are they? They're not conveying a sense of respect or appreciation for *your* perspective, are they? In their mind, belief is enough to establish "truth" or knowing.

Identified with mind, it's no wonder this happens. However, truth isn't found *in* the mind, and truth certainly won't ever be realized by looking *with* the mind. It's certainly never found in the writings of any book – this one included – no matter how highly regarded that book is. Your perspective may come from seeing what's actually real and true, but they won't be able to see or understand that as long as they maintain belief is enough to establish what's true. If your perspective is truly one of realization that comes from the heart wisdom that already knows – and not from a belief that's manufactured and held onto in the mind, you won't be bothered one bit.

Why would you need to defend what you *know* is true? Those who believe do this; they defend their beliefs. They tend to argue back and forth (often in a very subtle way) trying to convince the other that their belief is the right one. Let's be honest: How can we be objective when we've got so much invested in our belief? We can't. And there are those who vehemently defend what they think they "know." It's a valid indicator that they're operating from belief. It's not a bad or wrong thing, but it's incumbent upon us to know when we really don't know. They say, "You just gotta believe!" No, actually I don't. In fact, if I don't know, I don't need to deceive myself and believe that I know. I don't need to create a belief in order to feel in control.

Nevertheless, beliefs can serve as a bridge, but ultimately the bridge must collapse, leaving you hanging on for dear life. Because the bridge wasn't constructed with the proper materials, it wasn't designed to support over time. If a belief gets created spontaneously, without my intent, I can see through it – and discard it. But first, in order to see through it, I need to notice what my experience is as a result of that belief. I can peacefully rest in not knowing – and in that allowance of not knowing, and only until then, the known can reveal itself. If everything you presently "know" and believe in your mind still hasn't revealed the pot of gold (whatever that is for you) at the end of the rainbow, then doesn't it follow that the unknown is where your "answer" lies?

Millions of people have been slaughtered in the name of God and religion, practiced from belief –

in wars, inquisitions, political uprisings, revolts, ethnic "cleansings" and the like. Unless our consciousness is significantly raised, we are destined to repeat the same behaviors. We pay the ultimate price for such ignorance, becoming more desensitized to the true value of human life. More importantly, we remain in the dark to our true identity. Despite most acting as if truth and belief is the same thing, they are not. In fact, they are very different. Even if a revered and highly respected person believes in something – even has his own national television or radio show with a large following, it makes no difference.

Being lulled into a false sense of security (because you share the same beliefs as a person of "authority" or large group of people, however distinguished) doesn't validate your belief. Your security is rooted in an illusory story – and not what's actual. If it doesn't agree with actual evidence, there's no validity in the real world. At one time, highly intelligent and respected men accepted as scientific FACT, that the world was flat, and the sun revolved around the earth. Belief and faith doesn't establish truth or fact, regardless of how many people believe, or for how long they've believed it. Why do we pretend they're the same? Fear usually – and the potential discomfort we'll feel when our beliefs are exposed as falsehoods.

Please don't misunderstand me. This isn't about bashing beliefs. I'm not suggesting beliefs are to be avoided by any stretch. Nor am I implying that you shouldn't have them, so please don't infer that, either. How silly I'd be to suggest resisting what gets formed within us, naturally and spontaneously. In many cases, beliefs are functional and even necessary. For instance, most of us believe that it's a really good idea not to drive 100 mph if we don't want to pay for a speeding ticket. Most of us believe that in order to be successful at anything in life, we must put in the time and effort needed to accomplish whatever it is that we want.

Most of us believe that staying clear of the edge of a cliff with a five hundred foot canyon drop below is good for our physical safety and survival. Most of us believe that eating healthy and exercising is very beneficial to our overall health and wellbeing. And yet, when it comes to the more meaningful and important aspects of our lives, like realizing truth, enjoying the relationship with our selves and others, we tend to rely on belief. We've been taught to. Belief certainly has the ability to soothe and comfort for a while, but ultimately, like a house of cards, it must collapse. Beliefs almost always fall short – because they must. If it's truth we are after, we don't have the luxury of belief.

With belief comes doubt; it's just the way it works. Belief and doubt reside on two sides of the same restless coin. Neither is the "bad guy," and neither is to be resisted. Seen through, yes, but never resisted. Wisdom sees that what we oppose, we only strengthen. Many beliefs are survival based – and good for us. Like I *believe* that if I go skiing down the expert level diamond trail on the slopes, I'm most likely going to wipe out; I might even get seriously injured or killed. If I'm standing under a large oak tree in a lightning storm, I believe that I better find safer shelter, and quick. But when it comes to the bigger issues that require introspection and contemplation, belief has little ultimate value.

Faced with anything, I either presently know, or I don't know. Since I don't need to engage in self-deception, I don't need to rely on belief. Since I am willing not to know, belief doesn't get created to serve as a go-between. Generally, beliefs don't unite. Beliefs are divisive when we insist that our beliefs represent truth, but yours don't. This divisiveness can cause bloodshed – lots of it. Have you noticed once you believe in something, you generally stop thinking about it? You stop examining whether that thing you believe in is actually true or not. And that's okay, unless it's a belief that determines the quality of your existence, or how you meet each moment.

The majority of us approach the big questions in life by constructing a set of ideas and beliefs in our minds – or taking on what others "of authority" tell us about those bigger issues. We end up depending on them to tell us how life really is, instead of relying on our actual and lived experience to tell us what's really so. As you may have noticed, these explanations often end up being about as useful as a table with three legs. They just don't hold up. Because of their inherent instability, they must topple over. They ultimately fail to provide us the security we seek, because they *can't ever* provide the security we seek. If we look to belief to provide us lasting security, we're looking in the wrong direction.

Instead of seeing that beliefs don't ultimately deliver what we seek, what do we typically do? We go shopping! We go shopping for, say, another table, but this time, one with four legs and a higher quality wood like mahogany. We reason that surely, four higher quality legs (a new and "better" belief) must be more stable than three legs! For a while, this new table supports us, and we even invite others to sit at our table and experience it for themselves. They may like our table until it, too, must topple over – sometimes with our guests at the table. It can get kind of messy sometimes!

So, this works for a time, and temporarily provides us a false sense of security and comfort, until it doesn't anymore. Invariably, at different stages in our lives, if we are conscious, many of us discover that when it comes to our human affairs, beliefs are inherently unstable by nature. We see that if we deal in the realm of belief, uncertainty must eventually follow. With belief comes insecurity. This is the nature of belief, like a scorpion's nature is to sting. We see this by the pain or discomfort we experience as a direct result of believing in a particular thing when it doesn't hold up. Some beliefs are very comforting, and can be for a long time. Thus, we get duped into thinking they can be relied upon permanently. Since everything is in a constant state of change and flow, beliefs can't ever capture what changes.

When we look closely, we notice that beliefs get spontaneously created in our minds, so we can make sense of the world around us. They get manufactured in our minds so we can navigate our way through life. *Most of the time, we don't consciously create a belief – and yet, we take ownership of it as if we did create it!* If we can see this very important point, we are less likely to identify with belief. Instead of identifying with belief – and then acting from it, we can simply notice it's there – and without judgment or resistance, choose not to act on it. If we're really willing to acknowledge what's actual, our awareness of it often disarms and dissolves it.

The truth is, without beliefs, most of us would feel vulnerable and insecure. There's nothing wrong or bad about this. However, when it comes to the bigger issues in life, beliefs are very limited and self-fulfilling. We see what we believe, and we believe what we see – and so our life goes. However, before beliefs are created, there is an opportunity to see what's real and actual. All we must do is just look and *see* for ourselves what's actual, instead of assuming our belief is adequate, or representative of what's actual. The false cannot stand up to close examination. It's not meant to. If the false cannot stand up to examination, why would we ever NOT examine our beliefs that ultimately determine our experience? Either indifference or false evidence appearing real – fear.

Children believe pretty much everything their parents tell them. Since most parents neglect to teach their children the difference between "bad behavior" and the goodness that they intrinsically *always* are, it's no wonder we have such problems with low self-esteem. Being reprimanded as often as they are, most children grow up believing they *are* their behavior. And so, there's a big difference between having our child believe that eating yellow snow is bad, or walking on thin ice isn't such a great idea, and having that same child believe he or she *is* their behavior. Thus, when he or she acts out, they *believe* they are a bad person.

Sure, it is wise to avoid eating yellow snow and walking on thin ice, but deeper wisdom sees the greater importance of teaching our children the significant difference between his or her behaviors, and who they are as humans. If we want our children to love themselves as they are – and become productive members of society, we're responsible to teach them this essential distinction.

As small children, we are encouraged to believe in things like the Easter Bunny, Santa Claus and the Tooth Fairy. Seemingly innocuous, this conditioning invariably sets the tone and creates the mold for the way the child sees life. Parents who teach their children to believe without questioning, ultimately programs that child to turn to belief as something to rely on – the kind of reliance that just accepts on faith, without any examination.

After all, you better not pout, you better not shout, you better not cry, I'm telling you why ... Santa Claus is coming to town. He sees you when you're sleeping, he knows when you're awake; he knows if *you've* been "bad" or "good," so be good for goodness sake! The fat guy in the red suit and the long white beard is watching YOU, so if you want him sliding down your chimney, *you* better behave. If not, you'll wake up Christmas morning to find coal in your stockings! Innocent and harmless, eh? By the way, don't forget to leave him cookies and milk.

We have very little recognition of just how much our minds play in fantasyland. We won't ever get this recognition from reading a book, or listening to what other "reputable" sources say about it. Actually, there is nothing to "get." You already possess that which you seek – if you would just see it. How can we *get* what we are? Before we grasp onto any concept that tries to explain things, see what's being seen in your direct experience, already. It has absolutely nothing to do with belief. As humans, we have a remarkable ability to make things up, and pretend as if they're so. Fantasy, driven by imagination, gives us the ability to enjoy pleasurable experiences; we could say it's a functional necessity in order for the mind to escape what is. Fantasies and imagination require no belief in them in order to enjoy them.

That's the whole point; no belief is needed for us to escape, create and play in our minds. But when we start to believe in our fantasies, or worse... have faith in them, we usually set ourselves up for disappointment, or worse, devastating results. The tragic events that unfolded on September 11, 2001 are, in fact, a direct manifestation of having complete faith in religious belief. Promise of a pleasant afterlife was the reward for those who murdered the infidels, those against the will of Allah. And many volunteered for the cause. Sadly, we aren't even aware we're just killing our Self.

Generally, beliefs don't lead to the real wisdom that transforms a life. How can something unquestioned and accepted on "faith," in the absence of positive knowledge and proof, accomplish this? How can it be the right tool for the job? It's like expecting your four year-old to safely drive you home after you've become too sick to drive. It's not going to happen. We read or hear about the limitations, dangers and monstrous atrocities perpetrated due to opposing beliefs. We're mostly aware that our belief system determines our experience, but for some reason, most of us go about our lives in the same habitual ways, never really stopping to question. Since the tragic stuff doesn't hit home for most of us (it's happening to "others") our personal beliefs usually don't register as something urgent we really need to challenge and re-examine. Our minds entertain and believe in a whole host and variety of things that have nothing to do with truth or reality. Nevertheless, we continue on with the same formula, somehow expecting a different or better result. And life passes by, decades at a time.

What about religion or faith? The word (or concept) "religion" stems from *religio,* which meant, "to bind back very strongly to truth." Interestingly, every religion known to man – and every religion created BY man, was designed to be based in truth, but in actuality, is practiced *from* belief. Thus, it is approached *from* and *by* belief. And yet if you ask most people, they will say that their religion is "true," and that the precepts or scripture they follow are based in truth. Thus, at the core of religion is the promise and opportunity to *see* and experience truth. It isn't about collecting a variety of notions and beliefs *about* truth.

Religion, in and of itself, is not the problem. The confusion immediately arises when we approach religion from belief. Religion is commonly thought to be about belief – and consequently, it's almost always practiced from belief. Its chief concern is actually with knowledge, with knowing. Like religion, science is about getting to the truth of the matter at hand. The word *science* derives from the Latin *scire*, "to know." Science is about knowing, and not about believing. Science goes to extraordinary lengths to test it's beliefs – or what it terms, "hypotheses."

If science cannot prove the validity of a particular hypothesis after comprehensive testing, it's either thrown out or reformulated and tested further. Additionally, conclusions then must be tested by various independent sources to prove its validity. It's a very precise, unbiased and agenda-free method for arriving at truth; it's a method where man's thinking is totally removed from the process. While science is commonly thought to be about real and actual knowledge – and prides itself on not being dependent on belief, it is inevitably very dependent on it. Like fish need water, science needs belief in order to survive.

In fact, without it, it can't function, nor could scientific principles be applied in the discovery of what's out what's scientifically factual. In order for science to function, scientists must dissect the world in order to examine it. It requires that we create and construct versions of the world we experience based upon concepts. And while concepts can never capture or comprehend reality, conceptual models are necessary to come to what's really so. Thus, belief lends itself more valuably to science – and is far more dependent upon it than religion ever is, or needs to be. Conversely, for religion to be of real value to us, it needn't require belief.

"In science it often happens that scientists say, 'You know, that's a really good argument; my position is mistaken,' and they would actually change their minds and you never hear that old view from them again. They really do it. It doesn't happen as often as it should, because scientists are human and change is sometimes painful. But it happens everyday. I cannot recall the last time something like that happened in politics or religion." **Carl Sagan**

However, for centuries, all religions continue to depend on belief – and as a result, people run in all sorts of different directions, insisting their beliefs are "true," while the others are grossly mistaken. All the while, truth non-judgmentally rests quietly, watching the grand delusion go on. Consequently, we see religions at war with each other, each insisting that the other is "wrong" and "immoral." Religion fights science, too. It will claim science's findings can't be true because it doesn't jive with its dogma, its conceptual model of reality.

When faced with – or holding in their hands the reality of dinosaur fossils, and fossils of prehistoric man over a 1.5 million years old (Turkana Boy), one who believes in creationism will either say the bones are fake, or the age of the bones is mistaken. If they *are* real, they must be less than ten thousand years old. French philosopher Frantz Fanon aptly said, *"Sometimes people hold a core belief that is very strong. When they are presented with evidence that works against that belief, the new evidence cannot be accepted. It would create a feeling that is extremely uncomfortable, called cognitive dissonance. And because it is so important to protect the core belief, they will rationalize, ignore and even deny anything that doesn't fit in with their core belief."*

When we rely on Holy Scripture, Sacred Books, Sutra or any other conceptual source or "authority," we are essentially telling ourselves that, in and of ourselves, we cannot or will not arrive at truth. In other words, we unconsciously conclude we don't have the innate capacity to *see* what's actual. We conclude that we need to rely on belief, and/or rely on what someone else said, believed or witnessed. It's all hearsay. In doing so, we give up responsibility to find out for ourselves. Hence, we approach truth or reality from belief – and *believe* it's the right tool for the job. We tell ourselves that we can never truly discern truth from falsehood, or that it's for the special or chosen few.

We reject the very notion that every day common folk like us possess this ability, and that it's reserved for the monks or enlightened found in the caves and monasteries. We may even conclude that the enlightened and free are simply operating from belief, too – and that they're just more convincing! What's most interesting is that those who say this rarely ever do the inner work themselves. Those who say this rarely investigate and question all of it before jumping to hasty, unfounded conclusions rooted in belief.

If religion is fundamentally concerned with direct knowledge of truth, those who practice religion must see that belief isn't the thing that will assist them arriving at truth. We need to see that in order to really wake up to who we really are – and arrive at the truth – *and let wisdom bloom* – we must go beyond the mental constructs of belief, to the heart wisdom that already knows. That is, we need to arrive at where we already are, the space that is prior to mental creations – the awareness that encompasses all mental constructions – the awareness that radiates from the heart. Only when we stop leaving will we arrive.

All that's simply needed is to *see* what's already being seen. This may sound abstract, like a mystery wrapped within a riddle, but it's anything but. It's right here, in plain view. We just don't see it. Science can't actually reveal to us the real nature of ultimate truth. Instead, this is the ultimate role and responsibility of religion. Religion doesn't have in its operating manual ways to test and validate hypothesis, nor should it. It doesn't need, nor should it make use of, hypothesis and belief of any kind.

Provided that religion doesn't rely heavily on belief in order to arrive at truth, religion can be of real value.

Those who continue to identify with the mind's natural tendency to grasp onto something are much more inclined to say, "Yes, that's it – that's the truth and I believe it!" They don't yet *see* that truth isn't something we *can* grasp onto or believe in. In fact, ultimate reality or truth, being beyond belief or anything the mind can conceptually construct, isn't something that *can* be approached with belief or concepts. Although we try in vain, we literally cannot conceptually arrive at truth in any way, shape or form. We interpret those times, when our beliefs bring about an energetic feeling of truth in the body to *be* the real thing.

We conclude that since our belief *feels* true, then it must *be* true. Until we cannot see or sense any other way, we will continue to cling to our beliefs *about* reality, never realizing that they're simply fabrications that function as alleviating go-betweens. In our need to make sense of the world, we will cling to our conceptual models about reality, and therefore, never experience reality immediately and directly. Our need to control and feel comforted by our concepts will continue to overshadow our willingness to not know.

The paradoxical irony is that, it is only in our complete and absolute willingness NOT to know, can truth reveal itself as that which never left us in the first place. At some point, we must get in touch with our most fundamental impulse, the impulse to be free – free from our minds and free from our emotions. We just want to be okay with whatever arises. If the mind races and our emotions go on a rollercoaster ride, we want to be okay with that. The thing to *see* is, that whenever we ARE absolutely okay with the contents of our minds – and if we are absolutely okay with whatever emotions arise, both the mind and emotions settle down. Don't believe me; check it out for yourself. Resist the temptation to draw a conclusion that says you'd be in resignation mode, or that if you don't resist, you'll get more what you don't want. Neither is true.

This impulse to be free is expressed so beautifully in the numerous religions throughout the world. This impulse points to the open, innocent and pure heart and mind that embraces all, without any distinction or preference. It is a lover of what is – not a lover of what could or should be. Your true nature loves without condition or preference; it is a lover with eternal loyalty. Whenever we're able to retreat from the busyness of life and quiet our minds, we get an immediate and direct sense of this reality that we already are.

Unfortunately, in our fascination with the countless objects in our field of perception vying for our attention, our minds are rarely quiet. As a result, most aren't in touch with this inner impulse to be free. The truth is, that if this impulse were really looked into, it would liberate us. This impulse requires us to look within, to take our habitual focus off objects "out there" – and look at how things really are, not how we think or wish them to be. We often read these pointers, but we often gloss over them without investigating them. Belief in separation is the original sin – and every problem we have stems from this misunderstanding.

Adam believed he was separate from that which he sought – and this misperception has trickled down throughout the ages. We still believe we are separate from the truth – that there's truth, god, reality *and* us. This is the crux of our problem. The chief aim of spirituality – and religion for that matter, is to settle down, return home and realize that separation is a complete and utter illusion. *Be Still and Know* – and realize that separation doesn't exist. In fact, unity, not separation, *is* the fundamental essence of the nature of all things seen and unseen. Oneness is the ground of being that everything springs from. As the Ninth-century Chinese Zen teacher Huang Po said, *"The foolish reject what they see, not what they think; the wise reject what they think, not what they see."*

When we get "suckered in" by the mind and its beliefs, we face the direction that typically hurts; we remain confused and unsure. Since we've been taught since birth to believe what we think, this is a very natural thing that happens. How can it not be? Not only do we believe what we think, we take it a step further and conclude we *are what we think;* we let the dominoes fall! Sure, we can believe good and empowering things about ourselves, but what happens if we stop believing those things? What then? If beliefs change, as they often do, aren't we basing our security on something that comes and goes? What happens when others refute what we believe about ourselves? What happens when life and circumstance display something completely different than our beliefs about them?

Modifying or strengthening our beliefs is a band-aid approach. Questioning their validity is a rooting out approach. Fortunately, we are wired in such a way that illusion doesn't feel so good. If we weren't, we'd probably never wake up to what we are, and see beyond the limitations of belief to what's true. Fortunately, we are wired with the capacity to realize what's true, too. Are YOU your beliefs, or do you have beliefs? If you can notice the beliefs your mind entertains and clings to, how could you actually *be* those beliefs? If you can notice the actual formation of a particular belief, wouldn't YOU have to be fundamentally prior to that formation?

You sure would. If you keep looking, this alone could be the pointer that leads to awakening. Seriously. And it's not the mind that notices. Wisdom sees that we are not our beliefs. It knows

When Wisdom Blooms

that instead, we have beliefs. Wisdom sees that when we aren't feeling quite right, we must not be in harmony with life and the laws or principles of our own experience. As long as we're breathing, we continue to receive clues and indicators all the time. Wisdom blooms when we rest in the awareness that is prior to the formation of, and subsequent belief in, our beliefs. *Any time we aren't feeling quite right, we can be sure it is an indicator that we aren't in harmony with what's actual and true.*

Any time we aren't feeling quite right, we know we hopped on the train of thought and belief and went for a ride. Isn't this feedback fortunate? As I stated in my first book, "Born To Be Happy – How to Uncover Your Natural State of Happiness," the only time we ever really suffer is when we believe whatever is actually occurring, shouldn't be occurring. Since minds don't deal in simplicity, it overlooks this simple and transcending truth. Yes, that supercomputer you possess has real difficulty in simplicity. Pretty ironic, wouldn't you say? When we resist what is actually happening in any moment, we believe that something else "should" be happening. Is this ever true? No, it isn't. But since we believe it, we must suffer.

So what do we do when our conceptual models of reality don't ultimately support us? What can we do with the resulting confusion that must inevitably arise from belief? If we can't look to our beliefs to make sense of our world and comfort us long term, where do we turn to provide us that comfort and security? Instead of depending on our mental constructs (that have no substance or reality because they're literally made up and sustained by our minds) we can look in a different direction.

This "direction" is our actual experience in the moment, prior to belief, and prior to concepts. And that is to just *see* what's happening without labeling it. We must confirm in our own experience what's real and true, without relying on an outside source. Before we label something as "good" or "bad" or "right" or "wrong," we can just be with what is, with equanimity and neutrality – without any preference or bias. Wisdom sees that, in some instances, beliefs can appropriately serve as a temporary bridge to carry us across to the other side, the side of stability and clarity.

Like surrender, *seeing* takes no effort at all. If you think it takes a lot of effort and struggle, think again. Fear (false evidence appearing real) is typically the main obstacle. But when you see this "energy of emotion" is simply a result of erroneous thinking, temporary fear won't stop you. It's just a reminder we're not in harmony, that's all. Why make it any bigger than it is? We must be willing not to have it our way, and not to have it conform to how we think it *should* be, which is just more belief. Most of us *believe* that not knowing isn't a good thing, and something to be avoided altogether, because it must bring insecurity and vulnerability.

This is just another unquestioned belief assumed to be true. We habitually stop short of asking, "Is this really true?" When we stop short of asking whether something is true or not, obviously we aren't going to investigate our experience to confirm whether it's true or not! Why do we insist on relying on belief when we're capable of finding out what is actually so in our direct experience? If we can't discover what is actual, why must we create a belief? What's it like not to know? Isn't it spacious and peaceful when the mind doesn't get involved? Check it out.

If we want to live from our natural state of wisdom – and if we want to be in harmony with life in an intimate and transforming way, we recognize that two of our best friends are vigilance and discernment. We must recognize and discern what beliefs bring us pain, and be vigilant when they operate in our experience. Examining our beliefs is essential if we seek greater wisdom and happiness. The reality is, each and every belief held can be directly refuted by countless others. Doesn't this speak to the validity of belief? Truth is eternal and changeless – and can't ever be successfully refuted, no matter how eloquent or seemingly logical the argument.

In a moment of real clarity, we can see that, instead of placing our faith in our beliefs, opinions, past conditioning and anything else that comes from our minds, we can place our trust in our direct experience. That is, our actual experience prior to any concepts, thoughts about, judgments, resistances, desires, expectations and preferences. We place our trust in our being that already meets the moment as it is, and not as our minds want or prefer it to be. And we notice our experience.

Only when we are willing to drop all of our notions, assumptions and opinions about what we think we know in any moment, do we give ourselves the opportunity to really *see what's actual versus what's illusory*. If it's already happening, it can't be any other way. This one thing realized can change the entire world. The mind will try to convince us, that indeed, something *else* should or could be happening. And since most are identified with the mind, it's natural most believe the dictates of the mind! As the mind goes, we go.

In its infinite wisdom, it will tell us that something else can, should or could be happening – you know, because it "knows" best. But, it's *never* true. If it's already happening, why don't we see that it can't be any other way than it is? Why do we have such trouble seeing that this is the crux of our suffering? *Never* in any moment of anyone's existence has anything happened that shouldn't have happened. I realize some will have a huge problem with this statement, but nonetheless, it's true. The fact that your mind may believe otherwise changes nothing. *See* this and be free.

Once the barriers of ignorance are identified and seen through – and you refrain from replacing them with "new and improved beliefs," or buying into new ones that get spontaneously created, you find yourself living in the flow of life. Wholly unconcerned, yet intimately engaged, something of a higher order guides your activities. Fear and doubt leave your system, and you move when life moves you to move. And it's never conceptual; it's always experiential. That's when you know. And when you don't know, you look until you *see*. And if you still don't see, you rest in the knowing that, apparently, you aren't yet meant to see. You'll *see* when you *see*.

Doubts may come and go. But your own natural self, the one for whom the doubts appear is present and clear, and not subject to any of the doubts. That fact of being, which is the ground of the doubts, is the doubt-free reality. The awareness of doubt isn't in doubt at all. *Seeing* this, you effortlessly exit from of any possible doubts raised by the mind – because you *see* what's true. The mind may continue to have its doubts, but your being is present, beyond any and all doubt. Freedom is beyond belief. Do you need a belief to BE what you are? Know this by confirming it for yourself. When you truly allow yourself not to know, and when you let your actual experience blossom, wisdom blooms.

Chapter 2
Dead On Arrival

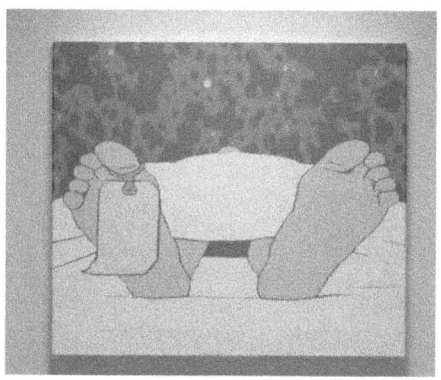

"Surely the memory of an event cannot pass for the event itself. Nor can the anticipation. There is something exceptional, unique, about the present event, which the previous, or the coming, do not have. There is a livingness about it – an actuality; it stands out as the illumined. There is the 'stamp of reality' on the actual, which the past and future do not have."

~ **Nisargadatta Maharaj**

No doubt you're well aware that human beings are wired to gain pleasure and avoid pain. More intimately, being human, you experience this tendency almost all the time, don't you? Just because we are hooked up this way doesn't mean that we have to live from this inclination, does it? In other words, must we live out our lives this way, especially *if we see* that avoidance for what we don't want and grasping after what we do want is a consistent recipe for experiencing the constant ups and downs of life? Fortunately, we sure don't.

Instead, we can welcome what comes our way, knowing that everything is in flux and that nothing remains – and see where that leads us. We always have the option to go back to our old way of being, right? You don't have to be highly intelligent (I'm not) and you certainly don't have to be special. None of us are – sorry to break it to you! You do, however, have to possess the earnest desire to be willing to look and see for yourself how your experience has a strong tendency to be pleasant when things go right and unpleasant when they don't.

In order to transcend this human mind's impulse to "avoid and grasp", we must look at what might happen if we simply welcome whatever shows up in our experience. While we don't have to be the sharpest tools in the shed, we do, however, have to be very observant – and without any agenda, willing to see what's actual. As long as our focus is on avoiding pain and gaining pleasure, we will always be subject to suffering at some point. By resisting what is (and placing our energy towards avoiding pain and gaining pleasure) we invite pain and potential suffering, only every time. It is consistent, reliable and predictable.

In the human experience, have you noticed that pain is inevitable and suffering is optional and unnecessary? When I first heard this many years ago, I got real curious and I had to know how and why this was so. Hearing that suffering was optional really intrigued me. I later discovered that *being human, we will never be free from pain, but there is a way to be free from suffering.* Those who don't feel any pain in this life aren't really engaged and fully present to their actual experience.

Enlightenment or liberation doesn't mean one is free from pain. It doesn't mean that we rest in bliss all the time, living beyond what the "unenlightened" experience. This is a myth that abounds in many spiritual circles, and isn't very useful. Enlightenment simply means to see things as they are, prior to thought or belief. If anything, even the most enlightened among us experience pain in some form or another, whether it's from the loss of a loved one or something else.

The difference is that those who are awake and free know that pain is part of the package of being human, so no resistance is offered to what arises; they allow pain to pass through as it's literally just the next experience consciousness is having.

Now granted, *seeing* this, so much untruth drops away, never to clamor for our attention anymore. Allowing any moment to be as it is makes for an even richer experience for the one who doesn't reject. It is *this* allowing that keeps suffering away, because the awakened know that resistance *to* pain is what causes suffering. Awake and free beings don't work against themselves. They know that whenever they are willing to have *any* experience, they are truly conscious, and therefore, free from suffering.

The nice thing is, when you really see how your experience unfolds, this allowing and welcoming begins to happen spontaneously and naturally. You don't have to consciously decide to welcome and allow. When you discern truth from falsehood, you find yourself living more spontaneously and non-judgmentally. There is an energetic movement that just happens on its own, without any conscious choice involved – *because* you finally saw what's true.

Old habit patterns that once hurt and divide are dissolved. Simply put, whenever we are willing to have *any* experience we are conscious, and therefore, free from suffering. Suffering happens when we unconsciously resist what's actually happening. What's happening is called reality.

When Wisdom Blooms

What you think or believe about reality is just that – just what you think or believe about it. Do our labels, judgments and definitions about reality *change* reality, or does it change our perception, and therefore, experience *of* reality? We can't change reality for reality never changes; we can only change our perception of it. What does change is everything that comes and goes in reality, like our thoughts, feelings, experiences, etc. Being in alignment with reality enables us to live in harmony with it. Consequently, we don't suffer because we're no longer in opposition to it. This simple truth escapes most of us, when in fact, it's right here, unhidden and in plain view for us to *see*.

When we believe that any experience we are presently happening shouldn't be happening, we invite and create more friction – and we actually hold in place what we *don't* want. We somehow go unconscious and allow ourselves to be deluded in thinking resistance is a good strategy to get what we really want.

Alternatively, when we know that any experience we are having is the only way it can be happening in *that* moment, we consciously allow for another possibility to arise in the next moment. If we really desire to have a different reality than the one we are presently having, we give up the battle. We no longer feed what we don't want with wishing it were different than it is. In this way, we just removed any energy that would continue to feed it and give it life. When there's no energy that goes into it, it can't continue to survive.

In this way, we don't unconsciously torment and confuse ourselves because the negative energy that feeds what we don't want isn't present anymore. Aside from a masochist, who would consciously choose to self-torment? Any experience we are having is *never* the problem. It is what we tell ourselves *about* the experience we are having that's the problem. Roman slave and Philosopher, Epictetus, conveyed this a few thousand years ago. Having a negative, pushing-away orientation towards any experience we are having must become divisive and painful. It is the secondary interpretation, an overlay we place upon what's happening that disturbs us, and not the actual event or happening.

Look and see if this is true for you – and don't believe a word you read here. Literally everything is energy with a distinct vibration to it – and inherent in every thought, belief, word spoken and action taken has a vibration. That distinct and corollary vibration determines our state of being, and how much ease or strife we experience. Every intention we have, and every intention that we evoke, carries with it a certain vibration that either leads to an expansion or contraction of our being. Our bodies are indeed sensing instruments of the divine, feeling and expressing directly from the level of consciousness it sprang from.

Wisdom sees we are wise to live from this realization and notice *what* are bodies are telling us. Wisdom blooms when we actually live in accord with that feedback. When we meet what is actually occurring with neutrality, acceptance, and even *gratitude*, we work with ourselves, not against ourselves. Gratitude arises when we see the truth of opposites. Once we REALLY SEE that we literally cannot experience joy, unless pain is also a potential experience, we have a much less tendency to react with resistance. After all, we all prefer less pain and more happiness, don't we? While I don't resist negative or unpleasant experiences, like most humans, I prefer pleasant ones – but I'm okay with unpleasant ones.

We see that joy and pain are two sides of the same coin; these opposite experiences are a functional necessity. Without them, we couldn't experience *anything*. In my book, *"The Dance of Imperfection – Living in Perfect Harmony with Life,"* I go into this in much more detail. When we see that to resist what's *already* happening only binds us to what we *don't* want, we untie ourselves from the bondage we never wanted in the first place. No longer are we shackled, because we know how it works in our experience. As the saying goes, what we resist persists, and what we focus on expands and grows stronger.

Argue with reality and suffer every time. We stop the battle and just intend for something else, while being okay with what's already arising in our experience. It's a recipe we can count on to deliver the ease of being desired. We have a wide variety of notions and beliefs about what freedom and truth is. We seldom *see* that it is these notions and beliefs that further distort and muddy our freedom, and in fact, keep us confused and contracted. What we say, think and believe about freedom can never lead us to freedom itself, because Truth and Reality can never be approached through these means. Reality and freedom can never be what we *think* it is. Reality and Freedom can never be what we believe, say or read that it is; it's always prior, underneath and all encompassing.

When we insist on our ideas and beliefs as being accurate representations for what is true and real, we only create more bondage for ourselves. It is well worth repeating because this truth is so powerful, liberating and transformational: the word or concept, being a descriptor and a symbol, is never the actual. Babies have no idea what words mean when they come out of the womb. We all know it takes years to learn the various labels for existence, and then to put them together into a storyline. Words have no intrinsic meaning. Words and concepts, being inherently limited, can only point to Truth or Freedom.

As it says in The Tao, *"The Tao that can be spoken is not the eternal Tao"* and *"The name than can be named is not the eternal name."* It can only be pointed to with language made of concepts – and language, being finite descriptions "about" things is inherently limiting and dualistic. Truth, being infinite, is ONE – and has only ever been ONE. It's not an object, despite our repeated attempts to make it one. And since it encompasses and precedes ALL (including your mind) it can never be adequately described or understood with the mind.

And yet, we actually think and believe we can accurately describe the Infinite Source of Everything, God or whatever you like to call it. It is beyond name and form. It makes perfect sense that there is a direct relationship between being more conscious and experiencing less inner division and suffering. We just can't feel good if we are divided inside. Inner division is painful, mostly because it's source is illusion. Naturally, the less conscious we are, the more we are divided; the more divided we are, the more we suffer. Rising above our conditioning (while including it) is needed if we want to express and enjoy are authentic selves.

Aren't we really here to enjoy and express who we really are? I sure am. If we want to transcend the collective consciousness that mostly deals in belief and separation – and the consequential perception of scarcity, competition and fear, we must see through illusion to what's true. If we want to transcend the inevitable experience of fleeting happiness that stems from making our happiness dependent on outside factors, we need to see through unreality to reality. Therefore, we are called to *transcend and include*, not transcend and resist. In fact, we can only transcend *when* we include all of it.

If it's more joy and freedom we want, we don't really have the luxury to say, "I want this experience all day, but I be damned if I have time for that crappy experience!" Instead, we must include all of it, the pleasurable and the un-pleasurable – but only if we want to truly enjoy our lives in way that's rooted in truth and reality. What we don't understand, we usually dismiss as pure folly, don't we? Isn't that human nature? So, if that is your reaction to the following statement, I invite you to reconsider. *What is happening in any moment is exactly what should be happening; what is happening in any moment is meant to be happening.*

The truth is, any other conclusion that we come to is insane. Why? First of all, can you prove that your assessment is absolutely true, that whatever is happening shouldn't actually be happening? In other words, can you prove that something else should or could be happening? If you're annoyed, just notice and welcome that, too. It is all appropriate and okay. Isn't it insane to resist reality, or what is? Secondly, check out your experience when you want your present experience to be other than it actually is. It never feels quite right, does it? In fact, it can be very painful.

It's simple, yet despite our actual experience of contraction and dis-ease felt in the body (that results from believing anything can be different than it is in *that* moment) we make it complex by believing what our minds tell us. We say that whatever is happening shouldn't be happening – and that something else *could* or *should* be happening. In and through every breath you've ever taken, in and through each heartbeat, and during each and every moment of your existence, no matter what you've gone through, it's never been true.

For anything to be true, it must be 100% true, not 99% true. If it's 99.9% true, it isn't true. We call things "true" that don't even come close to true, and we often call things that are mostly true, true. Sure, things can be relatively true, but not ultimately (or absolutely) true. But let's call a spade a spade, okay? If it isn't 100% true all the time, it isn't really true. It never was true, and it never will be true. Granted, there are thoughts and beliefs that are truer than others, more serving and beneficial than others, but no thoughts and beliefs are ultimately true. We just believe they are. The thought is never the actual – it just serves as a pointer to the actual.

What is true doesn't come and go, either. It must be present all the time in order for it to be true. Beliefs, opinions, judgments and assumptions change all the time, and therefore, come and go. We make them up as we go along, changing or altering them to suit our needs. There's nothing wrong with this, unless we become so invested in them, insisting that they're true. Can you claim without any doubt whatsoever, that in any given moment, something else should or could be happening? Can that be true – can that ever be true? No, it can't ever be true. *Any thought that is contrary and in resistance to what is actually occurring in any moment is false and DOA, dead on arrival.*

Anything we bring from the past is a dead thing that we give life to. Past, being memory only, is a dead thing. The only living reality is right here and right now, this present moment. Because our attention is life giving and supportive, what we give our attention and belief to, lives on and shapes our experience. When we cling to a belief, judgment or opinion that insists it can be different than it is, we essentially give a dead thing (illusion and lies) life. Literally, we put on "life support" that which is dead and unreal to begin with, and bring it into this moment. We prop it up as real – like the dead guy from the movie, "Weekend at Bernie's!"

When Wisdom Blooms

We resurrect what was already dead, and since it can work for a while (we can fool others like they did in the movie and carry around our propped up, dead illusion) we get tricked into believing it's a solid and lasting formula. Then, we live *from that lie believed in* – and illusion and confusion ensues. Consequently, we can never feel and experience the true contentment that we really desire because our foundation is built on sand, not rock. It's constructed on illusion, and therefore, it won't ever hold up. Wisdom sees that self-deception is painful, while truth telling ultimately isn't.

Since we aren't doing any of this intentionally, compassion knows everything is okay the way it is. The more we see this, the less it will occur in our experience. Therefore, beating ourselves up is the last thing we need to add to the situation. Compassion sees that yes, we constantly dupe ourselves into thinking a thing shouldn't be happening, because quite frankly, we don't want it to be happening! We sure don't mind something is happening if we *want* it to be happening, do we? That may sound very silly, and even painfully obvious. But what's sillier is to resist what's already happening. What's most silly is thinking what's already happening shouldn't be happening!

Wisdom sees how silly this *all* is (some call it the Cosmic Joke) and then compassion steps in, knowing it's just human nature doing it's thing, until it doesn't anymore. When we impartially see this entire cycle being played, we notice its momentum come to a halt. It's like our car coming to a halt because it just ran out of gas. Bringing a certain amount of levity to the situation can act as a dissolving agent, too. Laughter doesn't bind; it disperses and frees. When we look to our minds (and not our direct experience) to tell us what's true and real, we invite more suffering. In fact, absolutely every experience that you've ever had in your entire life could not have gone down any different than it did! See this and be free.

I was both shocked and relieved when I saw the truth of this in my own experience, and not what my mind told me. Seeing the truth of this goes beyond belief, and must be beyond belief. How many times have we come across this kind of statement, shrugging it off without really testing it out? I invite you to see how this is true in your own experience, too. If you do, your life will never be same. That's a promise. Like we said in the first chapter, the aim isn't to rid ourselves of beliefs, opinions and assumptions. That would be ridiculous because many beliefs are a functional necessity.

This isn't a book about bashing beliefs. If you believe it's not a good idea to walk across a congested highway of cars traveling over 65mph, would that be beneficial to your health? Of course it would, as you may be struck and die. But, I am "assuming" that since you are reading this book called, *"When Wisdom Blooms ... Awaken The Sage Within"*, you know this, and are interested in living more from what you know and realize is true – and not what you "believe" is true! Is this a safe assumption? Besides, this isn't so much about the obvious, physical survival stuff, like it's wise to believe swimming in shark-infested waters is bad for you.

"Getting rid" of beliefs, ideas, assumptions and opinions isn't really necessary, nor is it our aim. There is a much more efficient way that takes much less effort, and the effects are long term. Being one who prefers the path of least resistance, this got my full and undivided attention: Just see through these illusory concepts and notions as untruth, and they drop away by themselves. When we really *see* their unreality, they leave our system, usually for good.

Rarely, if ever, are we duped anymore. When we see that the sky really isn't blue, but only appears blue, our belief in a blue sky as actual drops away – yet we can fully appreciate and enjoy the soothing appearance of it being blue. When we see an old, limiting story we've carried around for so long isn't true, it drops away. We don't have to get rid of it; all that's really required is to see through our erroneous belief; it dissolves *in and through* that seeing. To see it as untrue is to let go. It's passive in that we don't need to "do" anything, yet it's effectively powerful.

Now, I am well aware that right now, your mind may be telling you a whole different story about this, so I hope you aren't throwing out the baby with the bathwater. If this is so, please consider suspending your judgment and read on as I will attempt to make this more clear shortly. We've been conditioned to typically think that (if we don't resist an unpleasant, unwanted experience) we won't get what we *do* want, right? "What, just lay down and take it? I'll get more of it then, wont' I?" After all, doesn't this conclusion seem, and even feel, logical?

Besides, haven't we experienced many achievements in the past with this attitude, that when we resist something, we drive it out of our experience? While it may appear this way on the surface, on closer examination, our unconscious strategy doesn't work long term. Further, we think that to allow what is to be as it is, we'd essentially be living in a state of resignation, passively allowing what we *don't* want to be in our experience? We conclude that, like the majority, we must "fight" for what we want – and do whatever it takes if we really want to attain a specific goal, thing or state of being!

Our minds will erroneously conclude that if we don't resist a thing, that it will continue on in our experience. It's as if we feel that our resistance is the fire extinguisher that puts out the fire. In actuality, our resistance is fuel that adds to the fire. We equate an attitude of passively allowing with being a doormat for all to walk on, inviting more unwanted and undesired experiences to come our way. I thought, believed and acted from this perspective for many years. It was only until I considered the possibility that maybe my strategy was counter-productive.

It was only until this strong doubt seeped in, that I saw my approach worked *against* the law of my experience. I saw that when I allowed what was happening *to* happen, as I intended for something else to happen, change occurred. I noticed what I didn't want left my experience rather quickly when I no longer resisted it. It's like I starved it. When I saw that believing the thoughts in my head wasn't the best formula (for peace and happiness) I made room for an altogether different possibility to arise in my experience. Pretty simple, yet it took me a long time to *see* this.

Despite the feedback I was constantly getting from these sensations in my body, my main pre-occupation was with my mind being in resistance to what arose as a useful an effective strategy. Until that realization, I was unconsciously creating more of what I didn't really want. And it was repetitive and unconscious, day in and day out. I noticed that when I became conscious, and allowed any experience to be just the way it was – whether painful or pleasurable, it never owned me; it never stuck around to torment me. I also noticed its life span was very short. Recognizing resistance to anything had to be present for suffering to arise, I stopped resisting!

When I dropped my agenda on insisting that any particular experience conform to how I wanted it to be, a delightful thing happened. Peace and contentment arose – and it stayed. Despite what my mind told me in the past (in regards to allowing and acceptance) this new orientation led to a much more peaceful existence, one that was real and not manufactured from my mind; it began to happen all on its own. Seeing what was real led to new patterns of energy to spontaneously move in ways more in alignment with life.

My experience confirmed this; it was self-authenticating – and things were never the same after that seeing. Fortunately, you can't un-see what you've seen. And once you really see, that seeing *is often* the letting go. So, you don't actively "do" surrender. It happens on its own when you *see* (with your conscious awareness) what's true. Letting go happens when we see that what we cling to must bind us. It's as if we are rewarded for seeing what was never true in the first place. When all else goes, truth remains. Truth always remains because truth, being right where you are, never comes and goes. It never left us, as it never arrived.

In fact, whatever comes and goes isn't real to begin with. Reality doesn't come and go. Thoughts, beliefs, opinions, feelings and experiences come and go in the ever-present reality. And since they all come and go, they can't be what you are. Instead of pumping life into a dead thing (a thought of resistance or assertion that something other should or could be happening) by giving it my attention and belief, I would let it die as soon as it arose.

"Let the dead bury the dead" took on a whole new meaning for me. I finally saw its real meaning. It is palpable, too. I could feel a visceral, but startling difference in my experience. I saw that life begets more life, and awareness surely begets more awareness. Contraction previously felt in the body was replaced by an open spaciousness of allowing that felt inclusive and freeing. The more I was consciously aware, and the more I wanted to see, the more freedom and joy I experienced. The more I consciously saw this, the more it was noticed in the next moment.

The more it was noticed, the more it took on a life of its own, without my intention for it to do so. It was like a snowball rolling down a hill, getting bigger and bigger, until at last, you had a solid foundation to make a big snowman. After being tired of being on the carousel of life, spinning around and never getting the ring, I became willing to see what was true. No matter the cost, it didn't matter. I was tired of the suffering and I wanted out. Regardless of what

I thought or feared I'd be giving up (and there was a lot of stuff that came up) I kept looking.

I somehow finally got to the point where I no longer cared about what I "thought" I'd lose; I wanted truth more. *I was done with bringing back the dead, giving life to the dead.* Subsequently, it was much easier to notice when a dead thing arose in my experience, as if it was saying from the grave, "Hey, buddy, give me life with your attention, will ya? Help me out of this hole." Noticing what was vying for my attention, and noticing how differently my life unfolded became enjoyable. When we're sick and tired of being sick and tired, something else moves in and takes over, but only when we've exhausted ourselves, surrendering to our situation.

When we stop dancing with the dead, we notice the dead don't bother us nearly as much. They begin to see that dance partners are few and far between – and we let them rest in peace. Incidentally, this is one of the ways in which grace works. Grace steps in only when we let it step in. It never forces its way in; it waits for us to open the door and invite it in. It waits for us to let go. As Jesus said, *"It is God and not I that doeth the work."* To surrender is to win, not to lose. On the rare occasion that I do get duped now, it is seen rather quickly and discarded, usually before pain arises.

When Wisdom Blooms

Instead of going to battle with what we don't want, wisdom sees that any time we oppose life we lose. When we stop insisting that our ideas and opinions are actually true, we make room for new possibilities to arise, possibilities more in harmony with our actual experience. In order to sit in a new recliner, we need to discard the old, worn one. We do this by *seeing* the old one no longer serves us. Clearing out the old, we make room for the new.

Fortunately for us, we don't have to continue living out our lives in ways that don't ultimately work for us. Being a conscious and aware species, with the ability to learn and adapt, we can see the error in our ways and choose different in the next moment. The real and original meaning of the word *sin* is to "miss the mark," and not meant to seek control by evoking guilt or shame through the more popular interpretation that has held so many down for centuries.

As long as we sincerely want to be free – and are willing to look until we discover truth more than our fear of losing things we imagine we'll lose, we don't have to miss the mark any longer. With this orientation, we will be a finder, not a seeker. The neat part is that with this conscious orientation of a sincere looking with the intent on finding what's true, we can't help but notice when dead and untrue things present themselves to us, clamoring for our attention.

None of it is a problem unless we believe it is. When we don't say and believe that it's a problem, we watch it pass through, like a fast-moving summer thunderstorm in the middle of July. And what's revealed is the shining sun, the shining sun that was always present, but temporarily obscured. As the Buddha said, *"Three things cannot be long hidden: The sun, the moon, and the truth.*

Chapter 3
Return To Sender

"As one lamp serves to dispel a thousand years of darkness, so one flash of wisdom destroys ten thousand years of ignorance."

~ Hui-Neng

Elephants are truly remarkable and beautiful animals – as are all of God's creations. They possess amazing intelligence, and an uncanny ability to remember. In fact, their memory is so good that it can be very difficult for them to decipher the difference between what's actually taking place, and what isn't. About a year ago, I saw a video clip online of the CEO of Go-Daddy killing a defenseless elephant in Africa, and being very proud of his accomplishment. As I watched in horror, the gunshots dropped the elephant. It made me really sad and angry, especially the way in which the villagers celebrated the death of the magnificent creature.

While I realize that it is much more acceptable in that culture – and what I deemed unacceptable was acceptable to them, I told myself I'd never do business with Go-Daddy again. He got a lot of expected backlash for this and incidentally, sold the company for a huge profit not too long after the uproar. Why does anyone reward these people? Apparently, we don't have to look too far to find those who don't really care about the peripheral stuff; "collateral damage" is acceptable as long as profit is involved, especially large profit. To some, I realize that I am being out of line here with my view, but such is life. Belief in scarcity has driven man to commit many atrocities.

As long as the "overriding outcome outweighs the means," questionable and self-serving behavior often becomes much easier to justify. But let's be honest, there are those who just don't need to justify or rationalize the means, and there's not a whole lot we can do about it. Ignorance is a powerful influencer, and the direct cause for so much bloodshed, is it not? You may be aware that when elephants are being trained by a circus, the trainer controls the massive creature by having a leg shackled with an iron or steel chain. After many months of being trained this way, the elephant not only becomes proficient in the tricks and activities that it's been taught to perform, but comes to believe it's always shackled, even when the shackles are removed.

Once it has been established that the elephant feels it can't get away, the trainer is reasonably confident it will stay put. Instead of going on a rampage or just leaving, the elephant doesn't go anywhere, because it still thinks it's shackled – or at the least believes it's still under the control and influence of the trainer. In other words, *it can't tell the difference between what once was, and what now is.* The elephant still believes it's bound, when in reality it is free to roam as it pleases. The trainer knows just how good the elephant's memory is, and uses it against the elephant, in order to control the elephant.

Enter human beings. Don't we have a very similar problem to that of the elephant? Don't we have an issue with distinguishing the real from the unreal, from truth and falsehood? Don't we allow our memory of the "past" to dictate how we perceive and act in the present? Don't we also possess the key to our freedom, while at the same time feeling imprisoned and shackled? Yes, we most certainly do.

In fact, if we aren't awake to what's real and true, we live our lives from the filter of the past –

which is literally from memory. We keep the past, a dead thing, alive with memory. The truth is, the past does not exist in reality except as memory only. What past is there unless you think about it? Is there one? No, there isn't. Before reading on, *see* this now. If we really look for ourselves, we see that there really isn't a past, unless we think about it.

Since birth, it has been constantly drilled into us that there is a past and a future. Neither has any reality except in our minds. Since the vast majority of us believe the thoughts in our heads, we feel guilt and shame about our past – and fear and anticipate an imagined future. This is the inevitable byproduct of identification with our minds. To be awake and free means to see and realize that *this* moment is all there is, and that anything else is a dream. To be awake and free is to see that time doesn't exist except as a mental construct. In other words, time is mind. It's always *this* moment.

To be awake and free means to live and see *this* moment is all there is. It is prior to thought, memory, belief or opinion – or our interpretation of it. Wisdom blooms when we no longer reference thought or memory to tell us what's true and real. Wisdom blooms when we live in the present moment – where it's NOT possible to suffer. *Wisdom sees that time is mind, and that we can't suffer if we stay in the present, where there is no time.* When we no longer reference the past as something real, we live in the one, true reality

– and nowhere (now here) else. This is the kingdom of heaven Jesus often spoke about.

Have you ever received a package or letter in the mail that you didn't really want by the time it arrived at your doorstep? Perhaps it was an impulse buy, and by the time it was delivered you had a serious case of buyer's remorse? I've done this many times – getting caught, hook, line and sinker by the persuasive presenter telling you it was the best thing since sliced bread! Remember Don Lepre, that dynamic, infomercial salesman back in the mid-eighties and early nineties? He used to do those thirty-minute commercials on television, pitching classified ads as a "simple and lucrative" way to earn money? He'd make earning money seem effortless by posting classified ads in newspapers all across the country for "pennies on the dollar." He'd post ads pointing to some product or service he was selling – and so could you!

The guy was very convincing and you couldn't order fast enough. Well, at least I couldn't. Incidentally, he recently committed suicide due to being in way over his head, apparently having all kinds of legal and financial troubles. Not knowing Don personally, I can't help but sense that intense guilt and shame may have sadly led him to end his life. Perhaps he couldn't envision living with a tarnished reputation, suffering jail time or paying big fines. We'll never know, but it's unfortunate that a guy with all that charm, talent and personality felt the need to take his own life.

So, what do we do when we don't want receipt of that package? We write with big letters on the front, "Return To Sender," don't we? Otherwise, we are stuck with it, right? Fortunately, *we* have the option to return to sender, too. Just as the post office, UPS or Fed-Ex allows us the opportunity to send back (without penalty) what we really didn't want in the first place – but only thought or believed we did – we can do a similar thing with our thoughts, beliefs and habitual patterns of thinking. Just because a thought or belief arises, telling us that something is "true" or desired, we don't have to act on it, do we?

We have the option to return to sender. In this case, the "sender" is our minds, the thing that usually rules the nest, telling us what's best or right. Our minds repeatedly tell us what we "need" in order to be content, safe and secure. And since the majority of our minds believe in scarcity, inadequacy and competition, we hear from it often! The good news is, no matter how convincing these thoughts appear to be – or how persistent they are, it doesn't mean we must take receipt of it.

And yet, if we aren't vigilant and aware, our boxes can get stuffed full. In our state of overload, we have a tendency of our lives becoming one battle after the other. When this happens, we lose sight of the truth that what we battle we only strengthen and sustain. If we are conscious and paying attention to the thoughts and beliefs that arise in us, we give ourselves the ability to see what's really true and real. If not, we will invariably take receipt of so much unreality, paying attention to and dealing with the consequences *after* the fact!

Very often, we don't even see what's *in* our mailboxes because we just can't keep up. Our mailbox (our minds) can be so filled with notions and ideas that have nothing to do with reality that confusion and pain pile up. If we *see* that the vast majority of what we entertain in our minds wasn't even created by us (but taken on board by assimilating what others think we should do) we are in a much better position to see just how ludicrous and unwise our minds can be. If we discern, we can learn.

Again, the mind and its beliefs are never the problem. It is when we *believe and identify with* the thoughts in our minds that problems must arise. When we notice we aren't even doing it, and that it's happening automatically and spontaneously, we give ourselves a much better chance of not getting caught up in it's perpetual web of lies and deceptions. The real meaning of the laughing Buddha is that he finally saw the nature of the mind and its ongoing inability to discern reality versus illusion.

More specifically, he saw through the craziness and insistence of the mind's belief that something other than what is happening, can happen. He saw that the nature of the mind *is* to resist what is – to resist that which is *already* happening was a consistent formula for suffering. Most important, he saw he wasn't the mind, and that he had a mind. As a result, he woke up *from identification with* the mind.

If you received a package in the mail you didn't want – and if you wanted a credit put back on your charge card, would you damage the package and write curse words all over the front in hopes of getting your money back? Would you resist and offend the sender, thinking it's an effective strategy to get reimbursed? Of course you wouldn't. Why would you want to decrease your chances of getting your money back, when all you had to do was write, "Return to sender" and say, "Thanks anyway, maybe another time?" Don't we innately know that kindness and nonresistance can only increase our odds of manifesting our desired outcome?

Likewise, if we don't want the thoughts and beliefs that arise in our experience to stick around and further torture us, we'd be wise to do the same and just thank it for sharing – without resisting it. Granted, we need to be aware of the inevitable and harming nature of the belief in untrue thoughts that arise *before* we can respectfully send them back, don't we? *We can only really "send them back" by first seeing they aren't serving or true, without resisting or avoiding them.* It is in the momentary gap right before we take receipt of anything that we can see what's real versus what's false.

Don't we often intuitively know and sense what's BS and what isn't, especially if we are conscious and willing to look and see for ourselves? I say yes, wholeheartedly. I think you'll agree that you already possess this intuition that has the ability to decipher when bullshit arises. We all possess, in varying degrees of sensitivity, an inner "bullshit-ometer" that goes off, warning us when we're being duped. If we don't always see what's BS at first, and if we don't always see what must ultimately bind us at first, that's absolutely okay and even appropriate – yes, appropriate.

We will see it the next time, or maybe the time after that, who knows? There is no timeline unless we impose one. Is our timeline even real, or is it just a self-imposed thing that runs us? The truth is, the less we make demands of how it should be – the sooner it (seeing what's true) will happen. In an uncluttered room, we are better able to quickly find what we're looking for. When we let go trying to search our mind for the answer, it pops us later when our attention is on something else.

I can tell you this truth without any doubt whatsoever: If you don't *see* whatever it is in any moment that needs to be seen (in order to be free of what binds you) you weren't supposed to see it then anyway. Why? Simply because you didn't! Truth is so simple that the mind has a very difficult time seeing it. As you'll read throughout these pages, minds deal in complexity, and rarely, in simplicity. Did your mind just have something to say about that statement? Did you believe it? Besides, we can only understand what we are first aware of, so there's no need or benefit in beating ourselves up for not seeing it *this* time.

If we are unaware in any moment, how *can* we *see* in that moment? If we are unaware in any given moment, were we really *meant* to see in that moment? No, we were not, so we can relax.

In the spirit of *returning*, let's return to the original topic of this chapter regarding memory, and how our minds see this moment through the filter of the past, and not how it really is. If we really see that past is memory only – and that there is no past unless we think about it – we are way ahead of the game, and in the minority for sure. Seeing these two things clearly, and without any doubt at all serves us in ways we literally can't even imagine. When I finally saw that the past is a mental construct only, with no substance at all – and that unless and until I perceived this moment without any judgment or resistance, I was seeing this moment *from* the past.

Consequently, I was distorting the moment by seeing it *from* the past, from my likes and dislikes – based on my past, and whether or not it conformed to my present agenda. Seeing the unreality of the past

When Wisdom Blooms

(despite the appearance of a past) freed me in ways that's hard to describe. No longer did I have any regrets about "my past," because in seeing there's only the present moment, belief in an actual past dissolved. With that dissolution, so did the negative feelings or thoughts I entertained about that "past."

And here is where the mind has a tendency to step in to argue: What do you mean there's no past? What do you mean that the past is memory only? If that's the case, what is it that gives me the overwhelming impression of time, especially of time past, and of all the things that were? These are all great and reasonable questions. While we can see that it is not possible to live *in* the past or live *from* the past, what is it that convinces us of things of the past? It is memory, and it is memory alone.

While we see that, in our direct experience, there is only an endless present, without beginning, middle or end, there is something that speaks quite clearly and vehemently of things that were – of things which happened moments ago, days ago, months ago and years ago. Again, it is memory. And while we cannot see the past, feel the past or touch the past, we can surely (and quite vividly) remember the past. But we only ever do this in the present moment. Recollecting the past is only ever done right now, is it not?

Memory alone assures me of a past, and if it were not for memory, I'd have no sense of time, either. After all, others have this type of recall of the past and have a clear memory of it as well! Here is where we make the leap and conclude that memory provides us knowledge of an actual past, even if we can't directly *experience* any actual past! And this is where the train leaves the track. We conclude that since we can remember a past, there must *be* a past. We conclude that since having a past feels so real, that it must be real, much like a dream we just woke up from that seemed so real.

We conclude that since we have a strong sense of the past, that there must be an actual past, too. I'm not suggesting memory isn't a good thing. If we didn't possess memory, we wouldn't know that the last time we crossed the road without looking both ways, we almost got flattened by a speeding mail truck. So what could very well happen the next time? We could be road pizza. If we didn't have memory, we wouldn't know that lighting a match in a room filled with leaking gas would be the end of us.

The mystics throughout the ages all agree that when we think of the past, all we really know is a certain memory of it – but that memory itself is always and *only* a present experience. We can remember an incident in our past, but what are we actually aware of? We aren't actually watching that event unfold presently (like *remembering* watching our thirteen year old nephew run eighty yards for a touchdown – go CJ! – but rather, we are watching a present trace or memory of what already happened.

We can only know the past in the present – and as part of the present only. When we *see* this, when we really see this, we see that we can never know an actual past at all. We can only know memories of the past, and those memories exist only as a present experience. *Therefore, when we insist that the "past" actually occurred, it was in truth, a present occurrence and not a past one.* At no point do we ever experience an actual past, because there simply isn't one – except in our memory. Since most of us identify WITH our minds and its functions, we believe in past as reality.

Again, what past is there unless you think about it? Similarly, we can never know or experience the future; we can only ever know anticipations or expectations – which too, are only ever a part of the present experience. Anticipation, imagination and expectation, like memory, are all present facts. They happen presently, and nowhere (now here) else. To see that the past is memory only, and the future as anticipation (both present facts) is to see all time existing now. To *see* the past and the future as nothing but concepts held in the mind, is to *see* the only reality there is – this present moment.

When we *see* this, and I mean *really* see this, we are free because it is not possible to suffer in the present moment. Suffering happens when we believe in a past or future – and when we see this moment from the filter of the past, and not as it is. Suffering only happens in time, and never when we are fully present without stories or agendas. Waking up means to wake up from the concept of time. Sometimes, on the rare occasion that I attempt to share this with those I care for, I invariably get a look like I am from another planet!

Now, I love these people very much, but for whatever reason, apparently they aren't ready or desiring to see this yet. And that's absolutely okay. The truth is, they don't *need* to see this, now or ever. There's no outside agency or force that needs or compels any of us to see this, despite it being open and available to anyone – at any time. At the same time, I must admit the desire does arise now and then to share this, because the lasting byproducts of this seeing are so liberating and joyous. It's like when we found a great restaurant, or saw a wonderful movie; don't we naturally want to share the good news? Since I'm not attached to the outcome – that they see what I'm pointing to – it's not a problem when I see that glazed look that wants to change the subject!

Others have a right to dismiss this as pure lunacy or "out there stuff" that can't possibly be useful to them. Unfortunately, what we dismiss we usually don't look at. Perhaps another day they will look, but either way, it doesn't ultimately matter. I have nothing invested in anyone seeing anything, but if it's truth you're after, we have something to talk about – so bring your empty cup. The mind cannot understand this, but what You Really Are *can and already does*. This can only be understood from within, with Being, and not conceptually in the mind.

When this is truly seen, it is understood energetically in the body. The results are astounding. In other words, the proof is in the pudding, and the saying, "The peace that surpasses all understanding" takes on a whole new meaning because it's your lived experience. It's verified and confirmed by the one who sees what's true and actual. Until then, the mind will continue attempting to reference what's real and true by accessing the concepts and beliefs it clings to – because after all, that's pretty much how we've been taught since day one.

In fact, those who create religion count on this knowing (that we'll continue to look with the mind and rely on belief), instead of our actual experience *of* God or Truth. That's not to imply they know any other way. So, we continue to look to our stored data banks of past "knowledge" to see how it measures up with what we are looking at now. It's literally a habit pattern, a way of thinking and being that continues, until we recognize it's not working for us. We get complacent with the "the same thing, different day" mindset. Until we're no longer content or satisfied with the status quo, or when we sense that there *is* more to see – and more that we *must* see, we won't look any differently.

If we want to live more from truth (than untruth that divides) we do well to bring our awareness back to this present moment – and *return to sender* (mind) the silly notions that catch us off guard and lead us down an unconscious road, a road that generally brings varying degrees pain that drives us into a roadside ditch. Don't be that guy or gal who ends up in a roadside ditch! The more present we are to the thoughts we entertain and cling to, the more we render ourselves powerful in the present moment, the only reality there is. Leaving the land of make-believe (where fantasy is our lived experience) and returning home is always an option that's immediately available.

And when you do, you instantly begin living from truth. If we notice that it's always a timeless now, we have at our disposal an endless opportunity to be in harmony with what is, and not what we imagine what is. The overriding and determining factor becomes *which land* do we really want to live in? Have we suffered enough from living in the land of make-believe, or are we resigned to live our lives the way we always do? There is no right or wrong answer here, and there is no should or shouldn't answer implied here.

That's what's so liberating about all of this. There isn't any punitive God watching over us, keeping score – like Santa. We are free to do and be as we wish, and yet paradoxically, the answer to this question will determine the direction our lives go. Which land we live in will determine the quality of experience – and so much more. If uncomfortable and unwanted feelings and sensations tell us we aren't in harmony with life, then not feeling quite right is a useful and valid indicator. It speaks to us each moment. The question is, do we listen? Do we even *care* to listen?

The activity of returning to this moment (by bringing your awareness back to this moment) to see what's actually happening is essential. This activity of coming back to now, of bringing our awareness back to this moment, is the same thing as *returning to sender*, that which we know doesn't work for us. If the only problem we ever have is to want something other to be happening, wisdom sees that to resist what's happening is counterproductive and painful. It really is that simple.

When we see this moment through the filter of the past and/or how we'd prefer it to be, we are in essence saying, "I really don't want this, so send me suffering." When we take the past to be real, in this moment, we can't ever meet this moment as it is, but only as we'd like it to be. We can't ever escape the byproducts of our interpretations. We can't escape the resulting experience that comes from the way in which we see and interpret. It is just the way it works

– have you noticed? We cannot touch, see or feel anything resembling a past or future.

In other words, in your direct and immediate experience, there is no time – no past or future. There is only an endlessly changing present, shorter than a nanosecond, yet never coming to an end, flashing in and out of existence faster than your eyes can see and perceive. How wonderful to realize that each moment really is fresh and new – and to be lived and experienced knowing it won't ever happen precisely this way again? If you can actually live in the past or future, you'd be the first human to do so. If you happen to figure it out, send me a postcard with precise directions on how to get there, okay?

Chapter 4
No Story, No Suffering

"Man cannot discover new oceans until he has the courage to lose site of the shore."

~ Unknown

Have you noticed that animals don't suffer emotionally or psychologically? They might get emotional for a moment, but they don't suffer. I live with a ragdoll cat and a chocolate lab, and I must tell you that it is so refreshing to live with beings that are so even-tempered, greeting each new moment with a wonder and curiosity. Watch your pet and notice how they meet each moment as if it was brand new. Each sight, sound and smell is brand new and not referenced from the past. Who needs a guru or spiritual teacher when you have a pet?

It really is beautiful to watch – and as you may already know, it's contagious. It has been said that our pets are better teachers than our human teachers, and it is very obvious why. They don't tell themselves stories about how things *should* be, and how things *should* unfold. They have no concept of that. Aside from desiring a treat now and then, or going for a walk, they don't go into a fit. When they don't get what they want – or when their preferences are being met, they don't make a big deal out of it.

When a dog feels pain, it yelps. It doesn't go on and on resisting the pain, or tell a story about the pain. Thus, it doesn't suffer. Granted, our pets don't think in the ways we humans do. They certainly don't tell stories, but that's the point. *Because* they don't tell stories or make demands, they don't suffer as we do. We can pinpoint our suffering down to the fact that it is our stories, notions and beliefs about how things ought to be that creates our suffering. Forgive me for stating the obvious again, but isn't it useful to know that we can only understand what we're first aware of?

In other words, if we're in a habitual trance-like state, new possibilities aren't likely to arise. *When we don't see that resistance TO pain causes suffering, we'll continue to resist inevitable pain.* We are creatures of habit and have a tendency to remain with the known, even if the known continues to prove hurtful. Many times, we prefer to stick with the known than venture into the unknown, even if we intuitively know our freedom lies in what we don't yet know.

I once believed a story that I couldn't possibly write a book like this (let alone three), because I believed I didn't have the necessary focus and discipline. I once believed a story that told me I wasn't enough, and that if you *really* knew me, you might not like what you saw, either. As a result, I walked around feeling inadequate and insecure. That story was a long time ago, but you get the point. The only thing we can ultimately do is live out our stories. And, well, sometimes those stories bring suffering because those stories *about* life rarely ever are in sync *with* life. Life is always in flux and always changing, so it's very difficult to nail it down with a static description of it. Besides, concepts and words about a thing only point to a thing, and never can *be* that thing.

If you can just see this – I mean *really* see this, then you are way ahead of the curve. Conversely, we can have empowering stories, too, and we live them out as well. So, if we are faced with no other alternative (when would this be so?) than to live out our stories, it's certainly a better option to make up a good story, as opposed to a not so good one. However, it is still merely a story we are living, which means we aren't directly engaging life as it is. However, there is another option that we can live out, one I didn't see until my late thirties. Apparently, I was wasn't ready to see, or not meant to see it until then – which is essentially the same thing!

This other option is by far the best. And its byproducts are organic and lasting. It's called *no story*, and it doesn't bring suffering because it has no demands or formulas. No one can refute it and there's nothing to maintain. Conversely, any story never intends to meet each moment as it is. It's only interested in desperately keeping alive your story. However, when you live without any story, you live impartially and without mental bias. There's nothing to argue with, including reality. Whether we are aware of it or not, most of us create and maintain stories about our lives so that we can feel safe, secure and in control.

Somewhere along the way, we picked up the idea that to come naked and free, without an agenda, is irresponsible and foolish. Just pick a particular aspect of your life and you will find several underlying stories that serve as buffers to reality, intermediaries between you and the moment. If we can see that we are engaged in our stories about life, and NOT life itself, we give ourselves the real opportunity to transcend our stories. You won't necessarily know how and why these stories were formed, but if you ask it (the story) what it tells you about life, it will.

Each story we have has a voice – and that voice is usually most willing to tell you how it perceives. Believing this voice, we forget that perception is NOT reality. Hence, we live out our perceptions. Our minds love to create stories that have no basis in reality, yet we believe we need them in order to navigate our way through life. They become our compass. You could call it a basic lack of trust. While habitual, it is a still a lack of trust in our own being – and a lack of trust in life, too. Both are essentially the same thing.

The reality is, life is so full of twists and unexpected turns, surprises and mysteries, that when we insist on our stories to explain things – or help us proceed, we often end up feeling confused and emotionally unstable. Our life then, becomes a game of managing our emotional states, up one day and down the next.

We rarely ever look to see whether our stories are true or not, and whether we really would be confused and unstable without them! When we approach aspects of our lives with a story about how it should be, or how it should work out, we literally *ask for* pain and confusion, because our stories seldom match up with how life actually unfolds! We actually think we can box up and compartmentalize aspects of our lives with explanations about them, thinking we can proceed *from* those explanations. Sometimes we put a nice bow on top for good measure, believing it will enhance or our experience, or act as a buffer to our experience.

We manufacture a conceptual reality and superimpose it onto our lives. However, if you were able to completely drop any and all stories about any aspect of your life, it would be literally impossible for you to suffer. Yes, you could be in pain, but that's different from suffering. You wouldn't have a sense of how things should be, or how things *should* work out. Whatever arises would be just fine with you. Whatever outcome would be just fine with you. This is what it means to be awake and free. You are a lover of what is, and don't resist what's already happening. Most minds would insist that this is an attitude of resignation and foolishness.

In truth, it is the true perception that delivers liberation. The Buddha called this, "Right Seeing." Liberation is our experience when we don't insist on our stories about life being adhered to. It's our experience when we don't insist on our personal agendas being fulfilled. In fact, life could care less about the stories we make up, and life could care less if our stories jive with reality. While we suffer from our unmet expectations about life, life continues on, unaffected and free. Remember when Mom or Dad would tell us, "Honey, life just isn't fair?" How right they were, and yet, don't we often insist on life being fair? It's just another belief we create about life (life should be fair) – and when it doesn't match up with our experience, we suffer.

Many times, instead of dropping our concepts about how things should be, we come up with a more clever strategy: When life clashes with our story, just invent a new story! That way, no more suffering and we get what we really wanted all along. As clever as this strategy seems, it's really just a cheap backdoor mind trick. It won't work long term. It may for a while, but inevitably it must fail. That's because when we fail to see that living from a story is ultimately a lie, we don't engage life as it actually is. Disappointment can only ensue.

We actually think life cares about our desires, needs and preferences! It usually takes a whole lot of suffering before we see that this isn't the case, and that something must be truly amiss in our perspective. We start to get a glimpse that just maybe the source of our problem is our interpretations about life, and not life itself. For so long, we don't see that we are reacting to (and living out) the projections we send out through time and space, and not what's actually happening.

We don't fully comprehend the ramifications of our mind's insistence that its conceptual creations actually represent reality and explain how things really are. We somehow believe that we need a secondary interpretation to show us how to be in life. Instead of responding to directly perceived reality, we can recognize we've placed an overlay, a conceptual barrier on the moment, as a way to soften how we experience reality.

We tell ourselves, "Life is just too painful and difficult as it is, so I must come up with a strategy to manage it." When we react to our secondary interpretations, and not directly respond to what is, we usually pay a price. And that's okay, until it isn't okay anymore. Paying a price can definitely serve as a wake-up call for us – to see we are looking in a direction that hurts. Wherever we look is what we'll experience. Simply put, choose the direction and you choose the consequence. However, whenever we suffer, we can use it as a trigger to notice the direction we ARE looking, and choose different.

Each moment is a brand new opportunity to look in the direction that heals – and then to actually look in that direction. In essence, when we don't feel quite right, we are forgetting that our own innate wisdom knows the way – if we would just trust it. Trusting in our own being is not something most of us have been taught to do. Trusting that our own inner wisdom already knows isn't something that most of us have been exposed to. Since we live among other humans that have been conditioned to look to their minds (instead of their hearts) to tell them what's true and real, we naturally do the same thing. We are creatures of both imitation and habit – even if it's not working for us.

Don't we have an inclination to imitate the strategies and approaches of those around us that we admire and respect? How many among us were raised in a culture where we *knew* conceptual understanding is only partial, and therefore, limited and not to be relied on? We've been told that "knowledge is power" – and that the more we accumulate it, the better off we are. When are we ever really taught that knowledge is often, in fact, a barrier that stands in the way of successful living? Instead, we take on board a belief that says, "We need to first understand a thing conceptually in order to proceed accordingly."

Implicit in this view is that our innate wisdom isn't enough and knowledge is king. Granted, to the mind that deals in conceptual reason and belief, this makes sense. While conceptual understanding can be very useful in a certain contexts and life situations, it is usually quite limited when it comes to the bigger issues in life. *Inner wisdom already knows, while our minds think it needs to attain more concepts in order to really know.* What would it be like to just show up in this moment, in an open state of discovery, without any story or agenda?

What might it be like to be in this moment, without any beliefs, conclusions or ideas – with a complete willingness not to know anything at all? Don't answer this question with a conceptual answer. Find out for yourself in your actual experience. Initially, this scenario may seem very scary, and yet, there are times when we do just this – meet the moment as it is. When we do, we notice that "we" aren't in the picture; "we" aren't part of the equation. We find that we are much more present when our agenda is absent.

In the absence of any agenda, we are truly present. In fact, whether we realize it or not, there are many occasions where we simply forget ourselves, where we are most present when we are absent. If we are honest with ourselves, we see that in order to fully show up in our lives, a dropping of any and all agendas, opinions and preferences is needed. Then and only then, are we really Here, meeting this moment on *its* terms, not ours. Besides, where has believing in dogma, scripture and other sources of "wisdom" really gotten us? Where has it gotten us, other than temporary and fleeting relief and a false sense of security – the kind that comes and goes? Doesn't that seem manufactured and unreal to you, and therefore, tell you something about its authenticity?

Possessing the perception that *"whatever wants to arise is just fine by me"* is the way of freedom, the way of enlightenment. This may seem a scary proposition to the mind. To come unarmed and without an agenda, may even seem weak and resigning. However, check it out in your own experience, instead of what your mind tells you about it. This pointer isn't for your mind. This is for YOU. Minds will go to great lengths to convince you something is true when it's not. And it's not a problem. You won't be successful if you consciously create a story that says, "I am just fine with whatever arises." This perception will spontaneously happen once you've seen through all you're your illusory stories, beliefs, assumptions, etc.

As long as we continue to identify with the mind, we won't ever see this. We just need to take that extra step, and look and see for ourselves what's actual. Having a good dose of humility will prevent us from thinking we are stupid. If we don't humble ourselves, we're less likely to look. Because we're identified with the mind, we fear what we'll tell ourselves about our intellectual capacity. We just create another story to live from. Unless we're willing to come naked and free, never will we see that it's all just a defense against nothing.

Not all stories are disabling. As we discussed, if we must create a story, we can create an empowering one. There's nothing wrong with this, at least not temporarily. Using what we need to use for a time isn't shameful, nor does it make us any less worthy. Life is game of seeing and not seeing. The more you see what's real, the less pain and division you experience. It really IS that simple. Like belief, a story can serve as a bridge, until we no longer need that bridge to get across to the other side. Sometimes that bridge collapses, and we are left clinging to its railings. It's a good indicator that we must go beyond belief, because we know that ultimate and lasting freedom IS beyond any story we can come up with.

When we insist that our stories, agendas and desires need to be manifested, our lives become problematic. Desire in and of itself isn't the problem. Many people are under the impression that the Buddha said that "desire is the root of all suffering." He never said this. Buddha said that, "attachment *to* desire is the root of all suffering." Quite a big difference! Being human, desires will arise and desires will fall. Nothing would get done; advancements in medicine and technology wouldn't occur in the absence of desire. Procreation wouldn't happen in the absence of desire – and perhaps you wouldn't be reading this now!

However, when we insist that our personal desires need to be met in order for us to be happy, we must suffer to some degree. Do we believe in order to be happy or content, our desires must be met? Do we really believe that fulfilling our desires is the key to lasting and real happiness? Does your intuition tell you that a life lived demanding all desires met can only be an empty life? Whenever we insist or demand anything, we can be sure that suffering will follow, like night follows day.

Life just doesn't work this way; life doesn't cater to what we desire. It's *we* who need to desire what life brings, for if we resist how the moment unfolds, *we* suffer. Desiring what Is, is the way of the liberated and free. Wisdom recognizes that having only preferences is the way to live in harmony with our experience. All of this can be experimented with and confirmed in your direct experience. Don't believe a thing you ever read here, and find out what happens when you insist on getting your desires met. See that wanting what you have is freedom. See that having only preferences is freedom. See that the truest freedom is not wanting.

In order to be vigilant against creating stories in our lives that invariably lead to division and pain, there are a few things we can do without applying effort or actual "doing." Telling the truth is one powerful way that takes no effort. Somehow, as a species, we've perfected pretending as a way of being – as if telling ourselves the truth is a scary thing to avoid. The funny thing is that truth needs no defense, while stories and beliefs do! Once we've aligned ourselves with truth, the armor naturally falls away.

No longer are we in protection mode, because we have truth on our side. We've become great pretenders, and it goes mostly unnoticed because it is such a common practice. Everyone does it, so it must be okay, right? Somehow, we've come to believe that telling the truth is a difficult thing to do, and that it usually brings consequences we'd rather not face. We may conclude that lying to ourselves (and others) is easier and less painful. We hurt most when we deceive ourselves. We forget that it's really difficult to be honest with others when we deceive ourselves.

Often times, what is true in a situation is that we really don't know – and in fact, really can't know. But we've been conditioned early on to believe not knowing is a bad thing, a weak thing, an unenlightened thing. The reality is nothing could be further from the truth! Uncertainty is an integral part of the natural order of life, and to deny this reality is to invite chaos and confusion. If we have the humility and earnest willingness to notice that it's our mind's function to resist the unknown (this present moment) – and that it's our mind that has a constant *need to know* – we are better able to tell the truth and admit when we don't know.

More critically, we are better able to SEE that we *can't* know anything in this brand new moment, because this fresh moment has nothing to do with what came before. Granted, it feels that way and our perceptions tell us otherwise. However, the reality is that this moment stands independent of the moment that just died. Until then, we will identify with our thinking minds (that needs to know) and continue to lie to ourselves, pretending we know when we don't.

We will play out our lives much in the same way as we did before. It's all one big charade.

When we are willing to see what's true, no matter what, we recognize that we can't possibly know. We can only imagine we know. When we disengage with the ego that pretends to know – and must know, when we see the ego's need to project a certain image, ego's grip is loosened. What we think is, and what actually is, are not the same. We overlook this fact all the time! If we drop all stories, we see that, in our experience, not knowing is quite peaceful and expansive. The experience of not knowing isn't what we've been told it is – or what we've imagined it is. You might find that it's spacious and peaceful – and where true and unlimited potential originates.

The unknown (no story) is so much more peaceful than ever imagined – and not something to run and hide from. *Whenever we're willing not to know, we refrain from identifying with the mind's unexamined conclusions and allow ourselves to be in an open state of discovery. If truth demands anything at all, it demands an open state of discovery and an innocent looking filled with curiosity and wonder.* Is this moment weak and without power? What does it need? Does it need our help or guidance? When we insist that we know anything in this moment (except for the fact of our own being, that we exist) we are in fact, bringing the past to *this* moment. We bring to life a dead thing and attempt to resurrect it.

When we think we know anything in this moment, we aren't seeing the reality of this moment. This moment has no story, and it has no suffering. It is devoid of anything stale or old. It is our minds that bring stories – and consequent suffering, to this moment. This moment literally need nothing other than your showing up to it, without an overlaying secondary interpretation of it. It doesn't even "need" us to show up to it. That's on us! Stay out of your mind, be fully present, and see this for yourself. Don't rely on another. There is nothing more liberating, I tell you. No story, no suffering.

Another thing we can do, instead of believing in a need to create a story around something (or notice that a limiting one is already in operation), is to just be curious about what is true in the moment. It is this orientation of curiosity and not knowing that is such a powerful and peaceful combination that baffles the mind – if you allow it. Be like your pet and show up innocently to this fresh and new moment. Act as if it will never repeat itself in that way – because it won't. It is the mind's habitual belief that it "knows" what's happening. This very belief causes so much boredom for the mind because it thinks it's the same old thing!

We're only bored when we come from the mind. The mind believes peace and security comes from knowing (or strongly believing in) something. This is no surprise (as the mind needs to know) and will go to *any* lengths to avoid not knowing! YOU are not the mind. You precede the mind, and therefore, you have a mind. Call it Awareness or Spirit that animates your body and mind if you prefer. Without referencing thought, what are you really?

You are the silent, aware presence that everything arises from and falls back into. Believing you *are* the mind is the problem – the problem that causes *all* problems.

This can't be seen conceptually, with your mind, but YOU can see this now. The mind's need to know at all costs often overshadows the more natural impulse we have of just resting in curiosity, examining what's really true or not. If we have a natural inclination to always have to explain things when we really don't know, we can use that tendency (when it comes up) as a trigger to just relax and be okay with not knowing. The alternative is just to be reactive and repetitive – and let the mind lead the way. As the mind goes, you go.

Life will unfold as it unfolds anyway, regardless of the way in which we would like it to unfold. If we really desire to live in harmony with life, and if we really desire more peace and less angst, we do well to pause in that gap, that gap right before we hop on that train of belief in our story. It is in this small gap where we can either go unconscious and suffer the consequences, or be aware of that gap (of no story) – and enjoy the peace that comes with resting in that.

Aware that we have options in any moment, and aware that we aren't automatons without any volition at all gives us the wherewithal to look in a different direction. With awareness, comes volition and choice. Trusting in our own innate sense of wisdom, our own being, takes us a long way. When we see that life has no story, and that life knows how to live better than our egoic minds do, we become more conscious. When we see that there's no separation between life and what we really are, we let go and naturally trust. When we believe we are separate from life, we naturally don't trust.

The great news is that the more we show up and remain in the here and now, we realize that no story was ever needed. We see that the moment lacks nothing at all – and it never does. *The more we notice that our being always and already remains in the now, the easier it is to just rest.* It was just our minds that told us that we're separate from the moment. And we believed it. In truth, there's just the next thing that's happening. There's always just the next thing that's happening. I don't mean to say "next" in terms of future next, but right now. As soon as right now is experienced, the next thing is experienced, right now. Sometimes the next thing that's happening is something that your mind says is good that it wants, and sometimes the next thing is something that the mind says is not good, and you don't want.

But either way, none of the thoughts about what's happening have any validity to them, positive or negative. A nonsensical notion – but it's nonetheless, true. Find out. Since seeing this doesn't require us to think rationally, or in a linear fashion, reason and logic don't have to factor in. In fact, in this case, they don't at all. What you think is happening doesn't equate to what's happening. What's happening is just what's happening, prior to the concepts our minds create.

We get endless opportunities to see and experience what is as it is, before or independent of, any story about it. No matter what it is, it's not a problem, until the mind tells itself a story about what's happening. Only when the mind talks to itself about what is happening, what has happened, or what may happen, does stress, anxiety or suffering happen. The mind has conversations with itself about what is happening all the time. The mind converses with itself about what it would like to have happen, or must have happen, all the time. And yet, when we turn on the evening news and discover that a serial killer heard voices in his head, telling him to kill, we say he's evil and insane!

We are all insane (in varying degrees) and fortunately, the vast majority of us don't hear voices that tell us to murder. The sooner we admit this, the sooner we can get on with the business of happy living. Thought itself isn't the problem. Stories themselves aren't the problem. Problems arise when we believe in our thoughts and stories to be accurate representations for reality. They never are. When the light of conscious awareness penetrates any story of ego-based suffering, the story no longer continues to be the final authority. No story, no suffering.

Chapter 5
When Wisdom Blooms

"Wisdom tends to grow in proportion to one's awareness of one's own ignorance."

~ *Anthony de Mello*

Ever since I was young, I've had a desire to know who I am, why I am here, and what is true. At times, it was bordering on obsessive. The older I got, I noticed I was more naturally drawn to spirituality than religion. Being an avid reader, I consumed everything I could get my hands on. I can honestly say that the desire to know the answers to these questions has been extinguished. Seeing that answers are for the mind that needs to know, and seeing that I am not my mind, those questions dissolved. This is not to imply I've reached some end point (there isn't one) or that I am no longer open to Life and all its beauty and wonder.

In fact, the opposite is the case, as I am very open to life; each moment is fresh and new. Besides, there's no such thing as "having all the answers." Books and listening materials played a big part in my journey. While the "answers" aren't found in books and tapes, I'd be lying to you if I said that they didn't serve a useful role, because they did. I can't tell you how many books I've read since my late teens that had to do with self-help and spirituality.

I read and gained insight from some of the more popular self-help giants; Tony Robbins, Zig Ziglar, Og Mandino, Dan Millman, Wayne Dyer, Deepak Choprah and Earl Nightingale. Being raised Roman Catholic in a moderately religious family, I read much of the New Testament and the teachings of Jesus, to some of the great Christian mystics like Meister Eckhart, C.S Lewis, Henri Nouwen, Mother Theresa, Peace Pilgrim, Brother Lawrence, Thomas Merton and Anthony de Mello. Perhaps my favorite all-time quote is from Francis of Assisi. Not only was he a lover of all life – especially nature and animals, he gave one of the most direct and accurate pointers to Truth, *"What you're looking for is what's looking."*

For about 5-6 years, I immersed myself in "A Course in Miracles", "Conversations with God", and Ernest Holmes' "Science of Mind". I enjoyed and resonated deeply with the writings of Vietnamese Buddhist Monk, Thich Nanh Hanh, to the Sufi poets Hafiz, Kabir and Rumi. In 1998, Eckhart Tolle's book, *The Power of Now* hollered at me from the shelves in Borders Bookstore – and it led to the end of seeking. From there, I was led to the 20th century Indian Sages, Nisargadatta Maharaj, Ramana Maharshi and Papaji.

I share all this only to illustrate that my journey was as varied as the teachers and teachings I was exposed to. I include them all in my heart as equally appropriate and valuable, and am deeply grateful for their unique input and guidance. Despite some teachers having more of an impact than others, none are more worthy than the next. Whatever teacher and teaching I was drawn to at the time was exactly where I was supposed to be at the time. Looking back, it is certainly mysterious how it all unfolded, yet plain to see that my own inner wisdom was guiding me in directions I couldn't fully comprehend.

I only knew one thing and it was this: I wasn't going to stop seeking until I knew I found home. Something within told me I would know when I knew, like when you know you're in the right place at the right time, or when you just know you've met the right person you'll spend the rest of your life with. I wasn't going to stop until belief was no longer relied on to tell me what was true. I wasn't going to stop until something within told me I had found what I was looking for. I knew it wouldn't be conceptual knowing – and that it had to be an experiential knowing.

Nothing less than a permanent shift in my being and the way I perceived would do. In the early nineties (in my mid-twenties) I walked on 1200-degree hot coals with Anthony Robbins, without burning my feet. While I felt no pain or burns from that fifteen-second walk, high-fiving a fellow participant *after* the walk was very painful! That experience opened my eyes to the power of my mind and the power of focus. From about the ages of 18 to 26, the majority of the materials I read and listened to were self-help in nature.

I even spent a good chunk of attention and energy with a humanistic movement called, "Lifespring" – a movement similar to EST and the The Forum. Over the next decade, when I had the strong sense that I was spirit having a human experience, the majority of materials I consumed were spiritual in nature. I am 47 now, and rarely do I ever pick up a book. If I do, it is for the sake of enjoying how others point to the one Truth, and to say, "Ah yes, that's it."

Again, it's not that I have all the answers. How deluded is that? Besides, there's no such thing as "having all the answers." It's just that the energy of seeking dropped away, along with the desire to read what others have to say about spirit. But here's my point: For years, I read and read about what others had to say *about* self-improvement, spirituality and enlightenment – and much of it resonated deeply within. But it wasn't until I really looked within, that I discovered what I was looking for. It wasn't until I looked in the direction that some of these people were pointing to, that real and lasting transformation occurred.

We can read and read concepts until the cows come home, but unless we look in the directions we are being pointed to, *from those who have already realized the truth of their true nature,* not much will change for us. This is what I did for so long; I didn't look. Once a book or audio was finished, for a short period of time afterwards, peace and flow was my experience. But not long after, my life returned to the status quo – and I'd feel disillusioned and confused. It wasn't until my later thirties that I realized why.

Seeing that there is only now, and that past and future are just imaginary concepts created in the mind, brought about a peace and contentment that surpasses all understanding. If things are falling apart around me, it's still okay. It's not a mindset, either. If superiority or judgment arises – or if arrogance arises (especially spiritual arrogance, like I *know* and you *don't*) I know that in that instant, I am identified with ego.

Being temporarily identified with ego that compares and divides – and not spirit that includes and unites, just by noticing it, it lets go. Meeting it disperses it. Laughing at it, as if to say, "nice try, ego" is all that's really needed. The beautiful thing is that often the seeing IS the letting go. Humility has a way of putting you right back to where you rightfully belong – right here, right now, eternally in Spirit, always in grace; no better or worse than another. Without grace, nothing is. Without grace, I am not. Inner wisdom is an ineffable, subtle thing. We all have it, and most of us have very little idea how to access it because we're so busy focused on the drama of life, and the things that come and go.

I am by no means a basher of the self-improvement movement. It certainly has a useful and beneficial role in the proper context, at least temporarily. Undoubtedly it has helped many, myself included, but I do see the inherent flaws in it. There's nothing wrong with leaning on something if we need to, just as long as we know we can't rely on it forever. If we break our ankle, we are wise to use crutches until we can walk on our own. However, the basic supposition in the majority of self-help programs, books and other materials, is that we need help and that the separate self needs repairing.

Self-help can be likened to a ladder leaning against a wall that goes up to a rooftop. And on that rooftop is where you want to be, or where your end goal is. The prize sits at the top, and you must ascend the ladder to get to it. Put another way, you don't presently have whatever it is that's on the rooftop. You must begin a process to learn the steps to acquire the information needed. You climb each rung, one at a time, until finally you reach the top – your end goal.

The assumption is that you don't already know what you need to know in order to attain the goal. Therefore, you need to purchase the information authored by someone who has already traversed the path. Tony Robbins was the master at this. He reportedly got everything he wanted in a short amount of time. After living in a 400 square-foot apartment, washing his dishes in the tub, he had an epiphany one day. If he just modeled the success of others, he'd have what they have. Simple enough, right? Why reinvent the wheel?

Just study Richard Bandler and John Grinder, the founders of Neuro-Linguistic Programming – or NLP, and you're off in the right direction. Ask the right questions in order to get the right answers, master public speaking in a dynamic way and never give up. As a result, you'll have what less than one percent has! Finally, write out your goals on the back of a map one day while traveling on a high speed train in Europe – and presto, a short, eighteen months later, the world is your oyster. Not too long after, you're flying around in your own private jet, doing speaking engagements worldwide for $100K a pop.

Now granted, much of this is tongue and cheek, and I'm oversimplifying here. I don't mean to suggest Tony is completely off his rocker or in-authentic, because I don't sense that he is. How-ever, teaching others how to live a life continually managing their states takes a whole lot of effort. The strategies employed are manufactured and must have a certain life span. And I don't mean to imply that many haven't already benefited from this approach – because they have. But when it comes to letting our innate wisdom bloom, or realizing what we really are, this approach will always fall short and fail to deliver – simply because it must.

When we seek lasting happiness with material riches, avoiding pain and gaining pleasure, when we base our contentment on things outside of ourselves, we set ourselves up for misery. Lasting contentment can *only* come from within, and from what's true and permanent. It's an organic approach based on life's demands, not ours. So, when I mentioned that I made the switch from self-help books and tapes to spiritual books and tapes, I said it was because I had a strong sense that I was Spirit – and not what I appeared to be, a separate human individual, amongst other human individuals, living in this world. With that sense came my own sort of epiphany in the form of a visual metaphor one night as I lay in bed.

I likened my life not to a ladder I had to ascend to attain something I thought would bring me lasting fulfillment, but to a rose, mostly un-bloomed, but here for the purpose of blooming. The purpose or reason for my life on earth then, was to blossom into what I somehow knew I already and eternally was, undivided Spirit, already unified, already whole and complete – and inextricably free. I knew that wisdom – not intellectual knowledge, was the power or energy that would reveal the shift I was seeking. I saw that knowledge served its purpose and was appropriate in certain contexts and life situations.

However, it was wisdom and truth that I was after. Intuitively, there was a sense that told me that I already *knew* what was essential to live a happy and peaceful existence. That knowing sense told me I just needed to see what was in the way of that wisdom and truth revealing itself as who I am. Simply put, I needed to provide the proper conditions for it to blossom. I knew that the more conscious and aware I became, the more that wisdom bloomed. I knew it wasn't a process of learning, because learning implied that I didn't already know. I knew that it was more a process of *unlearning* – a process of subtraction and removing what was covering over what was already known. I can tell you many years later that this metaphor has proved true in so many ways.

Although there really isn't any "journey" needed to arrive to the only reality – right now, my own spiritual journey has taken many twists and turns. As I look back, it is really quite remarkable how one teaching and teacher led to the next. I can't say that I'm still a seeker today because it's known that this moment is it – and this moment isn't lacking anything at all. And it's never completed. This moment is endless. In fact, it is never over as *this never-ending present moment* lasts forever, eternally. You may think this is my belief. It isn't.

Eternally doesn't mean forever in time; it means outside the stream of time and space, where there is no beginning, middle or end. Here's a good metaphor to explain this: Imagine listening to a group of people chant the word, "NOW" without ever stopping. Can you hear it? This is the timeless present, and everything (including thought, feeling and experience) arises in and falls back into this timeless now, in that chanted sound we call NOW. There is a real and lasting contentment here that resulted from taking a heart approach, and not a conceptual approach in the mind laden with belief and dogma.

All the books I read were mostly read in a conceptual way, from the discriminating mind that evaluated and compared – and not from below the neck, impartially and innocently, where true wisdom resides. I wasn't really looking in the direction I was being pointed, either. Apparently, I didn't see the importance at the time. I later discovered that when I read from my head and not my heart, I stayed at that level, in my head. Truth is never found or realized in the mind. If there's only one thing you "believe" or take on "faith" in this book – until you see it for yourself – believe this.

While this may sound confusing, I hope you at least get a glimpse of what I am pointing to here, because it *really is* critical to see. If you don't now, please do not be concerned. The realization will occur when it's meant to occur. No striving or pressure needed; this will only prevent you from seeing! This *seeing* isn't abstract in any way, but experiential and sensed in the body. Abstractions reside in and from the mind, but what we seek is beyond the mind, and therefore, can't be realized *with* the mind. Discovering that real transformation happens below the neck and not from the inherently limited, conceptual thinking is the aim here.

The philosophy *about* something isn't the actual, is it? Philosophy, comprised of words and concepts, only points to something far greater; it isn't the actual. What ultimate good is philosophy if we haven't realized what we've read or contemplated? If our "knowledge" stays at the level of our minds – and not our hearts, we won't benefit in the long run. *No longer being satisfied with NOT having an actual lived experience of what I read, ultimately led to experiential knowing.*

I wanted the real thing, and I became willing to look wherever I was being pointed. I mean, what benefit is it to us if our "wisdom" is based on concepts and beliefs – and what outside "authorities" claimed? If I didn't experience it directly for myself, what those authorities claimed meant nothing. If I didn't know it from within, I didn't know it. This dissatisfaction felt in the body, coupled with a burning desire to simply *experience* God or Source (and not just collecting thoughts *about* God or Source) was the catalyst for a different kind of seeing – one where real wisdom was accessed.

One day, I came across a question that hit me like a ton of bricks. It read, "What is your actual experience of God?" It wasn't, "what do you know of God", but "what is your actual and direct experience of God?" Reading that question became the moment when my course was forever altered. The manner in which I became so willing to look where I was invited to look took on a whole new dimension; nothing less than truth would suffice. It was that moment when I saw the inherent limits of religion and belief, concepts, scripture, sutra and dogma.

Since I didn't want more of what I was getting, I wasn't willing to continue to delude myself any longer. I knew a different approach was needed if I was to be a finder and not a seeker. It occurred to me to ask, "what's the point of being a seeker if I didn't have a sincere intent on finding?" I soon discovered that when I looked in the directions that were being pointed to (from *below* the neck, and not with my analytical and comparative mind that evaluated what it *thinks* it knows from past experience) that something energetic within was activated; I felt an actual and organic shift in consciousness that played out in my body and affairs.

And it wasn't conceptual in nature. When it's not conceptual, it has a real chance of being transformative and life - changing. There was no doubt present. If it *was* conceptual in nature, it had to include belief. And if belief was involved, a certain level of doubt had to be present. Time usually tells the real story. Over time, I noticed that doubt still didn't arise. I found that the realizations were experiential and organic, taking on a spontaneous life of its own – only known and understood from the inside out.

When it was suggested that I don't look with the mind, confusion often arose. I remember feeling confusion and thinking, "What do you mean, don't look with the mind…how else *would* I look, how else *can* I look?" So, the pointers can seem very abstract and confusing, tempting us to throw them out as a ludicrous waste of time. My suggestion would be don't throw the baby out with the bathwater. Just keep looking. Since most of us look to our minds to tell us what's true, of course it may seem ludicrous at first – *because* we don't understand it.

So, if there is confusion with this suggestion, just know it's very common. It does appear abstract, especially when approached by the thinking mind, but it isn't. This is a very different kind of looking – the kind that is rarely taught and the kind that doesn't rely on the mind. Besides, most of our accepted ways of discovering haven't really delivered on their promises. We've got nothing to lose, except everything that is untrue about us. And when everything that is untrue falls away, truth remains. This is *always* game of subtraction, not addition.

If your mind has something else to say about this, I invite you to suspend your judgment. Refrain from throwing it out as something not worthy of your attention, because in truth, there's not much more that *is* worthy of your attention – this type of looking, I mean. This kind of looking is way more transformational, and its benefits are lasting and real. One great byproduct is that once you've seen the truth of something, you can't un-see it. Once you've truly seen the truth of something, it can no longer have any power over you. Anything we're conscious of can never harm us; it's the things we're unconscious of that harms us.

What we're conscious of can no longer torture or cause us suffering because we don't give it life with our confusion or resistance. Just keep it simple and know that anything still in the dark recesses of our consciousness has the ability to divide us; anything seen and met out in the open light of awareness can't. Our job is to simply meet what's causing us division – and watch it melt away. Notice when the mind steps in to give its thoughts and judgments. When it does, just let it be. It's not a problem unless you make it one. Someone once said, *"The only problems we have are the ones we believe in."* How true.

This is a game of subtraction, allowing and looking to see what's actual. A good way to tell if you're looking with the mind, as opposed to your heart, where wisdom resides, is that you'll notice your mind agreeing, disagreeing and judging what it's looking at based on the accumulation of past concepts believed to be true. This is what the mind does – and this is one of its many functions. It evaluates what arises presently in relation to what already arose – and then compares both to its manufactured model of reality based in belief and separation.

In other words, when we are invited to look in a direction that is different from what we're accustomed to – and we find ourselves comparing it against our likes and dislikes, we can be sure we are looking with the mind and not the heart. The heart, being a lover of what is, looks on without preference or partiality – without discrimination or distinction, for it knows the way is the way of acceptance and inclusion – and not resistance, avoidance and comparison. You may have read this conceptual pointer before, but have you REALLY investigated and confirmed it experientially for yourself – as if your life depended on it? While your physical life may not depend on, the quality of your overall life certainly does.

If resistance or grasping is happening, it's a telltale sign you're looking with the mind. Wisdom sees that separation is the grand illusion – and notices it is the mind that separates and divides. Reality doesn't divide. What you really are doesn't divide. By dividing and believing in the appearance of separation, we feel this fracture in our direct experience – with an unmistakable felt sense of inner division. This isn't a bad or wrong thing at all. It is just a reminder that we are indeed, looking with the discriminating mind that habitually leans heavily towards what it's most comfortable with – even if it brings pain!

Minds resist the unknown at all costs; have you noticed this? When we aren't in harmony with life, our bodies tell us instantly. It's telling us that we aren't in harmony with what is. All that is needed is to be aware of it, and to see that we are looking in the direction of what's true. With our awareness, we turn and face the proper direction (like West if we wish to enjoy the sun-set) while dropping our insistence of playing out our habitual tendencies. And we simply notice the experience of that.

Most of us unknowingly suppress our natural wisdom that just needs to be approached in the right way in order to blossom. Can a flower blossom without sunlight, water and proper soil? Of course it can't. If you wanted to feed the pigeons while sitting on a park bench, would you aggressively throw breadcrumbs in their direction in hopes of attracting them, or would you nonchalantly toss them lightly in their direction, gently welcoming them? Our approach makes a big difference.

We are constantly exposed to countless ideas and strategies that suggest ways to access the inner wisdom we all naturally possess. We read, listen to and ingest those ideas from all kinds of people, but not much changes for us. It's disillusioning and confusing, and it can lead to resignation and despair. If wisdom is something we already possess – and NOT something we need learn, it follows that *how we orient ourselves* (with the intent of accessing this wisdom) is essential, wouldn't you say? If gaining access, or tuning into our own inner wisdom is something that brings more peace and meaning to our lives, paying attention to *how* we go about it, is also essential, wouldn't you agree?

As the popular saying goes, "if nothing changes, nothing changes." If we go about our business as usual, we will inevitably get more of the same, won't we? If we want to enjoy the sunrise, we must be facing east, or we won't enjoy that sunrise. Likewise, if we want to live from the wisdom we already possess, we must look in the direction that wisdom demands. While it is neutral and unbiased, it demands we look in its direction. Its attitude is like, "Hey, I am eternally here if you need me" – and never, "Hey dummy, look here, I'm getting impatient." It's worth repeating, so at the risk of being repetitive, here goes: If wisdom is below the neck and isn't conceptual, we must look from our hearts, not our heads.

When I finally saw that believing the thoughts in my head was a surefire way to suppress my natural state of wisdom, something happened. When I questioned everything that I thought was true, something else happened. When I was fully present in this moment, without any investment on "my way" being the outcome, something *really* different happened. This *something that happened* continued to happen as long as I kept with this kind of looking. Notice I didn't say, "mindset." The approach is from being that already knows; the approach is one that's intent on seeing what's true, uncovering what's already there – and not from an analytical mind that depends on logic, reason and the past.

When I met the moment, without any investment in things being a particular way, I noticed a feeling of spacious freedom that was very welcoming and inclusive. When I no longer believed the thoughts in my head, and was willing not to know anything at all, that spacious freedom was present again. I began to really enjoy the freedom that came about as a result of making no demands on the moment. It started to take on a life of its own, without my conscious intent. When I saw that life didn't need my help, an ease of being was felt I hadn't felt before.

When I saw that life really was so much more capable of living in an effortless way than I was, I was able to hand over the keys, roll down the window and just *enjoy the ride*. And then, another interesting thing began to occur. I saw that when I no longer referenced my mind to tell me what's true, and trusted in my own being to know how to live life, life flowed in ways I hadn't experienced before. This confirmed that there really wasn't any separation. And it often took the path of least resistance. I liked that because that was my style! I never bought into the popular notion that you had to "work hard" to achieve what you wanted. Wisdom and the path of least resistance, the one without a lot of striving and effort, always seemed to go hand in hand.

As a result, it occurred to me to just say YES to what was already happening. That seemed very sane to me; *rejecting what was already happening seemed like real insanity to me,* the kind that got lunatics locked up for good! So this seemed like true wisdom, and it was confirmed in my experience. When I no longer argued with reality, I felt relaxed and free. Surely this was wisdom! I was home, at last. Allowing what is, to be *as it is,* felt strange initially.

However, it soon became the norm. No longer did I buy into the belief that said I was "giving up or giving in" when I allowed something to occur that I didn't prefer. No longer did I believe that I had to "fight for" what I wanted (if at first my way) didn't manifest itself. This belief dropped away when I saw the truth of things, that resisting and fighting what was *already actually occurring* only prolonged what I didn't want. I was tired of the pain and suffering, and losing in life. I wanted to win in life; I knew that in order to win, I had to work with myself, not against myself.

When I dropped the fight, I began to win in a big way. Let me rephrase that so it's more accurate: seeing that opposing life was a losing situation, the fight dropped away. What a beautiful paradox, and in fact, I began to see that ALL of life was a beautiful paradox. I could just allow what was happening, *as* I intended for something more desirable to happen, if that was the case.

Life began to flow with such ease because I was living in harmony with it, trusting that life really does know best. I saw that sometimes life went through hell in order to come out the other side. I was okay with that, too, because wisdom told me that life knew better than I did – so if life chose going through hell that day, then going through hell that day was indeed the way. My mind, being a finite thing, couldn't comprehend the infinite.

Instead, I deferred to a different kind of looking and experiencing, because I finally decided to actually confirm for myself what the enlightened were attempting to convey. I discovered that I could not pick and choose what I liked and didn't like; I had to stay with the same orientation in all aspects of my life. I didn't have the luxury of saying, "Hey, I'm okay with this being *this* way in this part of my life, but I'm not okay with being this way with *that* way in that part of my life" – AND thinking I'd still be free. I had to include the whole lot – or I'd suffer. It was very consistent.

I noticed that there's only one thing going on. I noticed that I couldn't fool life, either. Being okay with life choosing the route through hell made for a short ride, a ride without many bumps and bruises. Sometimes it's necessary to go through the jungle to get to the land of paradise, but the key was being okay with being in *either* land. As a very good friend of mine once said, "It's easy to know NOT to get caught up in hell, but it isn't so easy to know *not* to get caught up in heaven." How profound. Both are okay with me, as both are temporary experiences anyway.

Without insisting on my preferences being met, or offering resistance to what is, experience would never torture me. Wisdom sees that nothing remains – that everything comes and goes. By allowing the natural and cyclical order of things to do its thing – and function the way it does, I was no longer resisting what was actually happening. And I couldn't suffer, either. That was the really cool part – noticing that I could confirm this for myself and not have to rely on others to tell me what was true. What a relief!

One of things that we are so enveloped in (and run from at the same time) is innately so full of wisdom. It is silence. Silence is often seen as the enemy, or at the least, something to be avoided. When we make friends with silence, we can't help but have wisdom bloom inside us. Wisdom is rooted in silence and silence is rooted in wisdom. Wisdom sees that silence is the ground of all being, and that silence is, in fact, what each moment arises from and falls back into. If you just look for yourself, you'll notice each sound you hear arises from silence and falls back into silence. Each thought you speak comes from silence, and then falls back into silence.

You see this in your experience – and not with your mind. Confirm this now. We can't ever escape silence, yet somehow we've concluded it's not always our friend! How many of us run from silence, the backdrop of each and every moment? How many of us look to be entertained and distracted with television, books, music, food, sex, drugs and alcohol, in order to keep silence, the ground of being, away? Aren't we seeking to forget ourselves with these forms of entertainment that occupy and cover up silence? Isn't that what we're really doing?

It's one thing to be entertained by something, and quite another to be distracted by something. It is our motivation and intent for engaging in these behaviors that determines whether these activities are healthy or not – and whether or not they're engaged in for the sake of pure enjoyment, or for the sake of running away from something we'd rather not face. Don't we already intuitively know that *we are* silence? Don't we already know that silence is an aspect or quality of who we are that never leaves us? Don't we know that it's an integral part of our experience, and that without it, we'd probably go mad? Can you even imagine a world without silence? I can't, nor do I want to.

Are you still present when thought and feeling disappear? You most certainly are. Doesn't that tell you that you can't possibly be your thoughts and feelings? Are you still present when the mind is completely still, like in meditation or deep sleep? You most certainly are. Doesn't that tell you that you can't possibly *be* the mind? Wisdom sees that when we run from the silence that we already are, silence must chase us. Wisdom sees running from what we can't ever escape only brings unnecessary pain and suffering.

It's not that silence is problematic. It's that in the silence, we are very aware of the thoughts that race around in our minds, so we go to great lengths to distract ourselves from that disturbing experience. If we'd just relax into the silence we already are, we'd see that silence is indeed golden. There is more wisdom in listening to the silence, and being receptive to silence, than there is in reading *everything* anyone has ever written or said about silence. Find this out for yourself and be free. Make friends with silence and discover that is has ALWAYS been your trusted friend all along.

Don't believe the thoughts in your head *about* silence. None of them are true. They only *feel* true, and become true for you, if you believe them. Notice all along, you've been running from the thoughts you have about things; you've been running from the thoughts you have about yourself. Stop mixing the two and wake up to what you really are. Beliefs, opinions and perceptions are all objects in your awareness. You are the subject that is aware *of* them. The Christian Trappist Monk, Thomas Merton said:

"Words stand between silence and silence: between the silence of things and the silence of our own being, between the silence of the world and silence of God. When we have really met and known the world in silence, words do not separate us from the world nor from other men, nor

When Wisdom Blooms

from God, nor from ourselves because we no longer trust entirely in language to contain reality."

Chapter 6
You Are What You Want

"Why run around sprinkling holy water? There's an ocean inside you, and when you're ready, you'll drink." ~ **Kabir**

Imagine a world where every human woke up one day, realizing that they already were what they wanted? And that they finally saw they were living their lives like a dog chasing its tail, exhausting themselves with fruitless attempts to claim what was already theirs by birthright. As a result, there wouldn't be a whole lot of seeking going on anymore.

Can you imagine the implications? Wouldn't there naturally be great relief and a lightness of energy experienced? Wouldn't we have a much more joyous human race if we knew we lacked nothing at all? We would, as a whole, experience much less suffering and strife.

Since we no longer saw each other as separate anymore, we'd naturally love and accept each other. Would that be a world you'd want to live in? I sure would. In fact, there are many who've realized this, but for whatever reason, they are in the vast minority. If we desire a world where peace and love isn't just a conceptual idea – but is actually realized and expressed – then don't we have a responsibility to wake up to the reality that we already *are* what we seek? If it isn't our responsibility, whose is it? If not now, when?

Would you consider that a worthy endeavor, one that may take a bit of earnest attention to realize? What would you give for this? Would you give up all your ideas, beliefs and cherished opinions for the opportunity to realize that you are what you want? Although it may appear a scary and absurd notion, nothing less will do. Not knowing we already are what we want is the human condition. It's not accidental or haphazard that it is this way. Why? Simply because it *is* this way!

Remember, truth is simple. It's the mind's role to complicate things and turn them into complexities.

Seeking and wanting implies that we don't already possess that which we seek or want. *Just because we believe we don't possess a thing, does it actually mean we don't possess that thing?* Can we really make that assumptive leap? Just because our minds tell us we wouldn't be seeking a thing if we had it, does it make it so?

For example, do you really believe that you have a limited or finite amount of love in your heart? Do you really believe (in reality, in truth) that you don't have enough love in your heart for the entire human race – and for all the creatures, both on land and sea, and in the sky? If you don't, let me be the first to tell you: You are mistaken. I hope I didn't just offend you; that is the last thing I want to do here. But I just can't support that belief, so I must take the risk of offending you. Just because you may feel, believe or think that you don't possess enough love in your heart for all of creation doesn't make it true.

Now, I am aware that some people have had traumatic and unloving pasts, sometimes with horrific things done to them. This often leads to justifying hearts closing down, but that still doesn't equate to the truth of NOT having enough love in their hearts for all of creation, does it? Real love, true love – the kind without any condition – is present in all of us, right now. Past experience or present circumstance matters not.

When Wisdom Blooms

The fact that many of us don't realize this doesn't alter this truth one bit. In fact, you were born with this capacity (or space in your heart) to love and embrace all of creation. Notice that I am using the words "space" and "capacity," and not using the word "potential" here. I *am* saying that this total and absolute love is already present within you right now, the kind that includes absolutely everything, without any distinction or preference. It's simply covered over by past fears, hurts, traumas and the like. Therefore, the experiences that you've accumulated over a lifetime, both good and bad, cannot harm or touch this capacity.

This unharmed, untouched "enough room in your heart already" condition is present in you, regardless of your thoughts or feelings about it. All it takes is a thought believed in to close our hearts down. Actually, hearts don't close; they are always radiating love and openness. There's no such thing as a "wounded heart". When minds are closed, hearts *feel* closed and wounded. If we close down to all, or most of the love present within us, then yes, we will feel (and even proclaim to the high heavens) that in no way do we have enough love within us for all of God's creation. Sadly, we may even conclude that if we don't have this love of self, how can we possibly have it for all of creation?

But again, does this make it true? Does this make it actually so? And how could you ever know this is true? Just because you don't feel it is so – just because you don't presently *feel* that love for all of creation? Here I am, some guy you don't personally know, saying that you already are what you want, and that you already are what you seek. Who am I to say this, you may ask? I am simply just someone who realized this many years ago desiring to spread the good news. I am simply someone who knows that, although I appear separate and distinct from you, I *am* you.

More specifically, the essence of what you are, what animates the body and mind *you* have is the very same essence animating my body and mind – and every other body and mind. Our bodies are indeed separate, distinct and different, but what animates and informs them isn't separate at all. What animated and informed Jesus, the Buddha, and Mohammed was also this one essence. We all have different intellectual capacity, different values and interests, but what animates and informs absolutely everything and everyone is the same singular essence.

Let's take less of a bite here and look at this differently, and on a smaller scale. Would you agree that in our deepest honesty, it is human nature to desire to love oneself unconditionally – and then love others in the same way? Would you also agree that, it is in fact the human condition that many of us have a real struggle with self-love, and therefore, difficulty with truly loving another? Isn't this what we most struggle with? And if this is so, don't we often go looking for love *because* we feel it's lacking within us?

Don't we have a tendency to seek out what we think we don't already have? Yes, we most certainly do. If you knew and realized that you were already the source of all that you sought, would you feel lack, limitation and angst? Would you seek these things outside of yourself? No, of course you wouldn't. Do you believe this is "pie in the sky stuff" reserved for the "lucky" few, or is there something within you right now that knows, on some level, beyond belief, that what I'm saying points to the truth ... that you already possess (in full) that which you want, that which you seek?

If you *do* think this is "pie in the sky stuff," does that make it so? It IS if you say it is. That's literally all it takes. We give untrue thoughts life all the time. It feels real in our experience, but it doesn't make it real. One unexamined thought can separate the worlds apart. And if you do think this is pie in the sky stuff, will you write it off as something unworthy of your attention? Will you continue to live your life believing what brings true fulfillment is outside of yourself, and therefore, only attained through a rigorous, looking "out there" search?

If you've noticed, there is common thread throughout these pages, and one in which can't ever be overvalued or overstated. It is a willingness to find out for yourself what is true in your own experience.

This is our aim. It is a voluntary suspension of what we *think* we know, coupled with a deep curiosity and investigation of what we hold as true. A willingness *not* to know what is true, until we *can* know, is essential. A willingness to see that not knowing is very peaceful and spacious place to be, and not something to be feared or ashamed of, is waiting to be discovered.

The other night, I was watching "Wicked Tuna" on the National Geographic channel. I had no idea these fish can weigh over 1,000lbs, grow up to twelve feet long and swim over 45 mph! Incredible. Anyway, one of the boats was fishing for tuna off the coast of Gloucester, Massachusetts. Along came a bigger, fishing vessel trolling for all types of fish, not just tuna. This vessel had a big net that was being dragged about fifty feet below the surface, ensnaring and accumulating all sorts of fish. In the process, it also snagged the anchor line of one of the tuna fishing boats, rendering it powerless and dependent for a time. I couldn't help but notice that this is the way we are as humans.

As we live our lives, we collect and assimilate all kinds of beliefs, ideas and opinions – most of which don't originate from within – and we too, become powerless and dependent for a time, sometimes for a lifetime. We take on, and scoop up, these ideas from outside sources – and act as if they are true. Somewhere along the way, we picked up the idea that not knowing means we are stupid or less than, when the opposite is actually true. All these stories are illusory and constitute our "anchor" that's snagged in the net.

Somewhere along the way, we picked up the idea that to reach out and ask for help means we're weak, when somewhere inside we know the opposite is true. It is wisdom that admits when it doesn't know, and it is wisdom that admits when it needs support. Only when it is admitted that we don't know (or that we can use a helping hand) can another possibility arise for us. We'll never live outside the confines of the box if we continue to think inside the box. This is what wisdom "demands," and this is when wisdom blooms.

Wisdom also sees that to not know is to know. We know that we don't know. That's huge, and something that's way undervalued and unappreciated in our culture! *When we know that we don't know, we are no longer deluding ourselves. When we don't delude ourselves, we allow something else to move through us. No longer are we pretending to know, because we finally have the courage to tell the truth.* With this orientation, imagine yourself standing in a room in a very dark house called, "I am what I want, I am what I seek."

The room is dark and you can't see. In order to see, you light a lantern, illuminating the room you're in. At *that* moment, just before you lit the lantern, you didn't know, you didn't see, and that was perfectly okay with you. After it was lit, you still didn't know, but you were much better equipped to see what was true or not, to see what was in the room. Because you turned on the light of awareness, you're better equipped to see how many cracks were on the walls and ceilings (labels that lie, unquestioned beliefs and assumptions) and what kind of floors were present. Your light of awareness (the lantern) instantly dispelled the darkness, and enables you to investigate each room (each aspect of yourself) in the house.

As the light is on, you notice something telling you (innate wisdom that knows) it's okay to admit to yourself you don't know, that you really *don't* see that you already are what you want – and that you're willing to keep looking to see if it is true or not. Besides, you have a sense that seeing this could be very significant. That's integrity, and that's the spirit in which all good things come. It also happens to be the orientation that eventually allows us to see what we don't presently see, allowing us to experience what we don't presently experience.

Otherwise, we're just being phony, and the phonies don't ever get to see what's really true. Phonies don't get enlightened, and phonies certainly aren't looking in the right direction. Those who engage in self-deception look for shortcuts that lead to the easier, less truthful way. The problem is, this way doesn't reveal what you really want anyway. Telling the truth isn't something to fear anymore – because like silence, truth is definitely our friend – and ultimately, what sets us free. If something *can* set us free, how can that something *not* be our friend? Why fear a real and true friend? If there is still some fear present, we don't let that stop us because we know it isn't based in what's really true anyway.

Truth isn't to be feared. It's when we believe the fears our minds fabricate (about what we have to give up or lose in order to realize that truth) that barriers arise. The mind has NO IDEA, but it thinks it does – and then we believe it! Anything we project will be seen to be true for us, because we'll imagine and create the scenario we cooked up. Then we'll conclude it was needed all along! How's that for a self-fulfilling prophecy?

In reality, it's just a random bunch of thoughts we've collected with our nets that we've come to believe and identify with. Nevertheless, just because we see them in our nets doesn't mean we're obligated to bring them on board, does it? We can let them go; we can release them back from where they came because we *see* they don't serve us. Why would we hold on to a thought that tells us we're inferior, when all it does is make us self-conscious in front of others? Instead of really questioning what specific evidence tells us this, many of us often remain stuck, acting as if it's just a "fact" of our lives.

However, if we are sincere in finding what's really so, the answer will be revealed to us. Remember, the false cannot stand up to examination! It can become a new habit – a new way of being. As long as we are open and receptive to being okay with whatever arises, it's almost always rewarding. If we truly have a desire to look at this concept that says, "You are what you want," then we must want to know the truth more than we want to feel good. If we don't, we set ourselves up for failure at the first sign of trouble.

Like the weather, feelings come and go – and therefore, are impermanent. When we place a high value and priority on that which comes and goes, we set ourselves up for disappointment and suffering, every time. When we place a high priority on that which must erode and wash away any time stormy weather appears, any time challenging situations present themselves, we set ourselves up for disillusionment and disappointment. If feeling good is our primary concern, we won't ever have the capacity or willingness to take the road less traveled, the road that ultimately leads to freedom. Seeking truth isn't always a smooth ride, and can play with our emotions.

Sometimes seeing through illusion is painful and sometimes it's a great relief. We must consciously decide that we're willing to face whatever comes our way, especially since we aren't ultimately satisfied with the status quo. If it really was that easy, so many have would have already taken that road and reported back on how easy it is! It *is* simple, but not always easy. This road does take a certain amount of courage – acting in spite of the fear, but it does lead to the Kingdom of Heaven. We must be sincere, and we must genuinely *want* to see what we don't presently see.

It is the unknown that we must enter, without any expectation or agenda. Expectations and agendas only obscure seeing what's true. Feeling good must be secondary, because we see that, like thoughts and experiences, feelings come and go – and are not to be grasped at or held onto – because they can't be grasped or held onto! Despite our past conditioning that places such importance and value on feelings being such accurate barometers for what's true and real, we see them for what they are – just energy of emotion, spontaneously arising as a result of how we're presently perceiving a person, place, thing, or situation.

When feeling good isn't our primary concern, we can defer to how the moment is actually unfolding, and not how we want it to unfold. When our focus is on feeling good, we can't help but try and manipulate our experience to suit our needs – so we feel good – and it never works in an authentic way.

It's a manufactured feeling, not an organic one. Thus, it can't last. When we're able to fully show up in this moment, it means we come naked and free, without expectation or insistence of our way being manifested.

So what do most of us really want? Whether it's realized or not, most of us seek the feeling of inner peace and self-love. We want to experience a sense of belonging and communion with others. A feeling sense of being at home wherever we are, and a feeling of being content in our own skin is what we want. Humans want physical security. In fact, it's a major driving force, and sometimes, the very thing that takes up most of our attention and concern – often to the point of obscuring the direct realization of seeing that we already are the peace and love we want. This isn't a bad thing, it just is. However, when it takes up most of our focus and attention, we have little left for seeing what's real and true.

But most of all, whether we realize it or not, we want Truth. *Essentially, every desire we have is a desire to come home, to realize and experience the wholeness and completeness that we already are.* Naturally, we seek what we don't think we possess, but at what point do we stop and say, "Hey, wait a minute, I'm not really getting anywhere; I'd better look at where I'm looking." Sadly, this recognition and stopping never happens for many of us. We go to our graves without ever really singing our song. We go to our graves never realizing who we really are.

We all want to realize the truth of who we really are, and then to live from that realization. Not conceptually, but experientially. However, when we set it up in our experience that we must have physical security in order to have inner peace, self-love and a sense of deep connection, odds are we won't ever realize we already are what we want. Truth demands all of it. If you put off feeling good as your primary concern, I can tell you this: If you look until you see, no matter what feelings arise, you'll have so many good feelings later on. They will naturally arise later, if your primary concern is discovering that you already are what you want, now.

Granted, this is easier said than done. But it doesn't take away from the fact of its simplicity. Besides, what's our alternative? If we want to see that we already are what we want – and live from that realization, that desire to see must be stronger than our need for security. I remember long ago reading Deepak Chopra saying that, security, both emotional and physical, is an illusion that can be taken away at any moment. Further, it isn't even real to begin with! I didn't believe him. Instead, I found out for myself. Deepak was right.

While it isn't always easy to see formless, intangible and invisible things like thoughts, beliefs and perceptions *as* illusory, it's not only very possible to do so, it's within our capabilities. Our direct experience, instantly, or over time, will reveal to us whether something can be relied on or not, and whether it's real or not. Our bodies will reveal to us the validity of anything in the form of flow, resonance, ease, peace, lightness, dissonance, being stuck, anxiousness, heaviness, etc. And so, when we *see* that our beliefs don't hold up through examination, or prove to have any supporting evidence, they often dissolve. What's true can't dissolve.

When we see anything as bogus, it drops away on its own. With our *seeing*, we just took the life energy away – and it dies. Have you noticed that nothing in our experience remains, and everything goes? Once this is seen, we can just control what we can control – and let the rest go. It doesn't mean that we don't plan for the future, or work towards living in comfort for our remaining days. It means that we do these things today, we plan these things today, without allowing our minds to run amok by projecting unwanted visions of an imagined future we don't want.

We pay attention to the needs of this day – and it is always *this* day. When the next day arrives, God willing, we pay attention to that day – which is *this* day. If we find this difficult, we can *return to sender* and say, "thanks for sharing, but I am staying in the endless present moment, the only reality." If we are meant to have food in our stomach, a roof over our head, and money in the bank *any* day, then it will be so. If not, we may indeed have a different experience. Either way, anticipating and fearing an imagined future (we don't want) can only intensify the possibility of it manifesting. This is critical to see.

In Matthew 6:24-34, Jesus said, *"Consider the lilies of the field, how they grow; they neither toil or spin; yet I tell you, even Solomon in all his glory was not arrayed like one of these. But if God so clothes the grass of the field, which today is alive and tomorrow is thrown into the Ocean, will he not much more clothe you, O men of little faith? And which of you by being anxious can add one cubit to his span of life?"* Listening to, and taking to heart the wisdom of Jesus when he said, "Give us this day our daily bread" … we are grateful for our daily bread, without concern for tomorrow's bread.

What is *bread*, but the very staple of life and symbol of all that we need to live and grow? "Anxiety is neither helpful nor necessary. It robs us of faith and confidence in God's help, and it saps our energy for doing good works. Put away your petty preoccupations for material things and instead seek first the things of God – his kingdom and righteousness." As we only ever get to live one day at a time, we live for today without fearing an undesired tomorrow. Wisdom sees that tomorrow isn't even guaranteed, and that now is the only reality. If we really are what we want and seek, then why is this truth so foreign to so many of us?

The 14th Century Christian mystic, Meister Eckhart once said, *"The eye with which I see God is the same eye with which God sees me."* If this is so, why don't more of us see and enjoy the glorious implications of this beautiful truth? For starters, we were never shown this, and we are rarely among those who have realized this. Lastly, it takes an earnest desire to question everything we think we know, and everything we cherish. Not many are willing to do this! With the invention of the Internet, it's not difficult to find these people anymore. These people are out there in the world. They are mostly very ordinary, humble and unassuming people. They could very well be your next-door neighbor, the clerk at the grocery store, or your house painter.

So take heart, it isn't anyone's fault that this is the way it is. Asking "why" this is so is just an attempt by the mind to understand and control. There is no why; it just is. There's nothing wrong with seeking out these people, whether it's on the Internet, your local bookstore or in your local community, *as you look within to confirm this truth in your being.* In fact, I suggest it. Remember, wisdom sees the good sense of using crutches for a time, until one can walk on their own. As the Zen saying proclaims, *"If the truth isn't right where you are, where else do you expect to find it?"* Truth, being present all the time, doesn't come and go.

Find out what you are, find out what doesn't come and go, and enjoy your life. Feelings, thoughts and perceptions are all objects in your awareness that come and go, so they can't be what you are. The activity of thinking, an object in your awareness, comes and goes. That can't be what you are, either. What you ARE is eternally present, and prior to all that comes and goes – and is the ground of being. Find out what remains, when all else doesn't, and the ballgame is over. The great Indian Sage, Ramana Maharshi once said, *"Let what comes come and let what goes go. Find out what remains."*

There is something so elusively obvious that I must mention it here. We've all had the experience of looking for something that we've misplaced. Perhaps it's our car keys we thought we placed on the table, or the pickle jar that we could have sworn we still had in the fridge. We search and search, but can't seem to find them. Eventually we give up and sit down, dumbfounded that they're nowhere in sight. All of sudden, they appear out of nowhere, sitting right there on the edge of the coffee table, or staring right at us from the top shelf of the fridge, where we suspected it was all along. They were never truly lost; they just appeared to be lost. We just didn't see them.

Similarly, when we assume or believe that we aren't already the truth, love or peace that we want, we are missing something so obvious that it *seems* elusive. Therefore, we conclude it isn't already present! Asking the right questions is critical if we are to discover what's true. Asking the right questions orients us to look in the direction where truth reveals itself.

When we assume we aren't what we seek, we fail to ask ourselves a few pertinent and revealing questions: Is the love that I want and that I seek, not already present in my experience, right now? Is the inner peace that I want and seek, not already present in my experience, right now? Now, you may not feel or sense the love and peace directly (and immediately) when you ask these questions, but don't allow that temporary experience make you draw the lasting conclusion that you aren't already what you seek!

I can assure you this: If you were to get quiet and sit in silence for a few minutes, days, months (or for however long it takes YOU) then that which you want will reveal itself as that which was never absent. If you're earnest, and you want it more than you want to feel good, it will reveal itself beyond the chatter of the mind, without any doubt or confusion. If at first you don't succeed, try again. If at first it doesn't reveal itself within your preferred timetable, keep looking. The fact is, it could care less about your timetable. It only cares about your sincere looking above all else. Your fears and apprehension don't matter. Bring them with, as you look. Don't wait for them to disappear, or you may wait forever.

Resist the temptation of believing you must take a journey to see this, and that it must take *time* to see this. It can literally happen for you in an instant, even right now. Drop all agendas and preferences and allow for anything to happen; allow for all of it to happen, in *its* way, not *your* way. Your agenda is totally irrelevant. If you make this finding your number one priority, above all else, you won't be a seeker forever. And when you do find, you won't regret any of the experiences you've ever had, nor will you be anxious of any future happening to come. Both will drop away. You'll finally know what Jesus really meant when he talked about being one with the Father, and what he really meant when he referenced the Kingdom of Heaven.

When you turn up the light up conscious awareness, go within, and finally meet yourself, you'll recognize that the love you've been seeking was (all along) right where you are – IS what you are. You'll recognize you never had to go out in search of it. Always start where you are. This fire has been lit all along and has been burning brightly. It's never been extinguished, even for a moment. Once you see this, you can then be a light unto others. As the Buddha once said, *"First be a light unto yourself."* Stop looking for blessings and be the blessing you already are.

There is a wonderful story that illustrates this point. You may have heard of it because it is a timeless classic called, "Acres of Diamonds," about a farmer who lived in Africa and through a visitor, became tremendously excited about looking for diamonds. Diamonds were already discovered in great abundance on the African continent and this farmer became so enthralled with the idea of acquiring millions of dollars worth of diamonds that he sold his farm to go out in search of these diamonds. He searched and searched the continent over and as the years slipped by, his exhaustive search turned up empty. Eventually he went completely broke, and in despair, threw himself into a river and drowned.

Meanwhile, the new owner of his farm came across an unusual looking rock about the size of an egg and placed it on his mantle as a decorative piece. A visitor dropped by one day and upon seeing the rock, became so excited he started jumping up and down. He told the new owner of the farm that the rock on his mantle was perhaps the largest diamond that had ever been found.

The new owner of the farm said, "Well, the whole farm is covered with them" – and sure enough it was. The farm turned out to be the Kimberly Diamond Mine, the richest the world has ever known. The original farmer was literally sitting on "acres of diamonds" until he sold his farm. Each of us is right smack in the middle of our own "acres of diamonds", if only we would realize it and develop the ground we are standing on before charging off in search of greener pastures. Is the love that I seek not already present right here, right now? Is the inner peace that I seek not already present right here, right now – before I go in search of it? Is Truth not already present before I go out in search of it?

Osho said, *"Drop the idea of becoming someone, because you are already a masterpiece. You cannot be improved. You have only to come to it, to know it, to realize it."*

Chapter 7
The Greatest Gift You Can Give

"What is true is already so. Owning up to it doesn't make it worse. Not being open about it doesn't make it go away. And because it's true, it is what is there to be interacted with. Anything untrue isn't there to be lived. People can stand what is true, for they are already enduring it."

~ Eugene Gendlin

When Wisdom Blooms

There is a peculiar and consistent phenomenon that human consciousness reveals. And it is this: Consciousness has a real tendency to forget that to be human is to be possessed with both strengths *and* weaknesses. We forget that human nature is, by nature, bound by time and limited by sensory perception. To deny these facts is to deny our very humanity. Failing to see that, by design, we are created with both a limited and unlimited nature, we often judge and condemn. In so doing, we cement the notion that perfection is a human potential, when in truth, it's merely an idea we've been taught to chase after, an idea that if attained would make us happier.

The fortunate few recognize that, in that chasing, "perfection" is always a moving target – and one that can never be attained. Throughout the ages, saints, sages and the mystics alike have expressed this experience of "not rightness" as a sense of being off kilter, off balance, fractured, broken or divided. The Buddha proclaimed in the first of his Four Noble Truths that "Life is suffering" – and to be mindful that suffering arises when we fail to include absolutely everything in our experience, not just what we *want* in our experience.

In my book, *"The Dance of Imperfection – Living in Perfect Harmony with Life,"* we re-examine our interpretations of what it means to be imperfect – and how those interpretations impact our experience.

Ralph Waldo Emerson said, *"There is a crack in everything God has made."* It is in this crack (what I refer to as "perceived imperfection" or simply, "weakness") – and it is through the absolute and complete acceptance of *this* crack – that wholeness reveals itself AS our true nature. Therefore, it is *in and through* that crack of imperfection where our opportunity resides, if we would just see it. It is in and through that crack of "imperfection" where our transcendence takes place.

It is only a thought believed in that tells us otherwise; it is only a thought believed in that separates the sun, the moon, the sky and the oceans. Until then, this crack of "imperfection" will continue to torture and divide, until we see the profound opportunity in each moment of our existence. When we accept ourselves with all of our strengths and weaknesses, we give ourselves the opportunity to truly show up and be supportive for another in a way that is authentic and potentially transforming.

When we realize the truth of our dual nature, we're able to embrace and include all of ourselves, not just the desired half. When we see that the inherent nature of our own limitations can't be any other way than it is – we render ourselves truly humble. It is in this recognition where we understand the nature of our situation. It is in this humility and understanding where we're able to be of real service to those in need. When we no longer *unconsciously*

When Wisdom Blooms

(and ignorantly) point out in others that which we don't love and accept about ourselves, we're then in a position to truly be a catalyst for a new potential.

Then and only then, are we really able to be a neutral sounding board for another who seeks a way out of their present situation. Then and only then, are we really able to truly be an agent for change – if change is desired. Wisdom sees human beings connect with each other in a meaningful way in the reality of their shared weaknesses, and not so much on the basis of common strengths. It is in this vulnerability and acknowledgement of our shared weakness that makes us alike; it is in our strengths where we're different.

Where we most connect and heal is in a space of mutual recognition and shared acceptance of our accepted limitations. We all struggle with varying demons, fears and personal grief, while doing the best we can with what we have. We are all "imperfectly perfect," or "perfectly imperfect" just the way we are. It is this unabashed acknowledgement of our dual nature that gives us the wherewithal to live our lives with self-honesty and dignity. Pretenders won't see this. Those unwilling to face themselves as they are won't see this. It is this self-honesty and willingness to face ourselves as we are right now, that creates a rooted connectedness with others that bind; these are the "ties that bind."

Like each wave in the ocean appears separate from other waves – but remains the same ocean, we are one and the same, despite appearing to be different and separate. Expressing our unique strengths and abilities, we naturally grow in different ways and directions, while maintaining the exact same source and substance of who we really are. We remain rooted in the same soil of our own down to earth and humble imperfection. And it is in *this* fertile soil that wisdom blooms. It is in *this* fertile soil where we live more from what we "know" is true, and less from what we "believe" is true.

The willingness not to know what's actual can never be overvalued. In fact, wisdom sees that not knowing is often the only appropriate response to a situation. When it comes to another's struggle, we are aware that to offer unsolicited advice may be equal to robbing them of what they need to experience for themselves. Regardless of the urge we may feel to give advice, no matter how helpful we think it may be, we just can't know what is the highest good for another. How can we know, unless we listen to our mind that might tell us what's best for another? Recognizing this, I won't try to impose my will on you, or anyone else.

Instead, I want to welcome you, just as you are. That's real love. Real love that comes from wholeness provides and engenders the space for something quite different to start informing our activities. Unless we're asked, real love lets you find your own way, in your time, because it's about you, not me. With our shared weaknesses as the common thread in the human experience, we can appreciate (and even be grateful for) another's strengths *and* weaknesses, rather than be intimidated by them. Sometimes the best and most appreciated thing we could ever say to another struggling is nothing at all. Just our nonjudgmental and compassionate presence conveys so much more than any words we can ever say.

This brings up a metaphor for me. Most men don't want to admit when they're lost, especially when they have a woman in the car with them. And if it's a new woman in their lives they want to impress, forget about it. No way, no how, are they stopping at a gas station to get directions! They will drive around, even in circles, attempting to give the impression that they KNOW where they're going. They'll attempt to convey that they're just "temporarily turned around" and not to worry because everything is still under control.

In fact, for as long as they can pull it off, most men will go to great lengths to continue the facade that they know where they're headed. They'd rather drive around for hours, lost, rather than swallow their pride and ask for directions. Arriving on time takes a backseat to the show they must put on. And the funny thing is, the woman almost always knows he's lost, but the man's need for keeping up the charade has a tendency to delude him into thinking he's successfully hiding the fact he's lost. Personally, I can't relate to this, as I've never done this. Yeah right – and I have some swampland in Florida for sale that you'll love; no alligators or crocodiles included, either!

My Mom loves to tell the story of how I got lost once (13 years ago, mind you) probably because she is well aware of the male ego's need to always know where he's headed! Anyway, with my destination ten hours due West, I somehow found myself traveling North for two hours before I realized I was heading in the wrong direction! Thirteen years later, there's still a response that says, "Hey, what are you talking about – I've got a great sense of direction" when she insists on telling the story! Today, it's much easier for me to pull over and ask for directions when I need to – but Mom, I still have a pretty good sense of direction!

Invariably, if you ask a man for directions when *you're* lost, he's usually happy to tell *you* how to get there. If he has a woman in the car with him, he's even more eager to assist. Aren't we naturally happy to give directions to a complete stranger who's lost? I mean, how many of us think, "Oh crap, what a pain this nimrod is; I've got better things to do right now than give this guy or gal directions." Not many of us. It makes us feel good to point the way to others who are lost.

When Wisdom Blooms

It makes us feel good to give directions to those who have lost their way. It may even be a subtle ego boost for us, giving us the opportunity to take credit for being able to assist someone in need. After all, we "know" the way and they don't. There's just something about giving guidance to another human being that feels satisfying. Women aren't immune to this by any means. In many ways, women are more willing to be helpful, and their motives may be a bit less ego-driven than men. It may seem that I'm making hasty generalizations here – and perhaps I am, but I'm simply trying to illustrate a point.

While it is very easy and natural for all of us to *give* directions, we often find it very difficult and unnatural to *ask for and receive* directions. All those years I was reading books and listening to tapes about spirituality, for some reason I just wouldn't look long enough in the directions I was being pointed. I may have glanced, but I certainly never looked until I saw. Consequently, I remained stuck in most of the same challenges I was facing.

We can conveniently chalk it up to the male ego as being the primary reason men generally have a more difficult time asking for direction – or looking in the direction suggested – but let's delve deeper and see if there might be more to it than that. There's something peculiarly consistent and predictable about human consciousness – male or female – when it comes to receiving direction from another. We generally don't want it because we think we know what's best for us. In our lack of humility, we don't want guidance because we conclude if we need outside help, it must mean we're weak. Coming from ego, how else *can* we feel?

This conclusion goes unquestioned, like so many other beliefs and assumptions we have. Our world can be falling apart all around us, yet we rarely consider examining the beliefs and assumptions we operate from. The truth is, wisdom knows that to admit we don't know is anything *but* weak. If we truly desire to be free, we must see that it's ALL an inside game – and that nothing outside of us can ever harm us without our consent.

Therefore, never are we a victim, unless we *play* the victim. Seeing that we are the final authority in our own experience (and that nobody can define who we are) is essential if we are to experience the "peace that surpasses all understanding" – the peace that never goes away, regardless of circumstance. Belief won't do this, only realization will.

Even though we are the final authority, wisdom sees the benefit of looking where another points, especially if that other has realized what we are looking for. Nevertheless, we are the only one who can confirm for ourselves what's actual in our experience. Second-hand knowledge or opinion is fruitless. Generally speaking, unless we specifically ask for advice and direction, we don't really want it.

Isn't this true in *your* experience, especially if it's unsolicited? How many of us actually welcome unsolicited advice from others, the kind that implies "you should be different than you are?"

Don't we almost always feel a cringing contraction upon hearing advice? We sure do – and the primary reason is this: the message being sent to us is we need to be fixed; we need to change because the way we are right now just isn't "right." In short, we should be different than we are – and thus, we can't be appreciated for the *way* we are. For example, I remember being told by a college friend many years ago that I said, "Who cares" a lot – and it bothered him quite a bit, and I knew it.

His assertion initially stung me, but later on I realized why. I saw that when it came to my relationship with him, it was true. I did say, "Who cares" quite a bit. There was a part of me that didn't like my attitude, especially since I saw myself as a caring person. My motive was to annoy him because I *knew* it bothered him. However, on closer examination, I noticed that the driving force wasn't that I simply wanted to annoy him, but rather, that I didn't appreciate him calling me out on a number of other things *he* deemed unacceptable and annoying in *me*.

Consequently, I wanted him to know that I wasn't hearing or acknowledging his judgments of me by saying, "who cares?" I didn't appreciate his condemnation and judgment. Today I'm sure I'd handle it differently, but it's where I was at the time. Thinking we need to point out to others what's "not right" about them, and suggesting ways in which they can improve themselves or their situation only alienates us from each other. Even worse, thinking it's *our* responsibility to point out how others can change only divides, and never unites. We fail to consider walking in another's shoes before we go doling out advice.

There's no real wisdom in division, only in unity. In certain circumstances we could certainly debate this. However, when it comes to connection with another, and being supportive of another, wisdom always resides in inclusion, not division. Even if our intentions are "good," taking the liberty to point out to another how they can improve rarely ends up being received in a way that's welcomed, or in a way that actually transforms and enlightens. Identified with ego, it's natural to be attached to conveying our "great wisdom." But who wants to feel like they need to be rescued or fixed? Who wants to feel as if they're being perceived as an incompetent fool – a project that needs desperate repair?

Only when a person is open and willing to hear an outside perspective, can a positive and lasting impact be made. Only when someone is openly receptive to feedback – or has *asked for* that feedback –

are they ready to *hear* and benefit from that feedback – because they've put themselves in a space where change can occur. Only when a person is ready and willing to see what's really so, and move beyond where they are – and not rely on belief – will they have the courage to look where they're being pointed.

Any time we condemn or judge another, we send the message (and restricting energy) they need to change or be fixed. We impregnate them with ignorance. Thus, we resist reality. It's a lose-lose situation – for both of us.

So what does all this have to do with wisdom blooming and awakening the sage within, you might be thinking? Well, everything actually. Any time we're acting out of ignorance, we're naturally suppressing wisdom. Any time we're acting from wisdom, we're naturally suppressing ignorance. Any time we remain in the grips of fear, and aren't willing to look in the direction of truth, we're suppressing our natural wisdom. If what we do to others, we also do to ourselves, it follows that we can never escape the energetic shaping component of how we perceive others, the words we speak to others, and the approach we take with others. This energetic component ultimately either enslaves or liberates.

In other words, if we convey to others that they need to change, be fixed or saved, we confirm within ourselves that at some point we needed to change, be fixed or saved, too. On closer examination, we notice that ignorance sees that repair is necessary, while wisdom sees that everything is absolutely okay as it is. Wisdom knows that whenever we hold back another, we hold ourselves back. Wisdom won't bloom because the energetic soil isn't properly prepared. Judgment, criticism and condemnation, all ignorant energies, carry a constricting energy. These energies naturally "dry up" the soil, and remove all the necessary nutrients and minerals for wisdom to bloom.

Allow me to repeat this very essential point: Don't believe a word you read here. Everything you read here – or anywhere else – is merely conceptual and only points to something else, but can be confirmed and validated in your own direct experience. The word is never the thing.

Does your intuition tell you that there is such a thing as *"the way things shouldn't be?"* I invite you to simply stop, and just be with this notion for a whole thirty seconds before reading on. (Right now, the "Jeopardy" song is playing while you do this.) Okay, what came up for you? Does it make any sense to you that there is such a thing as the way things shouldn't be? Have you ever really examined this widely held viewpoint that informs the majority of our moment-to-moment experience? What does it really mean when we tell ourselves that things or people shouldn't be the way they are? Have we ever really contemplated how this viewpoint shapes our experience?

When Wisdom Blooms

What are we essentially telling ourselves when we decide things like, "It shouldn't be this way," "This person shouldn't be this way" or "These circumstances shouldn't be this way?" Are *any* of these instances ever true? Can they EVER be true? In our insistence that a particular person, thing or circumstance shouldn't be the way they are – or the way it is, aren't we basically saying that WE are the final judge, jury *and* executioner of the universe – and that nature, the universe (or God) has it all wrong? Isn't this perspective full of self-righteousness and arrogance?

Wouldn't the main culprit then, be ignorance – the direct opposite of wisdom – that compels us to *be* arrogant and self-righteous? And yet, we do this all the time, don't we? We don't wake up each morning and decide to be this way; it just happens this way for most of us. Why? Simply because we're not aware – we're not conscious of what's going on. This is an observation and NOT a judgment, by the way. It makes sense that if we knew better we'd do better. Put another way, things can only be the way they are because whatever is can only come from the consciousness (or level of awareness) that manifested it.

Naturally, if we were more conscious, we'd live more in harmony with the flow of life. Life isn't insane, we are. Reality doesn't resist what is; we do. As I like to remind, "In order to understand, we must first be aware." We can't ever understand what we're not first aware of. Therefore, it follows that when we come from ignorance – the opposite of wisdom, we'll maintain and believe in the "this shouldn't be" perspective. And we live in a dream.

If reality is "what is," then how can the "it shouldn't be this way" notion ever truly exist? It can't. The only thing that gives this perspective life is the mind that believes it. If it only exists in the mind – and nowhere else, it isn't real. Ultimately, what it comes down to is simply an argument with reality. And *any* time we argue with reality (what is), we suffer. Any time we oppose life and insist on "what shouldn't be," we lose. What a wonderful and reliable consistency to count on and rest in! If we're looking for ANY security at all, this is it. We can rest assured knowing that whatever presently happens (it's always the present) is meant to happen, and can't happen any other way.

Why would we ever resist reality if we want to be happy and at peace? Isn't that insane? Why would we ever CHOOSE to make ourselves unhappy? We don't choose – but we can see that this "choosing" goes on by itself. When we become conscious and see what's really happening, we "choose" different by looking in the direction that doesn't hurt and divide.

Imagine for a moment that you're taking a leisurely stroll with your lover through a wooded trail paved with beautiful stone. You come upon a rather large tree root sticking out of the ground, right up through the stone path. At the time you notice this root sticking up out of the ground, your mind decides, "This root shouldn't be here; I was peacefully enjoying a stroll with my lover along this beautiful stone path – and all of a sudden, this root is sticking out of the ground, right smack in the middle of the path." You argue with reality – the root is there – right in the middle of the path, and you don't want it there. The reality is, it's just a root.

The root has no notion of whether it *should* or *shouldn't be* there. None of this makes sense to the root. Nature has no concept of what should or "shouldn't be" – and as a result, it never suffers. Our mind decides it shouldn't be there. Since we believe it, we feel justified in our thinking and justified in our annoyance – and there goes our peace and enjoyment. No more leisurely stroll! It's a convincing closed loop that has us believing in it, for a lifetime in many cases.

In doing so, we separate ourselves from the flow of reality (the root is there) with our *thought* that it shouldn't be there. That's all it takes. And you believed thoughts weren't that powerful? Think again. Thoughts aren't really the problem. Believing in them is the problem! On the face of things, this may appear to be a silly example, but this is exactly what we do with our circumstances and experiences and with others. There's a consistent outcome when we do this: we always lose – and reality *always* wins.

Wisdom sees the ground must be fertile and ready – and the conditions properly prepared, in order for sprouting to occur.

Wisdom sees that one of the greatest gifts we can give another is to accept them for who they are, holding them in a space of absolute non-judgment and infinite potential. This is the soil that engenders real growth. Wisdom sees that there's no such thing as "this person shouldn't be this way" … and that in fact, this person can only BE the way they presently are – and *can't possibly* be any other way then they presently are. This is so simple the mind overlooks this revolutionary truth. Truth is simple. It always is. If this is true for another, it must be true for you.

Wisdom knows that since everything is vibrating energy, including thoughts, beliefs, judgments and perceptions, negation and denial can only continue to strengthen and enslave rather than dissolve and liberate. Compassion knows a message that ultimately says, "You are broken and need fixing," is both counterintuitive and counter-productive.

Conversely, the energy that releases and frees is of a total and absolute deep okay-ness with what is, as it is. Since everything is intimately connected and inseparable, this must include the way we view another's situation. Thinking or believing that we're immune from HOW we approach and view others is a great formula for continued discord for us.

When Wisdom Blooms

The wisdom of no escape mandates that if we want the best for ourselves, we must also want the best for others. If I don't come from the energetic vibrations that frees and releases, then I'm further enslaving the both of us. If I don't come *from* wisdom, I can only teach ignorance. Consequently, instead of wisdom blooming, ignorance blooms. If I don't come from wisdom, I only keep you confined, unless YOU know full well that *acceptance of your entire present lot* transcends all. Wisdom sees that we can never fool God, the universe, nature, life or whatever you prefer to call it. Only the authentic get to pass go and collect $200.

When we allow another to just be as they are, without any need to change or fix them, something lets go. Not only do we free them, we free ourselves in the process.

What's good for the goose is good for the gander. Since there's no separation, there can't be any escape, either. When we truly see this, we can stop running! Why would you EVER run from that which can only chase you? When we give another the freedom to be exactly as they are, in that giving, we give ourselves a most precious gift as well, the freedom to be who we are, exactly as we are. *Because* we held them in a space of love and acceptance (and not judgment or denial) another possibility can be stimulated and lived from.

The fundamental truth of mutuality (that pervades all realms of spirituality) holds up. While it's true that in the giving we receive, we're only able to *receive* when we are truly willing to give. We can only experience release when we have released, when *we've* let go. In so doing, we pass on this gift of release, through our energy that frees. It is a palpable and spacious feeling felt in the body and mind. Naturally, you want more of it, but wisdom sees that wanting it keeps it away. In the gap right before you seek it, you realize you are it, already. No becoming needed. In that seeing, wanting dropped away – and therefore, so did seeking.

In that seeing, the energy that's created no longer confines, but releases. Wisdom sees that when no opposition to life occurs, new possibilities can arise. When you know you already ARE what you seek, that recognition brings forth an organic experience in the body – an aliveness that doesn't come and go – confirming what you've known all along. To seek is to deny its full presence already.

What we deny in us will never blossom in us. What we face and embrace must dissolve *in* and *by* our loving gaze – and bloom eternally. When we give the gift of freedom to another, we can't help but simultaneously give ourselves the same, wonderful gift. It is in the true giving that we receive, and it is in the true receiving that we give.

When Wisdom Blooms

We discover that the statement, "All is One" isn't just a conceptual statement to believe in, or a comforting statement to accept on faith. Instead, Oneness is something to be validated experientially. The good news is it's something we *can* validate in our experience, and is more authentic validation that all IS one – but only if we dispel ignorance with the light of awareness, and let wisdom inform us.

Absolutely everything in the manifest and unmanifested world is made of energy. Thoughts, feelings, interpretations, beliefs, trees, grass, cars, oceans, mountains, dogs, cats, food, houses and people all come from the same source. Despite it all appearing solid, nothing is solid. Absolutely everything in the manifest world flashes in and out of existence (each nanosecond, each instant) at such a high rate of speed that our senses literally cannot perceive it.

Truth is always beyond the appearance of things, and is literally never what we "think" or believe it is. What we think is, is always illusory. Quantum physics has finally caught up with what the enlightened have been conveying for centuries, and has proven that all energy is manipulated by our perception of it – how we observe it.

In other words, the observer and the observed are one. No separation. Just more validation that there is no separation, that you *are* the universe, that there is *no* escape, and that indeed, all *is* one. Wisdom blooms in this recognition – and when we live in harmony with this truth, and not just talk about it conceptually. Wisdom won't bloom when we pretend to know when we really don't. Wisdom blooms only when we go beyond the limits of conceptual understanding to the essence beneath and behind the appearance of things.

Without any judgment, denial or wishing anything was any different than it presently is, wisdom blooms because we tell the truth of our situation. No longer do we run from our experience. We face what is, as is. No sugarcoating, no hiding from, no compensating for and no rejecting. This is the spirit that transcends, the spirit that is the ground of all being, that which includes without preference or partiality. It's the ground of being that sees absolutely everything is appropriate and perfect, just the way it is. Whenever we find ourselves condemning another, we are directly faced with our own ignorance staring right back at us.

Ignorance isn't something to be avoided or ashamed of, but to be appreciated for what it is: a simple reminder that we aren't in tune with reality or truth – that our thoughts and judgments about another never define another. Instead, they are just that, thoughts and judgments about another, thoughts that define *us* as a person needing to judge. Ignorance expressed is a reminder that wisdom must arise with it, for they are two sides of the same coin.

When Wisdom Blooms

When we resist or condemn our ignorance, we suppress our natural state of wisdom. When we embrace our ignorance, our innate wisdom blossoms. Our innate wisdom blooms when it sees that, without our ignorance, wisdom wouldn't or couldn't bloom in our experience.

Anyone who has been fortunate enough to experience a very deep, unconditional love knows that real love transcends all circumstance and experience. With this love, you can feel the walls of separation and opposition come down in the acknowledgment of a deep connection rooted in this love. When we have awakened to the kind of love that transcends all experience, good and bad, a dramatic shift occurs in our relationship with life itself. No longer are we subject to what our culture or conditioning tells us *about* love; we go beyond and experience it for ourselves.

We know that no matter how respected the authority is, we can't ever rely on what others tell us. This is the love that has no opposite, but is present through absolutely everything all the time. Jesus knew this kind of love didn't discriminate or make distinctions. Both the prostitute and the King were equally worthy of this love. This truth is timeless, and being outside the stream of time, is just as relevant today. Wisdom blooms when we allow this truth to inform the words we speak and the actions we take. The greatest gift we can give another, then, is becoming more conscious ourselves.

More specifically, the greatest gift we can give another is to become conscious of what's really true – and not just what appears to be true. Our higher consciousness impacts the entirety of consciousness, if only a little bit. If in our ignorance we can only keep down and confine, it follows that in our real wisdom that sees, we lift up and liberate. Understanding that another can never be different than they are – and the notion they "should be different than they are" is literally insane thinking. When we rightly see another, we hold both them and us in a space where something very different can begin to inform our perceptions and activities.

Something of a higher order can move in and replace what was once of a lower order – but only if the ground is fertile with the realization that what already arises can't be any different, no matter what the mind decides or perceives. Truth is always independent of, and never depends on, thinking or perceiving. Like wisdom, truth stands alone and needs no defense. Wisdom sees that things are often very different than they were, even different than they will be, but they are never different than they *are*. Wisdom blooms in the full embrace of this simple, un-deluded recognition of this reality.

Stop dreaming. Wake up from the mis-identification with the mind. Wake up from the

When Wisdom Blooms

concept of time, and be what you already are. And let wisdom bloom.

No belief necessary.

The Dance
of
Imperfection

Living in
Perfect Harmony
with Life

Alex P. Keats

The Dance Of Imperfection
Living In Perfect Harmony With Life

Alex P. Keats

Right Now
Publishing

Right Now Publishing

ISBN - 13: 978-0615949130
ISBN - 10: 0615949134

© 2012 Alex P. Keats

All Rights Reserved. No part of this publication may be reproduced in any form or by any means, including scanning, photocopying, or otherwise without prior written permission of the copyright holder.

First Printing, 2012
Printed in the United States of America

Dedication

This book is dedicated to Susan, Molly and Puff. None of this would be possible if it weren't for you.

"Re-examine all you have been told in school, in church or any book, and dismiss whatever insults your soul, and your very flesh shall become a great poem, and have the richest fluency, not only in its words, but in the silent lines of its lips and face, and between the lashes of your eyes, and in every motion and joint of your body."

~ **Walt Whitman**

Contents

Introduction i

1 - A Perfect Misconception 1

2 - A Level Playing Field 25

3 - An Existential Discomfort 49

4 - Paradox & Confusion 68

5 - Beyond Seeming Opposites 88

6 - Addiction & Grace 113

7 - Hey, It's Just a Ride 139

Introduction

From my late teens to my early thirties, I was an active alcoholic. Somehow I didn't connect my depression and low self-esteem with my weekend use of alcohol. Not only did it bring a lot of pain and suffering for me, but for those who loved me as well. I traded peace and happiness for short-term highs that led to fifteen-year lows, sometimes devastating lows.

When I finally realized that alcoholism is a disease with signs and symptoms – possessing a morbid process – and that it takes over your will and ability to choose, something inside radically shifted. Where for so many years I experienced deep shame, guilt and remorse for behaviors that sometimes shocked me, it all dissolved in a deep realization that I wasn't consciously doing any of it.

I was powerless over the disease that held me in its grips. I wasn't to blame for my addiction, but I was responsible to get the support I needed. Seeing the nature of the situation, it made perfect sense why I did what I did; and it explained why I felt as I did.

It made perfect sense that my life never got on track. How could it? I was addicted to alcohol and its consequences – and I wasn't pulling my own strings. Finally seeing that I wasn't in the driver's seat, and that I wasn't intentionally destroying my life, something of a higher order moved in. Permanently.

It was no coincidence that when the truth of the situation was seen, real healing began – the kind that effected long term change. Low self-esteem was on its way out, and in its place, a complete acceptance of who I was, as I was, came flooding in. Some people would think alcoholism is an imperfection. I don't see it that way. Are diabetes, cancer and heart disease imperfections? How about stuttering, dyslexia, autism, depression and chronic anxiety? Are they imperfections, too?

Like alcoholism, they're just conditions we call "disease" or "disorder. Some would say that it's a matter of semantics, and that it's all the same, just worded differently. If that's the case, then why do we feel insecure and self-conscious when we perceive and therefore, label aspects of ourselves "imperfect" or "inadequate?" How else can we feel *but* insecure?

In other words, if we didn't perceive and label aspects of ourselves as imperfect or flawed, would we still feel less than and unworthy? No, we wouldn't. What about those aspects of yourself you don't really like? Are they really and truly imperfections? When we *see* what's true, when we *realize* that any aspect of ourselves is simply that, just an aspect, as it is, we liberate ourselves from our mind that insists we can be different than we presently are.

We liberate ourselves from feeling unworthy and not up to par, too. We overlook that while things are often different than they *were*, and often different than they *will be*, they are never different than they *are* in this present moment. Can we live outside the present moment?

When we see that as long as we continue to judge and condemn aspects of ourselves (and others) – as they are – we hold in place what we don't want. Our resistance and judgments are wasted energy that gives life to what we'd rather not experience. Since we can never escape our interpretations, misperception also gives life to what we don't want. It's felt in the body, indicating that we aren't in harmony with life and the law of our experience. What we perceive, we receive. Whatever we resist and condemn, persists and binds us. Whatever we face and embrace dissolves and lets go of us. Thus, our perception either enslaves or frees.

Truth frees while illusion enslaves. You have this capability of self-examination. Look beyond the appearance to the real. One insight realized can forever change your course. Absolutely everything comes from God, Source, Oneness, Life, The All That Is, or whatever you prefer to call it. When we don't perceive what is true, we feel a sense of lack and deficiency. It's just the way it works, have you noticed? We may even conclude our Spirit needs fine-tuning, when Spirit is already whole and complete! Spirit cannot be harmed. Spirit, what you eternally are, is untouched. It's our minds that need the adjustment, because it's the mind that can lead us astray.

Some will say we need to cultivate and enhance the different qualities of our being (that seem dormant) as a way to boost our self-esteem and lessen the impact our imperfections have on us. It's basically a strategy to take our focus off of our perceived imperfections and place it elsewhere. Granted, we often get what we pay attention to, but in this case, we're just rearranging the deck chairs on the Titanic. Compassion, gratitude, integrity, wisdom and humility – innate aspects of who we are – become *objects* in our awareness we seek to amplify. Distraction becomes our method, and creating and maintaining good feelings becomes our primary motive. It's a band-aid approach at best, never getting to the root wound.

While there's nothing wrong with the desire to feel good, it's a contrived and inauthentic strategy. The truth is, we don't have to enhance our inherent *subjective* qualities by paying special attention to them, nor do we need to develop them! This approach takes a LOT of energy – and we're often left feeling like a dog chasing its tail. Paying attention to the effects can get really dizzying; it happens when we don't address the causes. Instead of the direct, rooting out approach, we take the indirect, bypass route, delaying our arrival, sometimes getting lost for a long time. We make it complicated, when all along truth is simple, so simple in fact, that the mind overlooks it.

I'm kind of lazy, and it's not an imperfection. Since I'm usually looking for the most direct route, it comes in real handy sometimes. As a result of a natural inclination towards the path of least resistance, paradoxes have become a very close friend of mine. Once understood, they require no work at all! They're like laser beams, cutting right through the discomfort that illusion brings, like hot butter.

Paradoxically, the qualities we most want to experience arise more than ever as a direct result of rooting out the false. When we see through illusion, when we realize something was never true to begin with, falsehood drops away – and our most desirable qualities *spontaneously* radiate and blossom. Like nature, our spirits are already endowed with perfect qualities that naturally blossom when the proper conditions are prepared.

Seeing what's true is a game of realizing what's already the case, and never about developing skills or improving upon our inherent qualities. Distinguishing truth from falsehood *is* the fertile soil that allows wisdom, peace, self-love and gratitude to bloom. When we seek to cultivate and develop as a method to enhance our qualities (or distract us from negative self-perceptions), we're operating from the dream-state, forever manufacturing our experience. It's inorganic, and we live our lives continually managing our states, endlessly on the wheel of seeking pleasure and avoiding pain. It's a wonderful recipe for staying on an emotional rollercoaster.

All the while, life is in continuous flow, unimpeded – yet we believe we're separate from that flow. There's no such thing as flow *and* us. Oneness isn't just a concept to believe in; it's immediately available as the reality to be realized experientially. If we have any purpose in life, it is this. When we continue to identify with the erroneous perceptions of our minds (that divide and condemn) we remain trapped inside a fiction of our own making – and life inevitably hurts.

When we continue to believe that it actually makes sense to embrace our strengths, while rejecting our weaknesses, we'll never experience the true contentment our hearts long for. Most of us want to love and accept ourselves as we are, and pay it forward, don't we?

The truth is, we're already as worthy as the next person, regardless of our upbringing, intellectual capacity and social standing. And it certainly has nothing to do with how much money you make, how big your house is, or what you look like. At birth, each person is fundamentally endowed with the same intrinsic worth. It sure is a silly notion to think that you accumulate worth over the years based on your achievements or status – or even your value to society, don't you think? Unfortunately, many of us don't realize we're as worthy as the next guy because we've either been told we're not, or *because* of what we tell ourselves. Identified with a mind that compares, contrasts, judges and wishes it was more like others, it's no wonder we often find ourselves in an inner battle.

If we want to be on the receiving end of a spontaneous happiness that needs nothing to be happy, we must see through illusion that hurts and perceive reality as it is, not as we'd like it to be. If we want to possess an authentically healthy self-perception that isn't propped up and sustained by formulas and beliefs, we must work with and understand the law of our experience. Nature doesn't need to improve or foster anything, nor do we. It has no concept of improvement. Only a direct and aware, no-nonsense approach is contained within these pages. Can you handle the truth? I think you can. In fact, I know you can.

This has always been a game of seeing what's already the case. *The Dance of Imperfection – Living in Perfect Harmony with Life* is an in depth re-examination of our interpretations of the concepts we live by, an intimate exploration to clearly see how we've set the rules up in order to live authentically, experiencing the peace, joy and love we are. If we truly are free beings, then it makes sense to really see how we're playing the game of life. We may discover we've set it up only to lose.

Commit to discover like never before, the ways in which we put ourselves behind the eight ball, and identify the rules we've been playing by. If it's appropriate, we can change the rules in our favor and win, not just for ourselves, but also for those around us. No cheating necessary!

Chapter 1
A Perfect Misconception

"To be yourself in a world that is constantly trying to make you something else is a great accomplishment."

~ Ralph Waldo Emerson

In the free online dictionary, "imperfection" is defined as *the quality or condition of being imperfect, a fault or defect.* Some of the synonyms included: *flawed, blight, blotch, deformity, blemish, disfigurement, stain, deficiency, inadequate, insufficient and shortcoming.* Some examples of imperfections in a sentence were:

The Dance Of Imperfection

He detected several imperfections in the surface of the jewel. She tried to hide the imperfection in the cloth.

Back in the Elizabethan times, imperfection was defined conceptually as "crack'd in the ring", flawed or imperfect at the perimeter or edge. (It was limited in application to money and artillery). In the early 17th Century, diamond in the rough: *one whose unrefined and external appearance, or ungraceful behavior belies a good or gentle character and untapped potential.*

This expression derives from the disparity between a diamond in its natural state, before being cut and polished, and in its refined state, when it has become an impressive gem. Early Christian writings, especially Paul's, are replete with calls to perfection. Many are from St. Augustine in the Old Testament: *"Thou shalt be perfect with the Lord thy God."* Elsewhere, synonyms for "perfection" are *undefiled, without rebuke, without blemish, blameless, holy and righteous.*

Italy's *Leaning Tower of Pisa* first started out as a concept in the mind of man, unintended to lean after construction. We can find many parallels in our human affairs, and the way humans unintentionally lean towards illusion and not truth. There are several ways we can approach this concept we commonly refer to as "imperfection" – this concept that induces more bouts of depression and lingering insecurity than our current stock market.

One of those ways will be to take a closer look at how we interpret the concept "imperfection" – and some of the implications inherent when we continue to cling to our interpretation. Additionally, we'll look at, and re-examine, the inevitable consequences of *our* tendencies and leanings – and how they inevitably shape our experience.

We'll bring our conceptual interpretations out into the open, unreservedly and with humility – and clearly see, through an earnest willingness to investigate, how our actual perception of the concept "imperfection" manifests itself in our experience. Once we see that, we allow ourselves the opportunity to rework, or reorient ourselves (to the concept) in a way that works for us – if it's necessary for us to do so.

That being said, there *are* actual limitations in our abilities, intellect and emotional makeup that come with the package of being human, and there are *perceived* imperfections in these same areas that aren't based in truth or reality.

The trick is to discern those that are part of our particular makeup, and those that are made up and believed in. To the degree that we give our perceived imperfections attention and energy, to that degree do we also give them credence and continued life. When we give credence to our perceived imperfections, aren't we naturally left feeling vulnerable and insecure? It is this very credence that gives them

The Dance Of Imperfection

continued life. Isn't it always our thinking *about* a thing that makes us insecure – and not the actual thing? When we resist and judge those aspects of ourselves that we deem "imperfect," how else *but* insecure can we feel?

We've set ourselves up to lose, but we continue on with the game, hoping to win now and then. Don't we often conclude that *if* we're deficient in a particular area, that it must *then* mean something else? For example, *if* I don't measure up here, *then* I won't be able to successfully perform there? *If* I don't improve on this flaw – or eradicate this flaw, *then* I won't ever be truly happy. Is it our actual weaknesses that cause so much angst, or is it our thinking about our actual weaknesses that causes the angst? Is it possible that our thinking and perceiving is flawed and imperfect?

We tend to overlook that just maybe our perception is the real culprit, habitually leaning towards believing the thoughts in our head to tell us what's true. We pay attention to our perceptions, without considering maybe we'd be better off paying attention to the perceiver – and the validity of the perceptions. Most of our perceived imperfections are, in fact, just that, contrived and made-up notions created in our minds that essentially tell us something shouldn't be the way it is.

We then label that something as "imperfect," or not as we'd like it to be. I say, "contrived" because we have a tendency to, with a glass half-empty paradigm, compare our present character traits, abilities and personality with some imagined ideal, or to someone we wish we were more like.

In other words, we essentially tell ourselves that what we innately possess *shouldn't* be, and that somehow, we don't measure up when we compare ourselves to that ideal, or to another. We fail to recognize that what we're really NOT measuring up to is nothing other than a mind-created fantasy. If pressed, most of us wouldn't even be able to clearly communicate our standard of perfection – or what it looks like! We suffer from our own perceptions, and nothing else. Instead of directly experiencing who we are, *as* we are – we experience our interpretations *about* who we are.

Isn't this the way it works in our experience? If we don't possess the qualities or things we want, don't we conclude we must acquire that quality, and those things? Since most of us are not ultimately content as we are, the search or chase is on. Generally, we unconsciously set it up within ourselves that we won't be content and secure *until* we possess that ideal or state of perfection we imagine will bring us the security and contentment we seek. For some of us, what others naturally possess becomes a threat to us, and we find ourselves in a competition of sorts, covertly hiding what we feel is missing, and overtly compensating for what we feel is lacking.

We go into pretend mode, not living authentically – and with gratitude for the gifts that only we uniquely bring to life. Since our consciousness can basically only focus on one thing at a time, it's easy for us to forget that to deny our actual weaknesses is to deny our very humanity, our unique thumbprint. Due to our egos being somewhat (or mostly) fragile, we don't always want to acknowledge that it is in our shared weaknesses, and not our strengths, where we really connect with others in a meaningful and healing way.

After all, it is our strengths and abilities – and not our weaknesses – that makes us different. Instead, in our arrogance and ignorance, we cling to the ideas that limit us, professing that somehow "God messed up; I shouldn't have these flaws and blemishes – and I'd be happier if I didn't." On some level, we know that what we cling to can only bind us, yet we hold fast to our beliefs that claim what presently is, *can or should* be different than it is right now.

And it's never true, is it? Things are always AS they are, aren't they? They may be different than they *were*, and they may be different than they will be, but they are always as they are – *and can never be presently different than they are.*

Not seeing this simple truth, we hop on the wheel of suffering and tell ourselves a story that goes something like, "If I can figure out how to eradicate these annoying shortcomings, then I'll feel safe and secure in this world. If I can figure that out, then I'll feel good about the way I am – and *then* I'll feel good about contributing to the world and those around me!" We don't yet realize that fully accepting ourselves exactly the way we are *is* the way *to* transcend our insecurity and self-consciousness.

Only when we are able to unequivocally accept the way *we are,* with all our weaknesses – perceived or real, can we accept *others* for the way they are, exactly *as* they are. Sometimes we fool ourselves thinking there must be an easier, softer way. Wisdom sees that this mutuality is real love, the kind that gives just for the sake of giving and asks for nothing in return.

As *they* must, these misguided notions that tell us that we can be intrinsically different than we presently are become obstacles in our awareness. They become the ways in which we hand over our power to something that has no real substance or reality – our contrived and imagined misconceptions that inevitably divide us.

Even though we are already and always whole, as a result of our self-perception, we feel divided. These misguided notions are added layers that get in the way of our ability to show up authentically in the moment. Carrying a heavy burden of mis-

The Dance Of Imperfection

conceptions around, they prevent us from meeting the moment as it is. As *we* must, we inevitably suffer from these delusions and flaws in our thinking, but only every time! Since we can only ever really operate from the way we *see* things, we operate from "perfect misconceptions" that divide and fracture, until we don't anymore.

Until we decide we want something else, like a child put in a timeout for his behavior, we continue to put ourselves in a timeout. If we've literally had enough pain and exhausted ourselves, grace has a way of stepping in – but only if we're ready to accept that grace. No one can make us ready, and grace doesn't force its way in. Grace doesn't operate when we're still holding on. Unless we're willing to hand it over, grace won't step in.

In the meantime, each moment STILL provides a fork in the road, where we can choose to take the same direction as usual, or take the path that's not divisive and hurtful. Despite carrying around our heavy baggage of misconceptions (and erroneous interpretations) that divide and hurt, each moment is STILL fresh and new. But in order to recognize this, and in order to drop our baggage, we must be acutely aware of our present situation and perspective, don't we?

In order to drop that unnecessary baggage, we must be aware that we're carrying it in the first place. Since we sense that truth only reveals itself when we allow ourselves not to know, we give up our need *to* know what it looks like, and we give up our need *to* know how it will turn out. Wisdom sees that it is the unknown – and not what we "know," where our answer lies, where our freedom is. The known isn't cutting it. Wisdom knows our own being isn't separate from the wisdom of all life.

Thus, with faith and courage, we take the unknown road. Wholly unconcerned, yet intimately engaged, we courageously step into the fire of the unknown, knowing that "the way of perfection" doesn't even exist in this finite, human existence, at least not in the cultural sense we've come to believe in. We see that it exists only in the mind of the one who believes it. Until we see this completely, this layer won't drop away. Fully seen, it drops away.

Language consists of concepts that describe something in particular. If we can really see that the function of language is to describe something else – and not ultimately define that something else, we're facing the right direction. If we see that language is inherently limited, with dividing lines that point to where that *something* seemingly begins and ends, then we give ourselves a chance to transcend our restricting and damaging notions about what it means to be imperfect.

Further, if it has dividing lines, any concept must also imply what it is not. Most importantly, we

The Dance Of Imperfection

see it must be dualistic in nature, having an opposite like cold has hot, wet has dry, up has down, pain has pleasure, and left has right.

Hence, all language is dualistic and possesses a seeming opposite. All language is limiting in that the word is never the thing, but only points to that thing. Concepts can only be described in relation to its opposite. If you read my first book, *"Born To Be Happy – How To Uncover Your Natural State of Happiness,"* you might remember I posed the question, "Can you drink the word "water," or be burned by the word, "fire"?" No, of course not. The word is never the actual, and can't ever be the actual. Words are symbols that represent something else. Once this is clearly understood and *seen*, we can then safely conclude that, since the word "water" can't ever quench our thirst, the word "imperfection" isn't the *actual* state of imperfection, either.

Naturally, with every concept having its opposite, we would be remiss if we didn't address the opposite concept called "perfection," wouldn't we? And that the concept "perfection" can't be the actual state or condition of perfection, either, can it? If we really want to understand (and come to *see*) how it is that any concept interpreted can have such great influence in our lives, wouldn't it make sense for us to *really* look into it? I mean, wouldn't that be a worthy endeavor that's deserving of our real and undivided attention? I say YES, wholeheartedly – and I hope you agree.

If the word isn't the actual, then certainly the way in which we *interpret* a defined concept surely isn't the actual, either, is it? It's just our interpretation, right?

As it goes in our experience, we'd have no other alternative than to live and experience *from* that particular interpretation. Have you ever considered that your interpretation and perception of the words *perfection and imperfection* can (and would be) resolutely refuted by so many others? And wouldn't that particular acknowledgement call into question the validity of those interpretations – and the fact that it's a totally subjective thing?

If we really look, we notice that we aren't stretching it when we say that there are as many different ways to perceive a concept, as there are those who perceive that concept! When it comes to something so subjectively interpreted as the concepts, "perfection and imperfection," we see how this is especially so.

Another chief obstacle is our lack of knowledge about the nature of consciousness itself – more specifically, our lack of awareness *(the no-thing that sees)* about the nature of consciousness itself. If we take a look, we can see the incredible rapidity of movement in the moment-to-moment, instant-to-instant processes of our minds.

The Dance Of Imperfection

Faster than a supercomputer analyzing millions upon millions of bits of information, the implications of its rate of speed are far greater than it would acknowledge – and far greater than we might even be *able* to see, and hence, be *able* to acknowledge.

We see that consciousness automatically and spontaneously "chooses" what it deems best in each moment, relative to millions of pieces of data, dominated and influenced by patterns of past conditioning. It's quite obvious to me that the crux of the problem lies in our failure to clearly recognize that the greatest catalyst for conflict (both internal and external) isn't just our spontaneous and ongoing compulsion to evaluate and interpret concepts.

Believing in and identifying with those interpretations as being anything other than a delusional fiction is the main cause of our undoing, and the proverbial nail in the coffin sealing our experience.

Information comes to us second hand, and our descriptions and stories are always (and already) a step behind, describing what already came and went. While we live in the present, our thoughts reflect the past. It's as if we're reading today's newspaper (based on yesterday's events) and we try and nail it down, attempting to make yesterdays events present and relative. It's like trying to fit a square peg in a round hole.

Since absolutely everything is on the move and in flux, we can't ever nail *anything* down, but in our ignorance, we keep trying to grasp what cannot be grasped. And we wonder *why* attachment can be so painful! Desire isn't a problem; attachment *TO* desire is the problem.

Clinging to old news, we tie ourselves down, trying to cling to our own shadow. This is what illusion does, and this is what illusion has *us* do. And all the while, right in the midst of this goose chase, is the wisdom of insecurity that patiently waits for us to see the pure folly of trying to grab hold of what must disappear. Like a loyal and faithful lover, the wisdom of insecurity is always right where we are, gently beckoning us to just let go, reminding us that literally everything is on the move, in flux and never static.

Unconsciously living from our fixed, conceptual interpretations about flowing reality, we remove ourselves from the spontaneous flow and movement of life. Life is dancing one way, and we're dancing in another way. It's like we're dancing the jitterbug and our partner (life) is trying to waltz with us. Consequently, we're out of sync with life and we feel out of balance. Thus, we try and cultivate balance in our lives without ever addressing the source of the problem, our perception. Like the rabid dog's nature is to bite, it is illusion's nature to divide, fracture and hurt.

If we're honest with ourselves, we admit that we crave connection with life and others. If we're honest, we can readily admit that we often fear what we want most. In our fears and ideas about what's "best and right," we erect barriers to that union realized. In union, there's no separation or division.

Without belief in separation, there isn't anything vying for our attention, telling us there's a problem that needs solving. Without any separation, there isn't anything that stands apart from us that *can* give us any problem. It's only when we distance ourselves from anything, push it away or avoid it, does it come back to haunt us.

Without pushing away the opposite experience of the concept we call joy (pain), and without resisting or running from the opposite of what we call courage (fear), both experiences are okay with us because we know how it all works. The only thing that can cause us pain is when we believe our mind's interpretations. Until we REALLY *care about how our lives go*, we get more of what we don't want. Like a heroin addict, we can never get enough of what we don't really want.

Let's look at the evolution and various meanings of the word "perfection" in order to get a broader perspective, shall we? Granted, this book is more about imperfection than perfection, but I hope you see the value in delving a bit further in its opposite, in the hope of gaining a greater understanding of how avoiding or compensating for our perceived imperfections can only divide us.

Living In Perfect Harmony With Life

What is perfection, really? Is it actual or imagined? According to Wikipedia, "The oldest definition of perfection goes back to Aristotle." In the Book *Delta of the Metaphysics*, he distinguishes three meanings for the term, or rather three shades of one meaning, but nonetheless, three different concepts. *That is perfect*:

1. Which is complete – which contains all the requisite parts;
2. Which is so good that nothing of the kind could be better;
3. Which has attained its purpose

Could this early interpretation also point to a way of seeing, as in how the enlightened sages and saints have been attempting to convey for ages? Could this be a way of perceiving that suggests whatever is presently arising is perfectly appropriate *and* complete as it is – and in fact, cannot be other than it is? The Jesuit priest, Anthony de Mello, who went on to really investigate truth and reality in his later years said, "Enlightenment is the *absolute cooperation with the inevitable.*"

One of the chief aims of this book is to delve deeper into this way of seeing, and the real meaning the enlightened were pointing to – and what the enlightened continue to point to today. To Aristotle, *perfect* meant complete with nothing to add or subtract to.

The Dance Of Imperfection

The paradox of perfection – that imperfection or weakness is perfect – applies not only to human affairs, but to technology as well. Irregularity in semiconductor crystals (an imperfection in the form of contaminants) is requisite for the production of semiconductors. In regards to the realm of physics, the physicist designates as a perfectly rigid body, one that "is not deformed by forces applied to it." A crystal is perfect when its physically equivalent walls are equally developed.

However, the expression "perfect" is also used colloquially as a superlative (perfect idiot, perfect scoundrel, perfect storm). Perfectionism has also been construed as that which is best. In theology, when Descartes and Leibniz termed God "perfect", they had in mind something other than *model*; than that which *lacks nothing*; than that *achieves its purpose*; than that fulfills its functions; or than that is *harmonious*.

Along with the idea of perfection, Holy Scripture conveyed doubt as to whether perfection was attainable for man. According to John 1:8, *"If we say that we have no sin, we deceive ourselves and the truth is not in us"* and then goes on to say, *"Perfect love casts out fear."* The Christian doctrine of perfection rests on the Gospel of Matthew 5:48, *"Be ye therefore perfect, even as your Father in heaven is perfect."* Those who believe in a God separate from His creation might say that only He is perfect, and that He wants us to strive for perfection, even when we believe He didn't create us to *be* perfect! Some say that only true love is perfect. Spiritually, perfection is beyond measure, and ineffable.

Spirit is intrinsically whole and complete, while our humanity, consisting of personality, past conditioning and experience, is broken and incomplete. The 17th century philosopher, Benedict Spinoza asserted that there was no personal God, and perfection became a property of (even a synonym for) the existence of reality, or the essence of all things. The 18th century brought a world of change to the idea of moral perfection.

Moving away from religious to secular, perfection was a fundamental article of faith for the Enlightenment. Its central tenet was that indeed, nature was perfect; and perfect, too, was *the man who lived in harmony with nature's law.* Primitive man was held to be the most perfect, for he was closest to nature.

For the ancient philosophers, the essence of perfection had been harmony. The Stoics introduced the concept of perfection into ethics, describing it as harmony – with nature, reason, and man himself. They held that such harmony, such perfection, was attainable for anyone. Cicero wrote in, "On the Nature of the Gods" that:

"The world encompasses within itself all beings, and what could be more nonsensical than denying

The Dance Of Imperfection

perfection to an all-embracing being. Besides the world, there is no thing that does not lack something and that is harmonious, perfect and finished in every respect."

File the above description by Cicero away; we'll be revisiting it in more depth later. For the remainder of this book, let's set aside perfection, relative to the disciplines of physics, chemistry, mathematics, art and even aesthetics. Let's look at it in a much more practical way, a way that directly impacts our human affairs – as it pertains to our very lives.

I can only assume that you're interested in this topic as it pertains to your life – and the way you live your life. Can I safely assume this? If we really *look until we see*, we recognize that perfection is indeed, an idea arbitrarily created and defined by a culture (or individual) that seeks to identify ways to measure one's progress and level of success. In other words, we make it up.

We make up ways to measure how we presently are in relation to where we ultimately want to be. Unfortunately, we often make it up in such a way that works against us and *not* in harmony with the law of our experience. Sadly, it's a concept many of us have erroneously tied into measuring our self-worth, which in turn must directly impact our degree of authentic happiness. Real happiness doesn't come and go based on our circumstance or situation. Only manufactured happiness does.

Living In Perfect Harmony With Life

The reason why our interpretations about perfection have a tendency to be hurtful and divisive is singular in nature, resulting in a domino effect that spreads out into several, if not all aspects of our lives. The reason is because our made up ideas and therefore, interpretations *about* perfection (in regards to living our lives) have no existence in reality! What's real and true is permanent, and must be present 100% of the time ... and certainly not something created by the mind.

Hence, in regards to our very lives and the things we strive to attain – whether it's spiritual, emotional, mental, financial or physical in nature, there is no such thing as "perfection" except for the one we give it!

For me, when I really saw this, I felt both relief and a bit of shock. Knowing that for much of my life, I had been fooled into believing that perfection was an *actual* state or condition possible to achieve. I saw how believing in it caused more pain than joy, more stress than peace, and more insecurity than security. Not only did I see this for myself, I saw it in others as well – and saw the negative impact it had on them, too.

I had a sense that believing in the existence of perfection was all so arbitrary and handed down, like the worn out shirt you got from your older sibling. I noticed I couldn't help project my misconceptions onto those around me. Evidently, I wanted to keep the tradition alive by giving out hand me downs, too. Being ultimately ignorant, I had difficulty allowing others to be exactly as they were.

By being in bondage (as a result of my own views), I couldn't help tying up others *with* those views. If we want to hang on to our present interpretation of *perfection*, we certainly have that right. It's our life and we can live it as we wish. But if we ask, "What is my direct experience as a result of the way I view this concept?" Or, "How might my life be different if I viewed it in a way that works for me", we may be inspired to view our situation differently.

Besides, if I can't escape experiencing how I view life, why not work with myself instead of against myself? Alternatively, how might our life be different if we dropped the concept altogether? Would we rather be "right," or be at peace? If we see that we really do make it ALL up, why would we continue to cling to notions that ultimately bind us instead of liberate us? Is it simply because we are afraid of taking responsibility for our life? Do we need to look at a belief in a higher power judging us in some way? If so, is it true?

Can we absolutely (and unequivocally) know it's true – or do we merely believe it's true? Coming to this realization can bring up a whole host and variety of responses, ranging from fear, reluctance and skepticism, to laughter, relief and utter amazement.

Living In Perfect Harmony With Life

I'm certainly not asking you to take my word on any of this. In fact, I hope you don't. I highly recommend that you don't believe a *single* word you read in this book (or *any* other book for that matter) – but rather, find out what is true in your own experience. Until you do, you'll just be living from someone else's notions and experience, and not from your own organic realization where real knowing happens, where real wisdom blooms.

Humanity is meant to include strengths and weaknesses that typically translate as "perfect" and "imperfect." Whatever arbitrary thing we chase after must elude us. It's like our shadow, forever being one step ahead, never to be apprehended. How many of us continue to strive for an imagined state or condition of perfection, without realizing that it is one of the greatest illusions the world has ever known?

Isn't this part of the human condition, being duped into believing there is actually something called "perfection," and it's something we can actually attain? Is there a way we can better define this concept so that it works for us, and not against us – especially since we make it all up anyway? If you don't agree that we make it all up, and that "perfection" is an actual and real condition, what tells you that? Who told you that? Can you prove it?

What makes one person define or perceive perfection in a totally different way than another person, when looking at, creating, or experiencing the same thing? Don't we decide what is perfect, based on our likes, dislikes, preferences and opinions? In a free society that most of us get to enjoy, don't we GET TO decide what's perfect for us? Aren't we essentially the architects of our own lives?

Being that architect, what if we were to simply drop the concept altogether from our blueprint, so that it doesn't manifest and make its way into our finished product, our very life? What would that be like, to live without any concept of "perfection" at all? If we could, wouldn't that, in one fell swoop, wipe out "imperfection" as an actual condition, too? Wouldn't that be liberating for us?

Assuming one could reach a state or condition of perfection in any endeavor one chooses, how would one even know when they reached it? If they did know when they reached it, what would they do – celebrate the attainment by hanging up "their perfection shingle" outside their homes, proclaiming to the world that they finally arrived? How boring would that become? Won't the novelty and satisfaction of that state or condition fade away, just like everything else must?

What if, instead, we saw everything already perfect, as it is? That the attainment was in our seeing and perceiving – and was already a done deal? What would that be like?

Living In Perfect Harmony With Life

There's a poignant story from the Zen tradition you may have heard of. *There was a man of great stature in Japan who had a beautiful home, and a garden with such beauty that it would take your breath away upon seeing it. The centerpiece of the garden was a large beautiful tree.*

It was late autumn and the leaves were dying. One day the man learned that he was going to be visited by a number of government dignitaries – something that rarely happens, even to people of great status. He ordered all the servants in his home to prepare his home for the arrival of his guests. There were only three days before they arrived, and there was much to do.

The man insisted that while his servants focused on preparing the home and the meal, he would personally tend to the garden – his pride and joy. The man pruned every tree and bush with great attention to detail. He then proceeded to rake every leaf from the ground, until every single leaf was removed. Now, next to the man's home was a Zendo. One day, as the man was raking the leaves in his yard he noticed one of the Zendo's Masters watching him from one of the balconies. As a matter of fact, the Zen Master would appear on the balcony at the exact time the man would begin working on his yard each day.

He would sit and watch the man all day without saying anything. As the man would go into his home after working, so too, would the Zen Master leave the balcony and retreat inside. The man noticed this, and even took pride in the fact that the Master never corrected him.

The Dance Of Imperfection

Surely, he would correct me if I were not doing something in a less than perfect manner, he reasoned. So when the last day came and the man picked up the last leaf on the ground, he looked up over at the Master and said, "What do you think of my garden, isn't it beautiful?" Smiling, the Zen Master took a few minutes to look over the garden from the balcony. "The garden is very beautiful, but there is something missing."

The man suddenly became very concerned as his guests were arriving shortly. "What is it, Master ... what's missing, can you please assist me?" At the man's request, the Zen Master came down from the balcony and walked over into the man's garden. He looked around again, and after a while said, "Ah, I know what it is." The Zen Master walked over to the large tree at the center of the yard and shook it several times, until leaves began falling from the tree, covering the grounds of the garden. The Zen Master looked at the man with a smile and said, "That's what it needed – now it looks perfect."

Chapter 2
A Level Playing Field

"And I will show you that there is no imperfection in the present, and can be none in the future, And I will show that whatever happens to anybody it may be turn'd to beautiful results, And I will show that nothing can happen more beautiful than death, And I will thread a thread through my poems that time and events are compact, And that all the things of the universe are perfect miracles, each as profound as any."

~ **Walt Whitman** (The Leaves of Grass)

Whitman is one of my favorite enlightened people because of his remarkable ability to eloquently point to Truth by using the written word, usually in the form of poetry and prose. There is something in the above quote, that is the crux of this chapter – and in fact, that *something* is the thread that weaves throughout the entirety of this book.

Admittedly, I am wondering if you were alerted to this "something" in the first chapter. Remember we said that all language is both dualistic in nature, limiting in the sense that the word is never the thing, nor does it define that thing, but only points to that thing? In fact, it can only be described in relation to its inherent opposite?

We also said that, in terms of our daily human affairs, that "perfection" isn't something that actually exists in reality, other than the arbitrary meaning we give it? In other words, without referencing thought, the concept has no reality. Well, if this is true, then its opposite must not exist, either! And so, the concept "imperfection" then, as it pertains to our human affairs, has no existence in reality other than the one we give it. We see that the belief in the existence of imperfection is rooted in wanting the moment to be other than it is.

Belief in the existence of imperfection is the same thing as saying, "This person is lacking," or "This moment is lacking." And it's never true. Belief in the existence of imperfection is tantamount to saying, "Humanity (as God or Source created it) should not have been designed this way – with both strengths and weaknesses." As Walt Whitman aptly stated, *"there is no imperfection in the present and can be none in the future, and I will show that whatever happens to anybody can be turn'd to beautiful results."* If you were hoping to learn a different perspective on the popularly accepted assumption that imperfection is indeed an actual state or condition in reality, I'm sorry to disappoint you. I'm sorry to break it to you, but there's no such thing – and there never was!

It's like the mirage in the desert that appears to be real; it appears to be moving, but once you walk directly up to it to get a close look, it disappears. It disappears because it was never there to begin with; it only appeared to be there. On the other hand, if you came with an open heart and mind, I invite you to stick with me here. In time, hopefully you'll see the truth in the declaration that *perfection and imperfection* are concepts that have no existence in reality other than the one we give it.

If it only exists in our minds, it isn't real. Actually, we can say this about any concept. *As it pertains to our human affairs, what the concept imperfection points to isn't an actual condition in reality.* There is nothing lacking and there isn't anything in the universe that shouldn't be the way it is. That said, how *can* imperfection be a reality?

In other words, its existence is manufactured, sustained and maintained in the minds of those who continue to believe in its reality, whatever the reason

The Dance Of Imperfection

or payoff happens to be. Personally, I don't really ever utter the word *imperfection* – not just because I'm afraid to give it life, but because I know that it's no more real than the Loch Ness monster. As a result, I don't really have a sense of it, either. However, I do have a real and organic sense of "perfection" that isn't a result of any interpreted concept – and I see it absolutely everywhere I look. Because I see it everywhere, this sense of perfection has no opposite.

I'm aware this may seem like a contradiction. Whenever we try to comprehend things with the mind, contradictions appear to exist. However, this isn't a book intended for your mind. It's intended for YOU. As each chapter builds on the previous one, hopefully this point will become crystal clear. Since mind's function is to compare, contrast, evaluate, judge and maintain preferences, experiences will arise (or be called on) that aren't preferred or desired. If a situation calls for us to utilize and express our weaker abilities, we're not always thrilled to do so.

One day we'll see that, without any labels or descriptions, without being attached to preferences and outcomes, direct experience is radically different, and certainly more pleasurable. Without distinguishing imperfect from perfect, we notice that it is just energy moving through – and it's not a problem.

I must confess, before I sat down to actually write this book, a short conversation arose within that went something like, "Maybe the best way to write about imperfection would be the way the vast majority have already done and continue to do – and in line with how our culture views this topic. That way, you'd be appealing to the masses, giving them what they expect, generating the most attention – and people would certainly 'get it' and understand where you're coming from.

You could follow the same trodden path, and approach it as if it's an actual state or condition, and comfort the reader by encouraging them to accept 'the perfection of imperfection,' because after all, we're all beautiful train wrecks with a shared destination, right? Besides, flaws, deficiencies and inadequacies are part of the package of being human, and God doesn't make junk! We're all 'perfectly imperfect,' and there's great consolation in this fact!" Perhaps provide some dynamic time-bound, powerful tools and strategies (including reframing and mirroring) to better negotiate and live amidst these conceptual anchors that drag us down, and keeps us immobile.

Well, I just couldn't do it. Something wouldn't let me. As I contemplated this softening, cliché-laden approach for about a whole two seconds, I knew that I just couldn't bring myself to add to all the misunderstanding surrounding these two concepts that wreaks so much havoc in the lives of so many good people. In fact, there are mountains of it all over the place, giving it further life. Sadly, some of it is intentional, irresponsible and self-serving. We

The Dance Of Imperfection

certainly don't need more untruths piling up; there's more than enough already. In fact, we're knee deep in it, and frankly, it stinks! Besides, I'd just be lying, and I won't do that. It would be paramount to slaying just one head of the hydra, only to watch multiple heads grow back.

In truth, aside from food, air, water and shelter, we don't "need" a thing. There's no outside agency, there's no-thing external that insists or needs for us to see *anything* in particular, or to be any other way than we already are. Nevertheless – relatively speaking, in the hope of living a more contented life, we *can see what's real* and replace false ideas with ideas that point towards freedom. That's what this book is intended to do. Truth must be present all the time. Being 100% present all the time, what's true never comes and goes; it never leaves us. Through conditioning or "past" experience, we may have believed or felt otherwise, but truth is always right where we are.

It can only *be* right where we are, despite any appearance to the contrary. It's eternally available and present, right here, right now. If a concept truly just points to, and isn't the actual, what we *need* is more accurate pointing – pointing in the direction of Truth, and not in the direction of illusion that fractures. While the truth cannot be contained within this or *any* other book, the concepts or words you read here are intended to point you in the direction of truth, so that it can be revealed to you.

You won't find any band-aid approaches, end around or bypassing approaches here. Rest assured that this is a direct and immediate approach that doesn't involve a process or method – or the need to "cultivate" anything. Processes and methods have a beginning, middle and an end, and an unstable life span; it would be geared for your mind to try and "get" or understand.

While your mind may conceptually understand these methods, *you* wouldn't be freed from whatever the affliction is that ails you. What needs to be seen isn't anything the mind *can* see. Again, I'd just be re-arranging the deck chairs on The Titanic. All *methods that require time are for the mind, and since they're* rooted in illusion and not reality, any benefit can't last. Since it doesn't last, it isn't real. Since it isn't real, it must inevitably hurt. YOU don't need any "time" to see this. You can see this immediately, right now.

You *will* find an intensive, DIRECT and practical approach here (that can work for you) if you resist the popular way of looking with the mind. If you are totally confused right now, don't worry. Remain open and curious, with an earnest desire to really look until you see. If you allow the words to sink into your heart that already knows, a whole new experience can arise for you. If you find yourself

The Dance Of Imperfection

looking and agreeing, disagreeing, evaluating, comparing, judging or resisting, you can be sure you're looking with your mind. If it's truth you're after, mind ultimately isn't the most useful tool for the job. Granted, it *can* be useful in many instances, but not for realizing truth, or for freeing ourselves from what ails us.

In fact, most of the time, and in most instances, our minds are an obstacle to seeing what's true. In my book, "*When Wisdom Blooms – Awaken The Sage Within,*" I discussed how to know when we're looking with the heart as opposed to the mind. If you haven't read it yet, I will repeat it here: If ever we find ourselves looking with an intense curiosity that has no expectation of finding anything in particular, non-judgmentally and without any bias from the mind, we can be sure that's a good indicator we're looking with the heart. If we find that we are in an *open state of discovery* where we aren't evaluating what we're looking at in relation to the past, we can be sure we are looking from the heart, from our innate wisdom that resides below the neck.

Like a highly skilled and precise surgeon, we'll get to the root wound that still hurts and shine a light on it in order to get a real good look at it. In order to really examine anything, we need to look closely. The better the look we get, the more we can see it for what it really is. The closer we get to it, the more we'll be able to hear its voice. If we ask it what its story is, it will tell us. It's pretty open that way. We will look at and undress the old dressing (our interpretation of and belief in the concepts perfection and imperfection) and find out whether it's healed or not. If it isn't healed – if it's still an open wound, we can clean it and apply the proper cure that lasts until we do.

Truth seen (and taken up) is that cure, and once applied, it never needs to be cleaned or removed. Therefore, it doesn't need any new and sterile dressing, either. In fact, we're done dressing up the dream state! We'll re-examine what we *think* we know, re-examine all we've been told in school, in church or in any book, not just in regards to the concepts "imperfection and perfection", but absolutely everything we cling to, including ourselves. Innocently and without bias, looking in the direction where Truth can be revealed is our practice.

If you find some of the pointers repetitive or even redundant, it's for a reason. If you find some (or even many of the words you read here) paradoxical and contradictory, it's for a reason – and not a result of a confused author. Language is already filled with paradoxical statements and seeming contradictions. Using language that points to truth and freedom – and away from illusion, is even MORE FRAUGHT with seeming contradictions. If there is only one point in this entire book where I

The Dance Of Imperfection

ask you to just "trust me on this," it would be this point – that is, until you see this for yourself. The use of language naturally involves paradox and invites contradiction.

In essence, life is paradoxical and often contradictory. Whitman said, *"Do I contradict myself? Very well, then, I contradict myself. I am large and contain multitudes."* I love that quote. Not just because it illustrates my point here, but more importantly, it speaks to our essential nature as both human and spirit simultaneously, one without any separation. It speaks to both our limited and unlimited nature, to both our confused and clear nature. Never being just one thing, everything is connected – and despite any appearance, nothing is separate in reality.

Things can be both something and *not* that something simultaneously. Most people are free, but enslaved at the same time. Everyone is alive and dying at the same time.

So, like all words, the words and ideas presented here *point to* a greater and infinite reality, an all-encompassing reality that envelops both our limited mental and intellectual capacity, and our infinite spirit nature. This all-encompassing reality is larger than any conceptual framework we can come up with; it's larger than anything our minds can comprehend. Really *seeing* this, we do well to let the words penetrate more in our hearts than of our minds, where Truth never is found or realized.

The mind, being a finite thing, can never apprehend or understand the infinite, no matter how hard it tries, regardless of its approach. How can the mind (while a wonderful and useful tool, more powerful than any man-made supercomputer) understand that which produced it?

How can something finite with a particular shelf life – and will die with the body – possibly understand or comprehend the infinite source that created *it?* How can the finite mind, bound by time, understand or comprehend that which is timelessly prior, beneath and behind it? How can the mind comprehend that which encompasses it? It can't, but we endlessly try – with the mind! How's that for ironic?

Now, if you don't presently see this, then I imagine this may be confusing, but does that mean it isn't true? Does it mean you won't ever see this? Heck no. Let me rephrase that: If you continue to look with the mind, you won't see this. Haven't there been times where you read something, or saw a movie a second time, and it finally penetrated in a way it didn't before?

Can I ask you a question? Are you the mind, or do you *have* a mind? If you say you are the mind, then I'd ask, "If you can notice the mind thinking, how can you *be* the mind? Wouldn't you have to be

The Dance Of Imperfection

prior to the mind in order to notice it? What's aware of the mind?" *Hint*: it's not mind. It may appear that I'm getting off topic, but it's all tied in and non-separate. One thing greatly affects the other. Rest assured that I'm not going off on a tangent; there aren't any wild goose chases here. There's been far too many of them already. Besides, if you really *see* that you are not the mind, that you are the aware spirit presence prior to the mind, this whole issue of perfection vs. imperfection becomes a moot point!

You'd no longer identify yourself *as* the mind – and your identity with everything the mind latches onto would drop away. The ballgame would be over, and you'd be free from any concept, free from mind and emotion. Granted, you'd still feel and think, but you'd no longer be attached to these energies, and therefore, you couldn't suffer. There would be a spontaneous shift in identity (when it's "meant" to happen) as a result of seeing what's actually true.

You'd see that it's the mind – and not YOU, that latches onto concepts and believes in them in order to feel safe and secure. YOU don't need this security; YOU already *are* this security. As long as we continue to identify with our mind – as our real identity, it won't be seen. If this is confusing, notice that your awareness of confusion isn't confused at all.

There are many well-intentioned people who are unknowingly disseminating erroneous information to those who sorely want the kind of freedom that liberates. How many of us want short-term fixes to what's ailing us? Don't we really want permanent and lasting solutions to our problems and challenges? Yes, most of us do, but most of us won't ever do whatever it takes, either. And that's okay, too. No one is saying you "should" want it more than anything – and if they do, they're delusional. To those who want freedom at any cost, nothing less than the real thing will do. In the guise of wanting freedom, whether we admit it or not, some of us just want to be entertained and distracted from our lives. And that's okay, too ... until it isn't anymore. Only you can know what your real intention is.

So why aren't most of us getting what we really need, if we really want it? For one, we aren't listening to the "right" people! This isn't a judgment by the way; it's simply an observation. We must be aware and vigilant as to whom we go to for solutions. Nothing so big to see, is it? I'm not going to go to a homeless guy on the street for financial advice, am I? Would I go to someone very obese for my fitness and nutrition goals? No, I wouldn't. For the most part, we just aren't receiving the most accurate pointers from these unqualified sources. Like a domino effect, they end up simply passing along what's been handed down to them, without ever really validating their assertions for themselves. If it hasn't been realized experientially – and it doesn't come and go, then they only have conceptual knowledge.

The Dance Of Imperfection

With all the familiar clichés, buzz-words and catchy phrases out there, it can make a lot of sense to the mind. Since it sounds very reasonable, and *seems* logical to our minds, we conclude it must be right and true. We reason that since so many other good and intelligent people believe it, that it must be right! In so doing, we further sustain the illusion we actually want to see through. We unsuspectingly read concepts and look in directions (from other unsuspecting, well-intended people) where truth won't ever reveal itself. It's here, and it's not hidden, but we're not being properly pointed. The good news is, we *can know* if we're facing the right direction just by the byproducts of looking in a particular direction.

What is our experience as a result of looking in that direction and following the pointers of that particular individual? Does harmony and being in the flow last – or is it short-lived and fleeting? The proof is in the pudding, and our direct experience *is* that pudding. We can't fool ourselves, nor can we escape ourselves. Do we have more clarity or less clarity? Does doubt arise often? Have our previous insecurities significantly alleviated, or have they been removed as a result of the new perception? Are we still negotiating with life and/or spending a lot of energy on managing our states?

Unfortunately, most of these message bearers neglected to look and see whether their realizations have stabilized – and that the fruits don't come and go, before pointing others. Personally, I just wouldn't feel right perpetuating the dream state, because in truth, there's SO MUCH of that already going on – for centuries. That's exactly what I'd be doing if I went the popular and familiar route. Injecting illusion only spreads further illusion.

As life begets more life, so too, does illusion beget more illusion. Giving further credence to these concepts isn't necessary. In fact, giving further validity to these concepts is harming. No pat on the back deserved for me; I'm simply suggesting that, in addition to going within, that it's vital we notice *where* we go for guidance when we go outside of ourselves.

Where we go makes a huge difference actually, and is usually the difference between seeing and not seeing – and what comes with that seeing or not seeing. There's a felt and shared sense of responsibility that comes along with realizing the truth of something. I had to tell the truth because that's what integrity insists on doing. When we don't do what integrity insists, we feel some degree of angst. Therefore, I knew this (couldn't or wouldn't be a book) about making the reader feel better about their "imperfections" by simply accepting them, or about giving them alternate ways and strategies to cope with their own perceived flaws. The byproducts aren't lasting or useful – at least not in a practical way that serves long term.

The Dance Of Imperfection

This is about telling the truth, and having the courage to face our so-called deficiencies and inadequacies. This is about investigating them, instead of blindly believing in them, just because someone else said so. This is about inviting you to consider the very real possibility that through no fault of your own, perhaps you've been looking in directions where truth won't ever be revealed. This is an invitation to look in directions you may not be accustomed to looking. It may not always *feel* good, and you may experience varying degrees of fear, reluctance and other uncomfortable feelings, but so what? Sometimes truth and feeling good don't always go together. Yeah, and? Don't let feelings stop you – they're just energy anyway.

If feeling good is more important to us than realizing what's true – and enjoying the immense benefit from that – then there's a very good chance we're going to bail when it doesn't feel so good.

As we already know, because we've experienced it many times, sometimes the truth hurts. Let's not pretend otherwise, and be open to HOWEVER it shows up. If we stick with it, and make no demands of it, and look until we see, we'll notice the seeing is often the letting go. Isn't freedom *from* our minds and emotions what we really want? Don't we really just want to be okay with all of who we are, without being tormented by our own thoughts and opinions we have of ourselves? Haven't the most challenging situations in our lives typically led to the most learning and growth?

If there ever was a state called perfection – where, as Aristotle proclaimed, *"a completeness containing all the requisite parts, where it's so good that nothing of the kind can be any better,"* this is it. It's found in the perception of true seeing. This is my reality – and it has absolutely nothing to do with resignation or complacency. Anyone who knows me knows I'm no doormat. This perception sets us free, once and for all. No maintenance needed. And no, it doesn't "kill" your drive or motivation.

If this beckons you, please read on. I am very aware that just because you're reading this doesn't equate to you buying into it, at least not right now. Actually, I don't want you to "buy into it"… I don't want you to buy into anything here. I want you to *see* it for yourself, in your own experience, beyond belief. Belief isn't required and belief isn't necessary.

Nothing less can, or will, liberate you. There *is* an inescapable integrity required for one to be free; he or she must see for him or herself, without relying on belief or any outside source. This includes the most commonly accepted "authoritative sources" we can ever find. If you do see the truth of this now, that's wonderful, and I hope that in this seeing, you experience as much or more relief and laughter as I

The Dance Of Imperfection

did. To suddenly realize that it was all a "crock of you know what" was instantly liberating.

Seeing through the illusory concept called "imperfection" to the reality of its eternal nonexistence, a dropping away (or a dismantlement in the belief) happened of its own accord. It's as if we're rewarded for our willingness to see what's true. Not only did this seeing significantly impact the way I showed up in the present, but also for the way I viewed my so-called past. Knowing that *how absolutely everything unfolded* couldn't have unfolded any other way than it did – and in the manner it did – dissolved *any* leftover regret, guilt, shame and sorrow. If it couldn't have unfolded any other way than it did (and it was only my mind that said otherwise) why would I beat myself up for the things I did?

Why would I create and hold onto a limiting story that said, "It was *because* of my shortcomings that I messed up, or it was due to my flaws that I treated myself or another that way, etc.?" You can imagine the impact this had on how I viewed others as well, and the perceived things that were "done to me". I couldn't fully comprehend that all that stuff, all those negative experiences were still harbored and being carried around for years. I didn't see how believing in untruths significantly influenced how I met the moment.

"Oh, what a tangled web we weave, when we first practice to deceive." This web we've fashioned, literally over a lifetime, seems and feels so real. And since it feels so real, we conclude that it must be real. It may *seem* insurmountable, like climbing Mount Everest, without the aid of oxygen. It may *seem* impossible to find our way out of this deluded and sticky web we've created, but we don't stop at appearances.

Take heart, there *is* a way out. The way out is the way in; the way out isn't to eradicate the web or destroy the web. The way out is to see through the hypnotic web as being unreal, and without a shred of truth in it.

It's about looking beyond appearances to the underlying essence beneath and behind. *See* that the mind's function is to create problems, only to try and solve them. Then, and only then, will the web begin to fall apart and free us from its hold, revealing its true nature, nothing but illusion – through and through. I didn't fully see the direct relationship between how I felt about myself, and how I treated others. I had little appreciation for the fact that all that unresolved "stuff" was still alive in me – in the recesses of my mind, my DNA, my memory ... and ultimately, in every fiber of my being.

Like a veil lifted, now I could see. There wasn't anything between myself and what arose ... no stories, no agenda, just this and nothing else.

The Dance Of Imperfection

Finally *seeing* that there was no such state or condition called "perfection" allowed me to live without any felt sense of insecurity, psychological or emotional fear. Gone was any regard of "doing it right" or "messing up," because *how* I showed up – the manner in which I showed up, was already taken care of. How I showed up "before" and how I showed up now, was exactly the way I was *meant* to show up. All the energy that would have previously gone towards being concerned about screwing up or being embarrassed was transferred to just being in the moment.

No longer identified with the contents of the mind, there was an organic sense of transparency experienced. If you slung arrows of criticism at me, they wouldn't stick. They still don't. They'd go right through me, landing somewhere beyond me. Being energy without a fixed reference point, there was nothing solid for the arrow to land. What I am is eternally unharmed and untouched – and it has absolutely nothing to do with belief. If something happened that wasn't of my preference, it's okay. If something didn't pan out because of a particular inability or weakness on my part, it's okay. There's always another opportunity, and I noticed that any attachment I had to being "perfect" or insecure about my "imperfections" was gone.

I no longer label things as perfect or imperfect. Things are just as they are. It's really that simple – so simple that I hope you resist the urge to dismiss it. If I can see, so can you. And if you think that *this* is just some strategy or method to soften or alleviate your experience of your interpretations, I won't try and convince you otherwise. I may, however, suggest suspending your judgment until you look and see for yourself – but no one is saying you have to. You may want to hold onto the status quo for whatever reason. Granted, at times, I still strive to get something just right (dare I say perfect) but I don't identify with it or get caught up in it anymore. The end result is just fine by me. Besides, maybe I'll do better next time.

Either way, even though I'm not separate from my creations, they don't define me one bit. This moment is whole and complete, as it is, where all the requisite parts are included, because in fact, it couldn't be any other way than it is. Nothing needs to be added, and nothing needs to be subtracted, except in the mind that says otherwise. Since it was truly seen here, my mind no longer says otherwise. All along it was just a thought believed in. Since I was totally willing to really see for myself, something or no-thing (call it God if you prefer) allowed me to see. You have this very same ability. We all play on a level playing field.

We are all essentially the same, possessing the same faculties of attention and awareness, with the ability to discern what's true and what isn't. Aside from those with significant mental disorders and the

The Dance Of Imperfection

like, we really *do play* on even ground. Regardless of our conditioning or past experience, we've all been endowed with the ability to live from truth, not illusion.

No one person is more worthy or deserving of seeing this than another. No one person is better or more worthy than another, from the homeless man in the inner city, to the King of England. I do have deep compassion for those who've had rough and traumatic upbringings, where all kinds of abuse were considered "normal". If this was your case, you never deserved any of that, and absolutely none of it was your fault. As you are right now, you are perfect and complete, without imperfection or inadequacy.

That doesn't mean to walk around thinking you're God's gift to humanity, either. The fact is, we're all intrinsically the same, no better or worse than another. Stop believing your mind that may tell you a different story. It just isn't true. Stop concluding that because you still *feel* it in your bones, in your DNA and in your being, that it must be true. Of course it's still there – it's there because you still believe it to be real. There's great momentum in belief and illusion; it is a very powerful force. Your belief in its existence *is* the energy that gives it life. It really does have that power.

Most importantly, keep looking until you really see, because you can never know when it might happen. And when it does, tell me what you really think about these concepts called perfection and imperfection, okay? Can an eye that sees faultlessly find imperfection?

Whether or not you believe in the existence of imperfection, feel trapped within the sense of imperfection as a reality, to follow is a wonderful, little story ...

A water bearer in China had two large pots, each hung on the ends of a pole that he carried across his neck. One of the pots had a crack in it, while the other pot was perfect and always delivered a full portion of water. At the end of the long walk from the stream to the house, the cracked pot arrived only half full. For a full two years this went on daily, with the man delivering only one and a half pots full of water to his house. The perfect pot without the crack was proud of his accomplishments, always delivering a full pot of water. The cracked pot was ashamed and miserable that it was only able to accomplish half of what it was designed to do. After two years of what it perceived as bitter failure, it spoke to the water bearer one day at the stream.

"I am ashamed of myself and because this crack in my side causes water to leak out all the way back to your house." The bearer said to the pot, "Did you notice that there were flowers only on your side of the path, but not on the other pot's side? That's because I have always known about your flaw, and I planted flower seeds on your side of the path, and every day while we walk back, you've watered them. For two years I have been able to pick these beautiful

The Dance Of Imperfection

flowers to decorate the table. Without you being just the way you are, there would not be this beauty to grace my house."

Chapter 3
An Existential Discomfort

"Please, Doc -- nothing too aggressive. I'm kind of attached to my symptoms."

"Striving for excellence motivates you; striving for perfection demoralizes you."

~ Harriet Braiker

Growing up, I can remember being a perfectionist. In sports, I not only had to beat you, I had to do it convincingly. I'd settle for squeaking out a win, but I much preferred to win outright. It was the ego stroke I apparently needed. Losing to my older brothers on our backyard basketball court likely

The Dance Of Imperfection

had something to do with this compulsion. In the third grade, I remember being involved in the SRA reading comprehension testing with my fellow classmates. We had to read stories from laminated cards that we'd get from a box on the teacher's desk at the front of the room.

After reading stories, we'd answer questions to test our comprehension level. It really wasn't a competition, but I made it one. In a classroom of over 35 kids, it was you against me for the right to claim the prize of "The Best and Fastest Reader With Great Comprehension Skills!" You won by being faster than the rest of the students. Funny thing is, the girls didn't seem to care about competing. Even at such a young age, the girls had it right! Anyway, I decided that I won if I finished in the top two. You always knew who finished in the top two, because once you finished a lesson, you'd have to get out of your chair and walk up to the front of the room to get a new card.

I still remember watching my friend, Steve, head to the front of the class. He made sure you knew it, too. He'd bang his chair when he got up letting you know he finished before you. I could tell Steve viewed it as a competition, too. I can still remember the jealous feeling, watching him and another kid saunter up to the front. Obviously, this wasn't acceptable to me, so I made some minor "adjustments" in my approach. I started skimming certain sections in order to finish in the top two – and it worked. Aside from the teacher, no one would know my actual scores, so that wasn't a concern; finishing first and winning was.

When it came to playing board games at home with my siblings, I just had to win. Coming from a family of six children, there was a palpable sense of competition in the air. Being the youngest of three boys and being the second to youngest, I can assure you that I got my fair share of beat downs and humiliations that only the youngest in the family can identify with. But my saving grace was that I had a sister, three years younger. Annemarie would unsuspectingly become my prey, allowing me to be in the "w" column most of the time.

In the spirit of full-disclosure, I must admit that whenever I found myself behind, or close to losing in chess, checkers, backgammon, monopoly or battleship, I'd sometimes cheat when she wasn't looking – or when she had to suddenly leave for a bathroom break. I just couldn't stand to hear the words, "You sunk my battleship" ... "King me" ... or "Pass go, give me $200!" And all because I had to win – no matter what it took. Looking back with the benefit of hindsight, it was all because I'd go to any lengths to avoid that feeling of losing. More accurately, I sought to avoid what I told *myself* after I lost.

The Dance Of Imperfection

I hated confirming what I was feeling inside ... that I was insecure, imperfect and flawed, so winning was a way to minimize this sense. There was occasion that I'd lose ... mostly due to the fact my little sister never took her eyes off me and got "lucky!" Over time, she became wise to my ways. Now mind you, I didn't resort to cheating all the time. Nevertheless, it's amazing that at such a young age, the need to win was so strong. I was even desperate to the point I was willing to compromise my integrity to avoid hearing the voice inside reminding me of my inadequacies.

Many of us have a strong inner critic, and we believe what it says to us. As children, we believed it when our parents told us, "You're not a good listener." "Why can't you pay attention when I tell you to do something?" "Why can't you get good grades like your older brother?" "If you don't get your act together, you'll amount to nothing!" They may tell you it's "constructive criticism" and that it's meant to help you. Consequently, the implication was that you shouldn't be bothered by it! Most parents don't intentionally want to hurt us, however, the effects aren't always so good.

Hearing criticism from the outside only compounds what we hear and feel from the inside. And what we do to ourselves, we do to others. In our own blame and shame, we blame and shame others.

Then, we often make the conclusion we're not good enough, worthy enough, and deserving enough.

We tie our behaviors and achievements (or lack of achievements) to our self-worth and become concerned with making mistakes and messing up. We worry about what others think of us, and put a lot of energy into projecting an image of someone who really has it all together. We put on a happy face, never addressing the root wound. Coming to believe we are our behaviors and achievements, our self-esteem and relationships suffer. We continue to beat ourselves up, thinking it's a good strategy to improve who we are, when the opposite is true.

While we continue to experience stress, anxiety, sadness and low energy from believing the criticisms in our head, the option to recognize none of it is true waits to be seen. The option to experience ease of being, peace, happiness and increased energy is instantly available when we align ourselves with what's true.

We live in a culture that's increasingly obsessed with winning and perfection – and actively avoiding, downplaying and hiding "imperfections". Rarely is it about "how you play the game" anymore. Winning is what really matters, and winning in a dominating fashion is a bonus, one sure to get you all kinds of praise and adulation from your peers. It's the icing on the cake, the icing that ensures the envy of your fellow competitors. It's the layer of icing that validates the child's need to cover up his felt sense of lack and insecurity. There's nothing wrong with our kids being involved in playing competitive sports and making a real commitment to one or more.

However, when it becomes so intense that the coaches of our children are pacing up and down the sidelines, yelling at the referees to make the "right" call, or aggressively telling our kids how to "do it the right way" ... something has gone awry and our priorities need to be looked at. When the parents are screaming at the referees and umpires from the bleachers – and fighting with each other – something isn't right. This behavior even goes on with our five and six year olds playing! It's both comical and disconcerting.

More and more, our kids are suffering from the effects of such intense competition. The underlying message is that perfection is an attainable goal and it's your duty to achieve it. Sadly, this pressure on our youth is spilling out in a variety of ways. What was once a healthy outlet to compete and be social is now an intensely competitive avenue for kids to try and validate themselves and make their parents proud. It's manifested as the 12-year old traveling all over, staying overnight in hotels and playing in all kinds of tournaments in various organizations. Practicing 3-6 hours a day between games, sometimes with a personal trainer, isn't uncommon. No wonder so many kids are on medications these days.

I recently read an article online from the New York Times called, *"Risky Rise of Good-grade Pills: Strained students increasingly take stimulants to study and take tests to get into the top schools."* It went on to report that before getting out of his car in the morning to enter school, a particular boy would twist open a capsule of orange powder and arrange it in a neat line on the armrest console. He leaned over, closed one nostril and snorted it. Throughout the parking lot, he said, eight of his friends were all doing the same thing.

The drug wasn't cocaine or heroin, but Adderall, an amphetamine prescribed for attention deficit hyperactivity disorder. The boy said he and his friends routinely shared the drug to study late into the night, focus during tests, and ultimately get the grades worthy of being admitted to the high end, prestigious colleges and universities. The drug did more than jolt them awake for the early morning SAT tests; it gave them laser focus, tailor-made for the marathon of tests long known to make or break college applications. "Everyone in school either has a prescription or has a friend who does," the boy said.

At high schools across the United States, pressure over grades and competition for college admissions are encouraging students to abuse prescription stimulants. Forty students agreed to share their experience as long as they remained anonymous. Each of them emphasized that the drugs were not intended for getting high, but to work harder and meet the ever-rising academic pressures and expectations. We can only imagine where this drug use has led.

In this age of instant gratification and instant news and information, advertisers and media play a significant role in mirroring back our obsession with projecting the right image, wearing the right clothes, driving the right cars, living in the perfect home in an upscale neighborhood. You know, a huge mansion that's a few square feet less than the property it sits on, with the most expensive marble countertops, kitchen cabinets and appliances? The next-door neighbor's bedroom window is twenty feet away ... with the perfect spouse raising perfect families – like the Brady Bunch! In a nutshell, the aim is to project the right and perfect life, the kind that's the envy of others.

The goal is to make others want what you have in order to feel validated. Sadly, if we are honest, many of us admit to a degree of feeling content, but also to a superficial kind of satisfaction that ultimately leaves us empty inside. An insecurity regarding *being* that right kind of spouse, parent and friend, isn't that uncommon. Headlines in the magazines and papers on the newsstands, supermarkets and internet invariably convey the same message: dress like this and project this kind of image, hang out with these type of people, drive these cars and do your hair like this person and you too, can be perfect.

The faces and bodies of the people gracing the covers are perfect, but conveniently left out is the airbrushing and other various manipulations applied to make them appear that way. And since you aren't perfect right now, you must buy this magazine or product in order to learn how to be perfect! We really can't place the blame on any one entity. We're all complicit and it spreads like an insidious, infectious disease without any antidote. This seductive message that promises lasting happiness and fulfillment in perfection is sucking us all in. All the while, we have the antidote: it's called integrity and choice.

There is presently an epidemic of eating disorders like bulimia and anorexia that plagues our culture like never before. They are often the result of an obsession to be perfect, or to hide imperfection. Granted, past trauma can and often plays a significant role as well. Since I am not an expert in this area, I won't pretend to know all the particulars of these unfortunate disorders. Certainly, there are numerous factors involved and each case is different. However, not many would argue that an underlying impulse to be perfect is a real symptom and byproduct of these disorders. This generation has the distinction of being the most obese, too.

Overeating and/or overindulging are other manifestations of perfection seeking, or avoidance of a felt sense of imperfection – or both. It can be a behavior to distract one from addressing their perception of a lack of achievement in their life, or suppressing the shame they may feel about their lot in life. As I say this, there are those who are fine with being overweight. Nothing says you must be a certain way. It really comes down to why we do what we do – and what the consequences are. Not everyone has the same reasons for engaging in the same behaviors. I'm not suggesting any of this is inherently bad or wrong. We can live our lives as we choose.

Do you want a good way to condition your child to learn that image is everything and that what you look like is critically important? How about a way to almost ensure they'll end up basing their self-esteem and worth on their appearance – and have them forever compare themselves to others? Enter them into a beauty pageant for kids! Heck, why not encourage them be a model, too? To me, there's not much more ridiculous and potentially damaging than seeing a five year old (like Jon-Benet Ramsey) all dolled up in a gown, with makeup and eyeliner, earrings and hair all done up, belting out a Broadway tune on stage for the judges. Like any other situation, there are exceptions and each kid is equipped differently to handle situations differently.

Quite frankly, I really don't have many opinions (mostly because I know they mean nothing in reality) but I do feel this is a good way to damage your kid and condition them to perceive and judge based on appearances first. We already live in a society where image is king, and where projecting the "right and perfect" image is valued. Why pile it on? It's already in our collective consciousness, so we don't need to hammer it home, do we? We don't need to increase the chances of our kid growing up one day obsessed with plastic surgery because they just can't accept the way they actually appear, do we?

This message and promise to deliver perfection has no boundaries. It's rampant in the self-help movement in the form of books, seminars, retreats, DVD's and dating sites that claim to have the perfect match just for you! There's nothing wrong with dating sites, but let's be honest. This message is all over the place, infusing (and infecting) our culture and collective consciousness in ways that feel overwhelming and virtually impossible to meet. The implications and its effects are devastating to say the least. Somehow we've come to believe that more is better and that acquiring more, better or different than the next guy is a recipe for getting us closer to the perfection we seek – just like the magazines promise.

The Dance Of Imperfection

Underlying this drive is an unspoken agreement that we're competing with each other, and our end result must be better than the next guy if we want to win. All the big corporations and all the competing interests, driven by the media and advertisers that fuel our economy, are making out like bandits pocketing huge sums of money. Apparently, that's of higher value, isn't it? The quality of our relationships and how we view ourselves has become secondary.

What we live we teach and pass on – to our children and grandchildren. Our overall sense of well being usually takes a backseat to the message that profit seeks. The end justifies the means - and sadly, it works. Until we wake up to what's going on and really see its impact, we can only create more of the same.

In our striving for this illusory state of perfection, at best, many of us become comfortably numb, outwardly content, yet inwardly unsatisfied. We end up living a life of quiet desperation, wondering how we ended up this way. It was never part of the plan, and we certainly never envisioned it this way. As a kid, we never said, "When I grow up, I want to be the kind of person who unconsciously chases after the illusion called 'perfection' in all phases of my life. I want to feel a need to project a certain image and worry about what others think of me. In the meantime, I want to spend massive amounts of time and energy suppressing and trying to accept my perceived imperfections, because it's much more difficult that way!"

Life just happens, doesn't it? The law of our experience also dictates that the more unconscious we are, the more we'll get what we don't want. Since it's not part of our make up, and since perfection doesn't actually exist in reality, how else *can* we feel when we chase after something that's unreal? Conversely, what we run from can only chase us. We're in a real dilemma where we run from many things – and chase after many things simultaneously.

Inner peace becomes a "nice idea for others" who aren't nearly as busy as we are. We tell ourselves we don't have the luxury or time for that, remaining mostly unaware of the true source of our existential discomfort. We just need the courage to face an altogether different direction – and then head in that direction, courageously. But first, we must be aware of the direction we're presently facing. We spend so much time looking in directions where problems present themselves, so inevitably we spend so much time and energy trying to solve our problems. We often label them as "confusing", "irritating" and even "depressing."

For some of us, our lives become a negotiation with solving one problem after the other, an endless job of problem management. We identify with this occupation and don't even know who we'd be without them. When we fill out the box that asks for

The Dance Of Imperfection

our occupation on the IRS form, we write, "endless problem solver." Whether consciously or not, we label our problems "imperfect" – and certainly not "complete with all the requisite parts." Rarely do we consider that problems only exist in the mind – and not in reality.

Without referring to thought, do you have *any* problems? Without referring to the past, do you actually have a problem? No, you don't. Resist the urge to shrug off the utter simplicity of this direct recognition! Truth IS simple. Only thought tells you it's a problem. Put another way, in the absence of thought, is there an issue? No, there isn't. As Walt Whitman said, *"There is no imperfection in the present and none in the future."* We don't see that all of our problems are imaginary, and in fact, unreal. Situations in life are not problematic, regardless of how challenging. If we really look, situations are just that, situations and not problems.

Our so-called "problems" are created by the grasping and pushing away within the moment we begin to interpret, project, resist, compare, deny or judge a situation – transforming it from simple to complex. When we identify with this process – and take ownership, we stay mired in the very thing we *don't* want. Consciously, we tell ourselves we really don't want to experience this, and yet, unconsciously, we continue to feed this vicious cycle by negating what is.

Our ability to experience freedom from this downward cycle depends entirely on our capacity to notice the fact that we don't have real problems, only imagined ones! If we really want to be free from the tyranny of our mind, and the emotions that follow, we must be willing to see how it functions and what it does. We must be willing to consider (or just SEE) that we *have* a mind, and that we *aren't* our mind. If this is so, we inquire into why we keep identifying with the thoughts in our head? If we really want freedom, we must learn to embrace the heat of the fire, which we usually avoid at all costs.

We must be willing to experience the burning, the burning of pride, of arrogance, ignorance and limiting beliefs. We must embrace the burning of protecting ourselves from the unknown, what we fear and what we *think* we know. If we don't, we just get more of the same. If we don't, our freedom comes from the temporary moments where we've experienced something delightful, where we've read something from another that resonates deep within, or where we've temporarily witnessed breathtaking beauty in nature.

Granted, that's all nice as far as experience goes, but it's fleeting and doesn't remain. As with all experience, it must come and go, leaving you right where you were before – not knowing what's actual, and guaranteeing future angst. Our very freedom exists right in the middle of the heat of the fire and

The Dance Of Imperfection

nowhere else, before and after experience. When we recognize that it is in the midst of that fire where our liberation lies, we allow ourselves to welcome the fire as our friend, something on our side – and not something to fear. We must allow ourselves to be consumed by that fire.

All we have to do is recognize what's going on in our minds. It takes no great intelligence at all; it just takes an earnest desire to see and observe with an impartial awareness what's happening, as it's happening. When we ask ourselves, "What's the payoff here?" When we ask, "Is this really for my highest good?" – and have the courage to answer honestly, do we begin to loosen the mind's hold on us. Only then can we begin to understand that we'll never be free as long as we cling to the endless ideas and beliefs in our minds. Only then do we allow for another potential to arise in our experience, one where we're no longer in opposition to reality, but in harmony with it.

When we clearly notice the grasping and avoiding nature of our minds, we begin to realize why we have this existential discomfort that feels like an itch in our minds. It's an itch we often conclude can only be alleviated by attaining what we think will satisfy us, or avoiding what we think won't. When we see that nothing has ever truly satisfied the longing in our minds, and that nothing *can* truly satisfy the longing in our minds, do we give ourselves a chance of experiencing reality directly, and not filtered through our ideas about it.

When we notice that it's never been about what the mind says it's about, we give ourselves an opportunity to see that there's nothing to get. Only then do we give ourselves a chance to see that what we're really after has no form – and that it can't be grasped, attained or achieved, do we play by the rules.

Like the scorpion's nature is to sting, we are wise to understand the nature of our situation; we recognize that the nature of the mind is to grasp and chase after what doesn't ultimately fulfill ... and resists what it thinks wont' fulfill. Both movements only disturb, and never bring the formless peace, love and fulfillment we really want. This existential itch can only be rooted out when we notice these movements are inseparable from reality and the law of our experience. When we *see* these movements only hurt and divide, we can intend for something else, but certainly not before we *see*. Seeing that the mind is a master at labeling situations as good or bad, perfect or imperfect, and pleasant or unpleasant, we see that it only thinks in dualistic terms.

Seeing that situations are just that, and seeing that the mind labels them as good or bad, we see *how* we create our experience. When we identify with the mind, as the mind goes, we go. If we desire to be in harmony with life and ourselves, we notice that labels lie. We notice that whatever label we give something can't ever accurately describe that thing or situation. However, we notice how *it sets the mold and lays the foundation for how we experience* that thing or situation. If we label something "imperfect," inevitably, we won't be satisfied. If we view ourselves *in terms of* our perceived inadequacies, shortcomings and flaws, naturally we feel less than – and perhaps undeserving and deficient, won't we?

Labels lie and they lie all the time, especially when we see their ultimate use and function. The "problem" is we believe in them to be accurate representations for what they're describing. Instead of seeing aspects of ourselves (or situations we face) as the way it is – without any conceptual labels, positive or negative, we add an unnecessary layer on top in order to make sense of it. We mistakenly conclude that in order for us to understand something, we must label it. To label is to control. This is one of the many functions of our minds. The mind, in its lack of humility and ultimate ignorance, thinks it knows best and therefore, overshadows our being that really knows the deal.

While our being just watches on with impartial delight, even humor … and patiently waits for when it's called on, the mind continues unaware. The mind actually thinks that whatever conceptual model or label it comes up with is an actual and real substitute for reality – and this is never true. Although it may be very tempting to dismiss this observation, continuing to ignore its implications can have potentially devastating effects. Believing that our conceptions and interpretations are accurate representations for what's actually occurring, our knowledge becomes skewed and distorted.

Whether we realize it or not, feel it or not, disguise it or not, what we all want is truth. There's something within us that knows nothing less will satisfy. We erroneously look for it in concepts, belief systems and opinions – all creations manufactured and sustained in and by our minds. And yet it's never to late to *see* this. Resist the temptation to believe it takes time. It doesn't require a process or journey to see this. All processes and journeys imply time.

You can see this right now.

Chapter 4
Paradox & Confusion

"Have no fear of perfection – you'll never reach it."
~ **Salvador Dali**

"The dance of imperfection" doesn't involve doing any sidestepping movements, where we avoid or deny the challenges we face. As cool as it looks, it certainly doesn't involve shadow dancing, where we turn the lights out and watch our shadow (our particular challenge) dancing on the wall, forever beyond our reach. The "dance of imperfection" requires that we understand life is paradoxical. It invites us to see the inevitable confusion when we fail to recognize these paradoxes operating in our lives. Dancing with our perceived imperfections, face to face, we wholeheartedly embrace all that we are. In this way, suffering and/or confusion won't arise for us anymore.

In other words, we *dance*, elegantly and gracefully, with our unique and "less than ideal traits and abilities" that only we possess, knowing we are so much more than we appear to be. We dance with what we've been given, never apologizing or being ashamed of how we are – as we are. A paradox is understood to be an apparent contradiction, where two things appear to exclude each other – cancel each other out, but in reality don't. A practical example would be that in order to have a particular experience, one must not want to have that experience, or not strive to have that experience.

It reminds me of the quote from John of The Cross, *"In order to have everything, desire to have nothing."* Similarly, when you want to hold water in the palms of your hands, grasping won't do the job. If we remain open to the reality of paradoxes in our lives, we give ourselves the ability to see how they operate and unfold in our experience. We see that it is the nature of our human condition to be both saint *and* sinner – and not saint *or* sinner. It is this *both and* realization of our human nature (and not *either or*)

The Dance Of Imperfection

that allows us to transcend the confusion that arises from misunderstanding.

Failure to understand this has created so much suffering and confusion in the past – and continuing to deny this can only create more suffering and confusion. Living in a world of duality and opposites, humanity is limited, and yet, this limitation doesn't define us. We are infinite Spirit at the same time. In truth, our infinite and *real* nature encompasses and includes our finite, limited nature. If this is the case, wisdom blooms when we include all of ourselves equally – not just the parts we like.

Essential to living a life of relative inner peace and contentment is our willingness to be honest with ourselves. Integrity and living a life that won't be looked back on in regret go hand in hand. We can't have one without the other. Essential to living a life of inner peace and contentment is our refusal to deceive ourselves. A common theme central in all spiritual traditions in history has been to "Know Thyself". In other words, if you only do one thing in life, make sure you know yourself. In order to know oneself, one must not engage in self-deception.

In order to know oneself, one must be willing to see what's true, no matter what. If we are earnest in our desire to see through the false, it's much easier to tell the truth. Honesty with the self, about the self, is essential if we are to enjoy our lives so that we won't have regrets on our deathbed, wishing we could do it over. Life isn't a dress rehearsal – this is it. A mind that is being watched tends to become more humble. With greater awareness comes a greater capacity to live from what we know is true – not we suspect or believe is true.

    Humility has a way of showing us our preoccupation with our illusions. Humility is like having an extra guard on duty, flagging us when our pride is preventing us from telling the truth. Having a good amount of humility is requisite if we are to be honest with who we are, *as* we are. It allows us to see ourselves not in some enhanced, made-up light, but rather, under the bright lights, naked with warts and all. Real humility allows us the capacity to laugh at ourselves and not take ourselves so seriously. Real humility equips us to be less a victim of the mind, and more its master.

    Otherwise, we are just wound tight, aren't we? And more inclined to bring about (quite possibly the most damaging kind of dishonesty there is) ... denial of our mixed human nature, the reality of our "both and" make up. Refusing to acknowledge all of our unique strengths, abilities and character traits – and all of our *not so great* traits and characteristics speaks to our fears in facing what we deem "flawed" or "imperfect." What do we imagine will happen if we admit the whole truth to ourselves? Who would we be then? Could we live with ourselves, and if we could, where might this integrity lead?

The Dance Of Imperfection

Clinging to an unquestioned belief that we must hide aspects of ourselves, aspects that we're either ashamed of or embarrassed by, further solidifies our faulty interpretation. We fail to see that we're all in the very same boat, sailing along through the journey of life with very similar struggles simply disguised differently. We fail to see that most of us have demons inside – but with a different voice and face. By the wayside goes the realization that in our mutually shared acknowledgment of *all* that we are, real healing happens ... the kind that liberates. The Saints and Sages that we honor to this day we honor for a reason: they were willing to be honest with themselves about their dual nature, their *both and* nature.

They knew that the "either or" perception was illusory and didn't exist, and was the thing that brought about suffering. Being ignorant to what's true, we must suffer. These people did what Walt Whitman once said, "dismiss whatever insults your soul" ... without denying any aspect of themselves. They knew that in our brokenness, we are made whole, and that wholeness doesn't exclude those parts that are less desirable.

We can hear the words of the Sufi poet, Rumi in his poem titled, "Undressing."

Learn the alchemy true beings know.
The moment you accept what troubles

you've been given; the door will be open.
Welcome difficulty, as a familiar comrade.
Joke with torment brought by the friend.

Sorrows are the rags of old clothes
and jackets that serve to cover,
and then are taken off.

That undressing,
and the naked body underneath,
is the sweetness that comes after grief.

In my second book, *"When Wisdom Blooms – Awaken the Sage Within"* ... I noted that dogs and cats have no concept of perfection and imperfection. They have no idea that what is presently happening shouldn't be happening – or that it could be happening in any other way. As a result, they don't suffer psychologically or emotionally. They are as they are, without any inkling of improving, or the desire to make their circumstances better.

Dogs and cats are perfect as they are, just like nature. Like animals, nature doesn't tell stories, either. Nature expresses itself as it is, freely unencumbered, without any regret or longing. Granted, animals and nature don't have discriminating minds, but that's the point. The fact that we do reveals that it's our minds that tell us there's a problem! But here's the thing we can notice:

The Dance Of Imperfection

The fact that we possess a discriminating mind doesn't exclude us from being perfect just the way we are!

What's wrong with absolutely anything unless you think about it? What's wrong with right now unless you think about it? Again, resist the urge to dismiss this powerful pointer that can reveal the truth. Resist the temptation to habitually latch on to a conclusion that says something like, "It's a ridiculous notion to even entertain such a statement, and a notion that will only lead me to the land of resignation, where I'll be walked on like a doormat!" I hope that you don't infer this, only because this grossly unexamined inference is absolutely illusory and untrue. Don't believe me. Find out for yourself.

If we are to find a real and solid manifestation of perfection *anywhere in reality*, we can always look to nature. An elegant swan cleaning its mate as they float in a lake, and a cherry blossom tree in full bloom suggests perfection. A beautiful sunset displaying various colors at the opportune moment – and a vivid rainbow after a sudden and passing summer thundershower suggests perfection. The sound of the wind caressing the leaves in the autumn trees on a crisp, October day, and a pod of whales singing as they swim by a tour boat in Hawaii suggests perfection. While they aren't actually two, nature and perfection are wedded, like the bird in the sky, or like the infant breastfeeding in its mother's arms.

Living In Perfect Harmony With Life

Like the constant ebb and flow of the tides in continuous display and in enjoyment of itself, everything unfolds perfectly. Nature doesn't have to *try* to enjoy itself as it expresses; it just does, naturally.

Hear the words of Emerson as he said, *"These roses under my window make no reference to former roses or better ones; they are for what they are; they exist with God today. There is no time for them. There is simply the rose and it is perfect in every moment of its existence. But man postpones or remembers; he does not live in the present, but with reverted eye laments the past, or heedless of the riches that surround him, stands on tiptoe to foresee the future. He cannot be happy and strong until he, too, lives with Nature in the present, above time."*

When humans *try* to enjoy themselves, they almost always have a difficult time. It's a wonderful paradox, actually – and one that frequently leaves us feeling frustrated and confused. We might say, "I really don't understand it; I made all the necessary preparations and made sure all the conditions were just right. I tried to make you happy, and it was a complete failure!" We forget that in order to really enjoy something, we must allow for it to happen, naturally and spontaneously. The more absent we are, the more present we are – and enjoyment just happens.

When we're clearly addicted to something, say a chemical substance that's creating so much pain in our lives, we can only begin the road to recovery when we surrender – when we give in. Only when we acknowledge that we are slaves to that chemical do we give ourselves a real chance at abstaining from that chemical. Recognizing *and then accepting* our powerlessness over the situation, we render ourselves powerful and able to respond appropriately. Response – ability. Whenever we don't understand the paradox of a particular situation we're faced with, odds are we will continue to approach (or relate *to*) that situation in a way that will further ensure us being in bondage to it.

Instead of not making any demands on the moment, we have a tendency to believe we need to "add to or subtract from" the moment in the hope of having a "better" or more complete experience – or at least, one that's more in harmony with what we *think* we want. I say, "think" because isn't it true that often what we think we want, (upon further examination) isn't what we really want? Paradoxically, when we give up trying to alter or change the moment – or when we give up thinking we must have something in a particular way, enjoyment arises and confusion eventually disappears.

As a result, we often discover that what we really want shows up. When we clearly recognize that all of our striving for perfection is really about our desire to feel whole and complete, we allow for new possibilities to arise in our experience. When we see what's true, something lets go, and we're no longer bound. Until we break free of the unconscious, trance-like mode we've been operating from, we'll never experience our true desire – to *experientially feel* that completeness, where nothing needs to be added to or subtracted from. This is perfection.

The perception of this wholeness and completeness, whether we realize it, is what we're really after – and nothing less will satisfy. Since no label or description can capture reality, we suffer when we mistakenly label aspects of ourselves as "imperfect and flawed" – as opposed to seeing that these aspects of ourselves are "as they are." When this happens, we inevitably experience the fractured hurt and dis-ease that comes with labels that always lie. Like Winnie the Pooh stuck in the rabbit hole, man is forever stuck and identified with his lack of awareness and knowledge of himself, *until* he is willing to look beyond apparent causes to the real source within.

It's all so simple really, but our minds insist on complicating things, until it doesn't anymore. All we need to do is want a different possibility, and be willing to examine our direct experience, consciously tracing it back to the perception that led us astray. Then and only then, are we able to take a different path, a path that isn't divisive. Seeing clearly the nature and reality of our situation, we are aware that we live in a world that isn't perfectible; we're aware that we live in a world that often displays a *sense* of

The Dance Of Imperfection

incompleteness, a *sense* that something is fractured and unfinished.

Arising from this sense of discomfort is a sense of being wounded, with the feeling we won't ever heal. Having difficulty imagining future happiness, we believe our situation is permanent, pervasive and personal. Instead of looking to heal something that we aren't even quite sure is actually wounded in the first place, we can look beyond *the appearance of imperfection and inadequacy* – and look to the wisdom of insecurity. In a world where absolutely nothing lasts, where nothing remains, we see that we can't cling to anything at all – including our very life – *and* feel remotely comforted. Without pushing away the reality of the situation we find ourselves in, we give ourselves permission – we give ourselves license - to simply allow whatever's arising to be just the way it is; we know that it's all perfect and complete already.

And if we really look closely, we recognize that none of it is personal at all. If we don't yet see it, we look until we *do* see. Our comfort resides in true perception, not pursuing some state of perfection we think will comfort us. Working with the law of nature and our experience (same thing) we see the wisdom of *transcending and including all of it,* for we know that to resist any part of it is unintelligent and nonsensical.

Consciousness has a habitual tendency to forget that it is our orientation *towards* our struggles and challenges that creates the problems. We project onto others own feelings of inner frustration and disappointment – and we don't take responsibility for our experience.

We forget it's ALL an inside game, always and in all ways. In addition, our culture has a tendency to operate from the notion that the way to effect real psychological and emotional healing is to cover over the wound with temporary, band-aid approaches. We spend our efforts and energy on correcting the *effects* instead of the *causes* – through justification, rationalization, minimizing and a variety of other distracting methods. Whether our end goal is the pursuit of happiness, or the avoidance of pain, the destination is a shared one. That destination is an unfulfilled place where existential discomfort resides because we don't recognize the nature of the paradoxes we find ourselves in. We don't see that the cure for pain is *in* the pain.

We don't yet see that *what we run from can only chase us, and what we pursue can only evade us.* Try to make something perfect and it will forever remain imperfect. Try to have fun – and fun evades you. Nature is effortlessly perfect, and effort is perfectly imperfect. When it comes to how we see ourselves, effort presupposes we must do something to fix or change the way we are. Reality (and our unblemished true nature) is always right here, before

The Dance Of Imperfection

labels and descriptions – immediate, undivided and already complete.

When we believe our labels and descriptions can capture reality, we often experience contraction. Paradoxically, when we resist the urge to label and describe, we innocently meet the moment as it is and not as we wish. And there's no contraction.

When I was twenty years old, I had the good fortune of going on a family cruise to Bermuda to celebrate my parent's 25th anniversary. Riding a moped alone one day, I noticed a path in the bush on the side of the road that led to an opening with a view of the ocean. I felt compelled to pull over, park the moped and wonder over to the path. I continued to walk about two hundred feet until I found myself at the edge, where the island met the ocean. I sat down and began gazing out into the vast, clearest aqua-blue water I had ever seen.

I don't know how long I sat there, perhaps twenty minutes or so, but I was lost in the view, not sensing any boundary between what I was seeing and what was doing the seeing. There was just absolute and total peace in that still silence – and a feeling of being both totally absent and totally present at the same time.

I was taken back, never imagining I could have such a wonderful and compete experience like this. After a while, I remember saying to myself, "this is so beautiful and I don't want it to ever end." And it was in that exact moment (when I became aware of myself sitting there enjoying and being immersed in the view) that the experience ended. Instantly jolted, I was transported back in identification with a mind that was looking out at the scene. In my desire to hold onto the experience and make it last longer, it ceased. It was the first time in my life that I noticed that self-consciousness terminated the experience.

This reminds me of a famous Zen story we can all relate to:

A Zen master was making a painting and he had his main student sit by his side to tell him when his painting was perfect. The master was worried and the student was also worried because he had never seen his teacher do anything imperfect. However, that day things started going awry. The master tried and the more he tried, the more it was a mess. In Japan or China, the art of calligraphy is done on rice paper, on a certain paper, a very sensitive and fragile paper. If you hesitate just a little, for centuries it can be known where the calligrapher hesitated, because more ink spreads into the rice paper, making it a mess.

It is very difficult to deceive on rice paper and the master knew it. You have to go on flowing; you are not to hesitate, even for a single moment. If you hesitate for a split second, what to do? You already missed, and one who has a keen eye will immediately say, "It is not a Zen painting at all" because a Zen painting has to be a spontaneous and free flowing painting. The master tried

The Dance Of Imperfection

and tried and the more he tried, the more he perspired. The student was sitting there and shaking his head back and forth saying, "No, this isn't perfect." Consequently, the master made more mistakes.

Then the ink began to run out so the master said, "You go out and prepare more ink." While the student was outside preparing the ink, the master did his masterpiece. When the student came in he said, "Master, but this is perfect, what happened?" The master laughed and said, "I became aware of one thing, your presence. The very idea that someone was there to appreciate or condemn, to say yes or no, disturbed my inner tranquility. Now I will never be disturbed. I have come to know that I was trying to make it perfect and that was the only reason for it not being perfect."

Try to make something perfect and it won't ever be. Being self-conscious and exerting a lot of effort in the hopes of making something just right only distorts. Do it naturally and it is always perfect. Nature is perfect and effort and striving isn't. True seeing sees the perfection in all things, as they are. Wisdom sees the inherent beauty and completeness in everything God has made. It is the evaluating, comparing mind that labels things imperfect and flawed. Whichever you identify yourself with determines what you see, and therefore, what you experience.

Conventional wisdom would try to tell us that if perfection is an actual and attainable state, then imperfection, too, must be an actual state that can be avoided or removed. This "wisdom" implies if we are to accept and embrace those aspects of ourselves (that we don't particularly like or appreciate) that those aspects will become more apparent in our daily experience.

In other words, we think they'll have more of an influence in our daily lives if we don't suppress, run from or resist them. Conventional wisdom and conditioning would try to tell us that the way to deal with pain (or that which we don't like) is to deny its existence – or at the least resist its presence in our experience. That way, it reasons, its life span will be short and the impact minimal. It then infers that embracing and welcoming is for passive wimps, for those who don't get up and "fight" for what they want. In truth, "Blessed are the meek, for they shall inherit the earth."

Since this kind of "wisdom" comes from the mind that resists what is, and not from the heart that already knows, it's no wonder things go awry. While we continue to identify with the mind and its distorted view, we won't ever escape the byproducts of those views. The antidote and the restoration of true perception lies in understanding the paradoxes we continually find ourselves in. The antidote is to accept and embrace these paradoxes so *that we don't continue to give life to* the kinds of experiences we'd prefer not to have.

The Dance Of Imperfection

A fitting poem by *Rumi*:

<u>Silkworms</u>

*The hurt you embrace
Becomes joy.*

*Call it to your arms
Where it can change.*

*A silkworm eating leaves
Makes a cocoon.*

*Each of us weaves a chamber
Of leaves and sticks.*

*Silkworms begin to truly exist
As they disappear inside that room.*

*Without legs, we fly.
When I stop speaking,*

*This poem will close,
And open its silent wings ...*

If we want to remember something that we're temporarily forgetting, we don't want to stress and strain and search our mind for the answer, right? We all know that the answer comes when we let go of needing to know in that moment. If aware, we say, "Oh, I will remember it later if I stop thinking about it." Sure enough, the answer pops up later when we aren't thinking about it. If we are meditating (or sitting in silence as I prefer to call it) for the purpose of rest or relaxation and find our mind racing, don't resist this movement of thinking. We can't relax by forcing relaxation, can we? Rather, we just let the thoughts go by like clouds in the vast, empty sky, watching our mind – and let the quiet stillness reveal itself.

If we want something gone from our experience, it *only* dissolves when we let it be there in the first place. Offer it no resistance and watch it leave. If we lean towards being the lazy kind (and would rather be more productive) fully allow yourself to be the lazy kind until something else moves you. If you don't worry about how to know when to move, you'll know when to move – but *only* if you welcome laziness to be present.

If we want that baby crying on the airplane to stop driving us nuts, we stop telling ourselves the baby shouldn't be crying – and watch the annoyance diminish or go away. Don't let your interpretations and conclusions *about* concepts become so real that you mistake them for *being* the reality – and not just symbols for the reality. Don't confuse the symbols and the things they aim to represent; don't marry the two, as they are forever meant to be divorced. Indeed, the "map is not the territory" and the map can only describe a territory in such a way as to help

The Dance Of Imperfection

us traverse that territory, not to mistake them as being the same. Granted, it's a useful tool but our perception of the map can never equal the territory.

If you have a real challenge accepting your perceived limitations or "imperfections" in your life – and they're renting a whole lot of space in your head, then stop believing the thoughts in your head that tell you that you should be different than you are. If we want someone we really care about to "change their ways" or "see the light" ... see that it's more about our need for them to be different than they are. When we offer no resistance and judgment to them as they are, over time, watch what happens to them.

One of the greatest gifts you can give another is *your* higher consciousness and unconditional acceptance, the kind that dispels ignorance. Work with yourself, not against yourself. By working with yourself, you effectively work with others. You are the ultimate and final authority in your experience – and what you live, you teach. But hey, don't believe me.

In closing, a verse from **The Tao Te Ching:**

> *To be whole, let yourself break.*
> *To be straight, let yourself bend.*
> *To be full, let yourself be empty.*
> *To be new, let yourself wear out.*
> *To have everything, give everything up.*
> *Knowing others is a kind of knowledge;*

Living In Perfect Harmony With Life

Knowing yourself is wisdom
Conquering others requires strength;
Conquering yourself is true power.
To realize you have enough is true wealth.
Pushing ahead may succeed,
But staying put brings endurance.
Die without perishing and find the eternal.
To know that you do not know is strength.
Not knowing that you do not know is a sickness.
The cure begins with the recognition of the sickness.
Knowing what is permanent: enlightenment
Not knowing what is permanent: disaster.
Knowing what is permanent opens the mind.
Open mind, open heart.
Open heart, magnanimity.

Chapter 5
Beyond Seeming Opposites

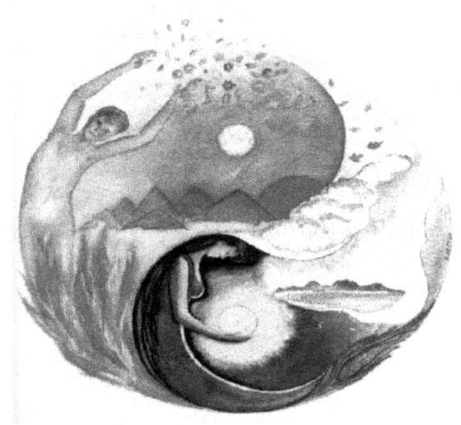

"Now the two primal Spirits, who reveal themselves in vision as Twins, are the Better and the Bad, in thought and word and action. Between these two the wise ones chose aright; the foolish not so."

~ Zoroaster

Man's ongoing dilemma has been misidentifying his own intellectual conclusions as reality. These inherently limited assumptions and suppositions are the end result of an arbitrary point of perception based on (and a direct consequence of) his past conditioning and habitual patterns of thinking. We see what we believe and believe what we see ... and then we often wonder how we create our experience. Understanding comes from operating from the appropriate context, asking the right questions and looking in the direction where the "answer" or truth can reveal itself. Sometimes, there isn't an answer – and that's acceptable for the one who doesn't need to know. It's acceptable for the one who knows that in order for truth to be revealed, one must be willing *not* to know.

If, on the other hand, we are to declare something as true or real based upon hasty and simple examination, we invariably end up with a distorted conclusion that hurts. Our conclusions don't mean much if, as a result of those conclusions, we end up feeling confused, alienated and incomplete. Our conclusions don't mean much unless we're willing to take the next step and question if they're actually true. Otherwise, we forever remain feeling isolated from the completeness and wholeness of Life and live from a fiction of our own making. Life isn't divided. Man's perception is divisive. Consequently, in a world without division, man divides.

Until man sees that there are no causes in the observable world – and that the world he sees and observes is the world of effects, not much will change

The Dance Of Imperfection

for him. Unlike any other species, humans have developed language as its primary means of communication, both spoken and written. We all know that it takes years to learn the various labels for existence and eventually string them together into a story that makes sense. Babies have no idea what words mean right out of the womb.

Words have no intrinsic meaning. They're just sounds and symbols that point to life's happenings. The words "happiness" and "joy" mean absolutely nothing to the aborigine in Australia. By nature, language is both dualistic and divisive, and sends us on all kinds of wild goose chases. Let me rephrase that: It is our translation *of* language that sends us on all kinds of wild goose chases – and not language itself.

If I classify something based on its appearance and function, then things that don't appear and function just like it are said to be something other, or "not" that – and classified as something else. I draw the line between *this* thing and *those* things that aren't just like it. If this tall thing with leaves that grows out of the ground is different in appearance than anything else, I might call it a "tree." Anything that doesn't appear and function like a tree is not that (a tree) – and I might call it something else, like a "rock" or a "bird" or a "mountain." There's the parasite and the host; there's the infection and the cure; there's addiction and recovery, and there's Hitler and Mother Theresa.

Like life, we can never quite pin down language; it is forever in flux and never carved in stone. The Greek philosopher Heraclitus said, "We can never step in the same river twice." Due to the constant flux and flow, new water is always rushing by, never being the same water. We speak of language as if it is something fixed and true – and something that we can rely on to tell us what's so. However, believing we always perceive language correctly is like thinking we can step in the same river twice.

We use, hear or read the same concept numerous times, but *we seldom seem to question why it is that the meaning tends to change over time.* Doesn't its meaning alter depending on our understanding and level of awareness? Doesn't its meaning change depending on who the perceiver is?

For instance, aren't there occasions when your interpretation of a profound insight or passage is different from when you were previously exposed to it? Of course it is. Doesn't this speak to its ultimate (and relative) accuracy and true function? In other words, the one who perceives is the one who draws their own meaning; the interpretation changes relative to where that perceiver is in terms of their level of awareness. This being the case, wouldn't this pertain to how we see ourselves, too? If one day we have a difficult time accepting a certain personal characteristic, but the next day we could care less, what does that tell you? That just maybe we make it all up?

Additionally, implicit in language is the notion that concepts are *either or* and not *both and*. Being wired to avoid pain and gain pleasure, humans naturally resist the "bad or unpleasant side" of the conceptual symbol called *joy*, of the conceptual symbol called *comfort* and of the conceptual symbol called *life*. Pushing away the certain realities of their opposites – pain, discomfort and eventual death – is a reliably effective formula for continued angst and anxiety! Please check it out for yourself; you are the final authority! Until we see that *any* movement we make is a movement away, and of resistance, we are destined to function like washing machines stuck on the "repeat" cycle.

In our abiding trance-like state of misunderstanding the true purpose and function of language, we unwittingly invite unpleasant experiences. We thank God for all the "good" and pleasant things that come our way, calling them "blessings" – and yet we don't ever consider thanking Him for the "bad" and unpleasant things that happen to us. And this is exactly where we go astray. Incidentally, this is also where the New Age Movement goes astray.

Have you ever really pondered why life comes in opposites? Why everything you deem worthy and of value is one of a pair of opposites? Why each decision you make is between opposites – and every desire you have is based in polar opposites? We see how spatial dimensions are opposing – up versus down, left versus right, long versus short, inside versus outside, here versus there and top versus bottom. We notice the things that have greater importance to us personally come in opposites as well: pleasure versus pain, good versus evil, comfort versus discomfort, acceptance versus resistance, freedom versus enslavement, God versus Satan, Heaven versus Hell, truth versus falsehood and life versus death.

The more subjective "eye of the beholder" qualities come in opposites, too: beautiful versus ugly, smart versus dumb, strong versus weak, success versus failure, and dare I seemingly contradict the central theme of this entire book and say, perfect versus imperfect? Every time we make a decision, we draw a boundary line between our options to choose from. When we desire something, we draw a boundary line between the pleasurable thing we desire and the unpleasant thing we don't want – and then move towards the thing we do want.

To sustain a particular belief means we draw a dividing boundary line between what we believe to be true and what we don't believe is true. To sustain

The Dance Of Imperfection

a particular energetic feeling sense of insecurity over some aspect of ourselves, we draw a boundary line between secure and insecure. Thus, we tell ourselves we won't ever feel secure until we improve upon, fix or change our weakness. All of these dividing lines are not boundaries at all. In fact, the boundaries we perceive are entirely MENTAL – and have no more existence in reality than Snow White and the Seven Dwarves!

If peace and self-acceptance is what we're after, we don't have the luxury of pitting one side against the other side. We don't have the luxury in believing in – or stopping at - the appearance of things. We must go beyond the appearance and look to the essence *behind* the appearance. On closer examination, we notice that delineating a boundary line doesn't distinguish anything but an inside versus an outside. Imagine a circle you've just drawn on a piece of paper. Better yet, please take out a piece of paper and do this now. And in that circle, you've written the word "inside." Right next to the circle, on a blank sheet of paper, you've written the word "outside." Notice that the opposites of "inside versus outside" didn't exist until you drew the boundary of the circle. That is, the boundary line created the pair of opposites, did it not?

Simply put, to draw a boundary line means to create and maintain opposites. To draw a boundary line means to distinguish this from that – and then we believe "this" and "that" are forever set apart. With this recognition, we can begin to recognize we live in a world of opposites because our lives are spent drawing and believing in opposites! We live in a world of opposites that create conflict and suffering. Where we decide to draw the line is precisely where the war takes place. The more entrenched that battle line is drawn, the more bloody that war becomes. The same thing that gives you pleasure gives you pain. The more that pleasure is absent, the more that discomfort is present. The more I try to maintain pleasurable states, the more I fear uncomfortable states.

Having a death grip on a need to be successful, the more I naturally fear failure. The more I steadfastly cling to life, the more frightened I am of my inevitable death. The more I strive for happiness, the deeper my sadness has a tendency to get. The more I pursue trying to project my most perfect self, the more obsessed I become with hiding what I'm insecure about. The more I am concerned with how others view me, the more insecure I feel – and the more I try to hide those aspects of myself I deem less worthy. To the degree that I value anything at all, to that degree do I become obsessed with its loss, and so on.

This orientation only ensures that I live my life in a contrived manner, attempting to manufacture and sustain some ideal image I've cooked up for myself – and hope it lasts as long as possible. Since it never matches up with reality, it can't last – and I must suffer the consequences. Illusion hurts, and the division we create is the wood-chipper we walk right into, tearing us apart. No longer am I in harmony with life because I've placed a conceptual barrier between my experience and whatever arises. In other words, my problems are with the boundaries I create and believe in, and the opposites they *must* create. In so doing, I remove myself from the flow of life – and I feel that removal in my thoughts, emotions and experience.

And the cycle continues – until what's feeding the cycle is exposed and seen through. Believing the boundaries to be real – after all, everyone else does – we never seem to inquire into its actual reality. More specifically, believing our *mental* boundaries to be real, we assume the opposites are forever separate and divorced from each other – as if they are pitted *against* each other. Coming from this place, we imagine that our lives would be more peaceful and enjoyable if we could just get rid of the negative and undesired halves of the opposites! We'd be in heaven, here on earth, and have no problems. If we could just get rid of all of our unhappiness, restlessness, insecurity, sickness, spiritual and financial poverty, how great life would be!

In our imaginings, we don't recognize that "Heaven" isn't just the "good" aspect of the halves, but the transcendence of both halves – and "Hell" is a conglomeration and abundance of the "bad" half of the pairs of opposites. If history is indeed a great teacher, why don't we learn that centuries of avoiding and pushing away the undesired half (and clinging to the desired half) has NEVER been an effective formula for genuine and lasting happiness?

Despite all of our remarkable progress and advancements in medicine and technology, it's pretty evident that our culture is more anxious and discontented than ever. Our unconscious and habitual way of seeking happiness is to somehow get rid of one of the opposites - and it never works. There's nothing inherently wrong with progress or improvement, unless we depend on it for our satisfaction and ultimate contentment.

Believing that the goal of our experience is to only attract what we desire invites further anxiety and dis-ease. Not only does it go against the nature of how our experience works, it implies that the opposite formula, avoidance of the undesired half, is also wise. In the guise of taking "full responsibility" for our lives, we think we're being irresponsible if we allow the "bad" half to stick around in our experience. Ironically, it is this resistance to the undesired half that makes it stick around. Thus, we don't see the forest for the trees. Believing we create and attract our physical diseases is harming, causing a wide variety of feelings like anxiety, guilt, shame and despondency.

Having the notion that God is a partial and biased deity (that rewards and punishes us for our self-centered tendencies) only strengthens our belief that moving away from what we deem "bad or wrong" is a useful strategy. Our bodies are equipped with five sensing instruments that tell us whether we're in harmony with the "outside" world, but somehow we underestimate its value, and instead, defer to the mind to tell us what's so. Once we defer to the mind to tell us what's so, we get a whole new set of sensations to experience – and they're usually not in sync with reality, either!

Isn't it peculiar that we have a natural inclination to place a higher value on believing the thoughts and conclusions in our heads more than the instant feedback we get from our bodies, moment to moment?

Minds think dualistically; there's no debating this. All concepts are inherently dualistic. Because minds think conceptually, mind can't help *but* think dualistically. It believes it's either this or it's that. When we want this, we don't want that. When we embrace this, we must inevitably resist that. When we resist that, we must experience a certain amount of discomfort – *from that*. Wisdom sees that the nature of absolutely everything in the manifest world is "both and" ... not "either or"... so we are wise to not only include both, but welcome both – but only if we don't want to suffer! Your lover's sensitivity is both a liability and a gift. Your need to make things "just right" is both draining and admirable. The whining, two-year little boy or girl is both adorable and a pain in the butt most times, are they not?

On closer inspection, we notice something we may not have seen before. While it *appears* that experience seems to arise alone, the opposite experience (although much more subtle) also arises. In other words, every experience arises in dualism, and in unison. We recognize that there isn't any separation between the opposite experiences, regardless of what our mind tells us. Thinking conceptually, we see that dualistically is the *only* way the mind *can* see experience – "this" way or "that" way, the "good" way or the "bad" way, the "right" way or the "wrong" way.

However, when I want to experience rest and quiet, at the same time, I don't want to experience unrest and noise. When I like or prefer quietness, at the same time, I don't want to hear noise, at least not to the extent that might compromise the quietness I seek. When I prefer to enjoy quietness, my mind simultaneously dislikes noise. They arise *together*; mind can't see this, but YOU can. While one half is very obvious and easy to feel, the other is very subtle and difficult to feel, but they still arise together, at the same time. When I want to be alone, arising in that

The Dance Of Imperfection

wanting to be alone is also the desire not to have company. When I insist on performing a particular task to my idea of perfection, also arising is my need to avoid actions and results that I deem "imperfect." When I fail to notice that this is how experience must unfold, I suffer to a certain degree.

My peace and security comes from *seeing* the necessity of both halves arising simultaneously, in order for experience to happen at all. Seeing this, gratitude naturally seeps in, even for the undesired half. Wisdom blooms when I recognize that this interplay and ongoing dance in nature is not only a functional necessity, but apparently possesses a check and balance system. If *this* arises, then *that*, too, must arise simultaneously. Wisdom blooms when I dance in harmony with that system, without needing to add or subtract anything. In an engaged yet detached manner, I don't identify with either arising. I rest in Spirit, that which gives rise to both – and I am free in this timeless moment. In this resting, all is balanced. In this resting, I notice balance is the reality.

With life comes death. In fact, without death, there could be no life. Human birth is the birth of opposites, of man and woman. The beating of our hearts as they open and close, pumping blood throughout our bodies and brains – and the muscles in our lungs that breathe in and out, are both necessary and vital movements operating in perfect harmony in order to for us to live and function.

Similarly, we look up and then we may look down; we turn right and we may turn left; we laugh and then we cry. We feel sad only to later feel happy; we love and we hate. The point is that *if* we have the option to do one thing, we must have the option to do the opposite thing.

This is how our world operates and this interplay is what informs our minds, letting us know what our options are. The entire world is a direct manifestation of these opposites, and in fact, couldn't exist if it not were for these pairs operating in unison all the time. Life is an intimate interaction and adventure of opposites – a dance if you will – where day turns into night and night turns into day. It's an amazing and ongoing dynamic, where the light shines and reveals everything, only to later have the darkness descend and hide everything.

High tide rolls in, hiding the rocky jetty that separates the beach from the adjacent one. Six hours later it recedes to low tide, revealing clams, starfish and seashells down by the waterline. This waterline appears to be a boundary – a dividing line between the beach and the ocean. However, the lines that appear to be dividing lines are precisely where the ocean and land touch each other. These lines *both* join *and* unite just as much as they divide and distinguish. Lines and boundaries are not the same thing; these lines are not boundaries! These "dividing lines" equally represent the place where the ocean and land meet.

It is indeed this constant ebb and flow that "makes the world go round" – and it is our understanding and orientation *to* this flow that determines the quality of our experience. If we fail to recognize and fully embrace that we can't have one experience without the other, and that we can't have this particular strength without its opposing weakness, we resist our experience. This resistance comes in the form of running toward or away from the moment, vacillating between pleasant and unpleasant emotions.

If we fail to see that in order to have our own unique set of strengths, skills and abilities that only we have, we won't see that we must also have our own unique set of weaknesses and "less than ideal" abilities, too. Consequently, we just may discover gratitude arising for all of it, as it is.

If we do see this, we can better understand and appreciate who we are, AS we are. How might your perception of your "imperfections" be different as a result? Would you have a different experience? Would it be possible that, as a result of seeing what's real, that believing in the existence of "imperfection" might drop away? You bet! If you think that this is just a sleight of hand, waving-away strategy that aims to soften and placate, think again. If you think this is just a matter of semantics, think again. If our strengths can't ever be "perfect," how can we ever rightly call our weaknesses, "imperfect?"

Jesus was one of the few teachers in all of the religious traditions that claimed to be both human *and* divine. Knowing he lived in a relative world of duality, Jesus didn't look to avoid any human experience. In fact, he saw the kingdom of heaven as right here, right now – right in the midst of any and all experience. Although perceived to be the Son of God, he definitely had his moments where his humanity came through. Some examples of his humanity were when, in a rage, he overturned the moneychanger's table, and as he was nailed to the cross he yelled out, *"My God, my God, why have you forsaken me?"*

In his moments of distress, Jesus couldn't help but express his human side, simultaneously possessing the capacity and consciousness to ultimately transcend his circumstance. His life was a living example of one who didn't adhere to the mind's collective insistence in the popular distinctions of "good" and "bad" … "perfect" and "imperfect." His life was a clear example of one who lived beyond the mind-body experience, making such statements as, *"I am in the world, but not of it."* Looking beyond appearance to the essence, Jesus didn't use labels that lie. He knew better. He knew "the way" to awaken and be one with God was to see that the true nature of things wasn't "this or that" – or "black or white." He conveyed this by saying such things like, *"Blessed are the meek, for they shall inherit the earth"* and to the unbelieving Jews that saw only their limited nature, *"Ye are Gods, I tell you."*

His undistorted vision was rooted in something far beyond what the mind could ever understand and comprehend – and certainly beyond what the collective consciousness believed in at the time. When he said, *"I am in the world, but not of it"* we realize that Jesus saw that the way to be freed from the pairs of opposites, one had to have the direct and immediate realization that Spirit is NOT good versus evil, or pleasure versus pain, or life versus death. Jesus knew that Spirit is that which gives rise to the opposites … impartially and with equanimity.

Therefore, Spirit is not the "good half" of the opposites, but the ground of all the opposites. Our "salvation" then, lies not in identifying with or chasing after the pleasant side of dualism, but to rest in the Source of both sides of duality, for that is what we are.

"Let this consciousness be in you that was in Christ Jesus." "I the Lord make the Light to fall on the good and the bad alike – I the Lord, do all these things." As a result of his true perception, he knew his oneness with God – and since he knew he was *both* human *and* divine, he made no distinctions and judgments about himself.

Since he didn't judge himself, he didn't judge others. Each person he encountered was perfect, whole and complete – no less or greater than he, including the man sentenced to death by stoning for his sins, and the prostitute shunned by the locals. He made statements like, *"Greater things than I will you do"* ... and *"Let he who is without sin cast the first stone."* Sadly, Jesus' open teachings were considered a threat to the people of his time and he paid a huge price for sharing what he realized.

While we don't usually recognize this, in our constant judging and evaluating things as good or bad, right or wrong and pleasant or unpleasant, we essentially separate our selves from what's actually happening. In the form of concepts, assumptions, beliefs, judgments and opinions, we erect a seemingly solid wall of separation between our self and what's actually occurring. No longer are we intimately engaged in the moment, experiencing it as it is. Instead, we experience life's moments through the filter of our mind that's always describing what's happening in relation to its familiar and preferred story. In our ignorance, we divide and fracture. As Neale Donald Walsh accurately noted in Conversations With God, *"In the absence of that which is not, that which is, is not."*

My brain contracted in confusion when I first read that statement almost 15 years ago, but I noticed something else arise within that confusion. There was a sense of knowing expansion, albeit a small one – and that's what I ran with. It's made all the difference, and a huge one at that. I never thought I'd live one day welcoming the "negative and undesired stuff" in my experience. Paradoxically, seeing how it all works, you notice the negative stuff hardly arises anymore. Thought and the mind can never comprehend this – but YOU can. What is presently arising can't be any other way than it is.

Wisdom already sees this as clear as day, but the masses believe it is lunacy. Mark Twain said it best, *"When you find yourself in the majority, it's time to pause and reflect."* Wisdom knows that when we battle anything, we lose.

The wisdom of no escape invites us to see that we can't ever escape the way in which we interpret anything. It comes with the package, like the west wind down the New Jersey Shore brings greenhead flies that bite. We can easily confirm this for ourselves. Simply put, it goes like this: We interpret the moment based on our beliefs and conditioning; we feel or experience that interpretation in our bodies, in the form of uncomfortable emotions like contraction, anxiety, depression and dis-ease, or to the more enjoyable and preferred comfortable emotions and sensations like openness, lightness, resonance, peace, happiness – an overall sense of well-being. This happens all by itself. And yet, there's another option available that the awakened know: If we refrain from labeling our experience in terms of our biases, likes and dislikes… we meet the moment as it is.

It becomes simply energy moving through, and not something we need to run from or grasp. Instead of working against the law of our experience, the awakened know if what we pay attention to expands, we are wise to see the intelligence of paying attention to the "good half," while accepting the potential of sensing the "bad half" arising, for they can't be separated. The cool part is that once this is finally seen, without any doubt whatsoever, this too, happens by itself. In other words, choosing to pay attention to the more ideal half isn't needed; because you saw through illusion, flow happens – and you're in it. In truth, you *are* it.

Sensing the much greater wisdom in our hearts than our minds, we trust in our being and let it to guide the way; we allow it to dictate our next move. No longer coming from the dictates of our minds, we access a deeper wisdom that allows ourselves to be in harmony with life and its natural perfection, as it is. As a result, we're no longer concerned with what it looks like or how it will turn out; we're able to meet the next moment in an uncluttered and unfettered way. It's that simple.

Wisdom sees that if we just allow experience to be as it is, without labeling it, something else begins

The Dance Of Imperfection

to happen. The wisdom of insecurity invites us *not* to cling to anything, not just because what we cling to we're bound by, but because absolutely nothing remains. Similarly, there's wisdom in no escape, too. When we understand that whatever is arising cannot arise and unfold in any other way than it actually does, wisdom blooms like the sun-drenched flower after a prolonged period of rain and clouds. *When we open our eyes and understand our situation, without any bias or agenda, wisdom moves within us – dancing with and to whatever's arising.* We find ourselves moving in rhythm to the circumstances and conditions of our lives, even if they appear asymmetrical and chaotic.

Inexplicably, we find ourselves responding to life in a way that we only imagined before. There's a flow present now, a flow that we always suspected was there, but didn't know how to align ourselves with. And with this flow comes greater ease, less stress and struggle. No longer opposing life, no longer seeing ourselves as "imperfect" and in need of fixing, we feel like a bird just let out of its cage. Our shackles are broken in two. Where we were once bound, now we're free. Like an orange must produce orange juice when it's squeezed, compassion oozes from us when we're squeezed, spilling onto those around us.

We discover that there's an ultimate reward for no longer engaging in self-deception; there's an ultimate reward for having absolute and full integrity. It's called freedom – freedom from the tyranny of the mind's ongoing insistence that it is the sole arbiter of reality, and that its unique view is the genuine article. No longer identified with the contents of the mind, we are freed from the negative emotions generated *by* that identification. And you laugh your head off. You laugh at how long you fooled yourself – and you revel in the feeling of a great burden that's been lifted. Suddenly you know why the Buddha was laughing so hard. You feel gratitude and relief. Once you really *see*, you never un-see.

Life then, is a celebration and a glorious opportunity to express our divinity, to choose whatever aspects of ourselves we wish to experience, while embracing those parts of ourselves that we'd prefer be hidden on the sidelines. In that embracing of both halves, the less desired half has a natural tendency to want to stay on the sidelines – and that's fine with us. If these aspects do end up presenting themselves from time to time, it's not a problem unless and until we make it a problem. Living in a world of opposites that arise together, we are grateful. We are fully aware that if misery wasn't a potential experience, we could never experience enjoyment. But first, we must look until we see.

Without pain and suffering, there is no joy and happiness. Without the willingness to feel insecure and vulnerable, there is no chance to experience the security and stability that comes from true understanding. Without hate, there's no love, and without sadness, there's simply no happiness. In other words, *we work with ourselves* because we know and accept the reality of our situation and how our experience unfolds. If we couldn't experience the so-called "lower" aspects of ourselves – those that we used to deem "imperfect" or "flawed," then in truth, we literally wouldn't have the ability to express and experience our natural strengths and gifts, either. I am here to express and enjoy. How about you?

The restoration of true perception lies in knowing that ultimate reality is a union of opposites. This knowing comes from seeing what's true in your direct experience – beyond belief – and beyond what others have told you. Therefore, the solution to the war of opposites demands the giving up of all boundaries – and not just the chaotic dance between the opposites against each other. Cutting out the root cause of our battle with the opposites is equal to seeing all boundaries as illusory. In Western terms, being "freed from the pairs of opposites," is the realization of the Kingdom of Heaven on Earth, despite the majority of the popular theologians and evangelists forgetting this.

Mainstream religion would have you believe that Heaven is a state of all positives, without any negatives, and not the true state that Heaven is the realization of "no-opposites" or "not-two-ness." In The Gospel of Thomas: We hear the words of Jesus when he said, *"When you make the two into one, and when you make the inner like the outer and the outer like the inner, and the upper like the lower, and when you make male and female into a single one, so that the male will not be male nor the female be female, then you enter the Kingdom."*

In my denial of the bad half, not only do I encourage it to stick around, I suppress the good half – what I prefer – from arising. When life knows we've seen it's a game of inclusion, the more our experience will accurately reflect that understanding. Seeing this, we welcome all aspects of ourselves, as they are. We watch the old existential discomfort that naturally arose from ignorance, dissolve from our experience. In its place, we can't help but notice the much greater sense of genuine gratitude arising for ALL of it, as it is – and not just the desired half.

The nature of reality and how it operates in us is simple – beyond all mental comprehension. If you don't yet see, do not be concerned. You will see when you see, as long as you continue to look to see what's actual. Always start where you are, not where you think you should be. There is no one keeping score; the more relaxed you are, the better off you are. There is no one workable approach for everyone here; there isn't a one-size fits all formula, either.

The Dance Of Imperfection

Nonetheless, this is an intimate and fruitful dance well worth dancing. Just put on your dancing shoes.

Chapter 6
Addiction & Grace

"O Lord, help me to be pure, but not yet."
~ **Saint Augustine**

When I was in the drafting stage of writing this book on imperfection, it occurred to me that it wouldn't be complete if I didn't discuss addiction. I mean, don't we see our addictions as imperfections? If you don't see the relationship between battling imperfections with addiction and grace, it is my hope that you soon will. Although I could very easily write

The Dance Of Imperfection

a whole book on the subject, I felt for the purposes of this book, that dedicating an entire chapter on addiction would suffice. Since we know that every concept and experience has an opposing side, grace will be discussed as it relates to addiction, and how it arises in conjunction *with* addiction. Keep in mind that I don't have any degrees or letters behind my name in regards to addiction, but I do have a PHD in battling them!

The majority of them (especially the more harmful ones) are in my rear view mirror (knock on wood) but I still have a few I'm willing to share with you. I literally have no shame about any of them and some may have a problem with that. Oh, well. I am human and they come with the package. It is my sincere hope to shed some light on the nature of addiction – as I see it – and how grace, the most powerful force in the universe, fits in.

While the words here certainly don't classify as authoritative by any means, they accurately reflect my experience with both my struggles with addiction, and my acceptance of what arises with it, grace. Mere conceptual understanding won't ever deliver us from addiction, but it *can* help us to appreciate the transcending power of grace. And so, I ask you to read these words in a way that allows them to penetrate your heart and mind, resonating with you in the way it will, in your own experience.

What does it mean to be addicted, and when do we know we're addicted to something or someone, as opposed to when we're truly passionate and deeply interested in something or someone?

How do we distinguish love and need? Is there such a thing as a "healthy" addiction, or are we just fooling ourselves in an attempt to simply continue the behaviors we have a love/hate relationship with? When we think or hear of the word "addiction" we normally think of it in terms of being hooked on a chemical substance like heroin, cocaine, marijuana, prescription pills and perhaps the most damaging drug of all, alcohol.

It's interesting that the most "socially accepted" drug listed above, alcohol, is the one that does the most damage, ruining more individuals and families than all the others combined. Do you suppose there's a direct relationship here? I sure think so. As I mentioned in the introduction, I am a recovering alcoholic. I will never forget the morning of October 22, 1999. After a night of heavy drinking that started early, I awoke to not only a major headache, but to something within me that just knew it was over. As I stumbled into bed that night, I didn't intend on surrendering the next day, and yet it would be an understatement to say that I wasn't very open to surrendering.

I was totally unaware that the events of the next day would forever change me deeply.

The Dance Of Imperfection

Something ineffable (but very palpable) descended upon me, arming me with a deep realization that I had reached the end of the line – and that I was utterly and completely defeated. Somehow, I had finally reached my lowest emotional and spiritual bottom. To continue drinking was paramount to death, at least emotional and spiritually. At 35, I just wasn't ready to die.

I don't have the greatest memory, but I remember that morning as if it was yesterday. I always sensed that surrender had to be the way out, but until then, I wasn't ready to hand it over. That morning, in my absolute devastation and brokenness, the wholeness of reality washed over me in waves. I felt completely held in its infinite and unconditionally loving embrace – and I knew I'd never be the same again. There was a deep compassion that welled up within me. Indeed, grace happened and it clearly wasn't a result of any conscious decision or anything I earned. In every single fiber of my being, I knew my desire to drink was lifted. The desire to engage in the behavior that brought so much pain was removed – and it never came back.

Not everyone has their desire to drink lifted, so I have great compassion for those who can't shake the obsession to use. Grace made me humble. When you see the reality of the situation, humility is really only the appropriate response. Like any other alcoholic, I know I'm one drink away from inviting those destructive behaviors back. I can't take any credit for it, so I don't. In fact, I can't. I didn't do any of it.

The reality is addictions aren't just limited to substances, chemicals and foods. We're addicted to things like control, fear, projecting a certain image, staying at a certain weight, approval, work performance, success, love, infatuation, sex, and sex on drugs. Many are addicted to certain patterns and ways of thinking, including negativity and pessimism. If we look and see, we notice we get certain payoffs. In our insecurity and vulnerability, we're even addicted to perfection. Some of us are addicted to avoiding our perceived imperfections, running from them or compensating for them in a way others notice. We become obsessed with being preoccupied with aspects of ourselves we'd rather not face, and then wonder why we can't ever fulfill our deeper desires we sense will bring us the contentment we seek.

In this age of technology and instant information at our fingertips, many of us are addicted to Facebook, television, music, video games, mobile devices and porn. In the last decade, I have "picked up" a few addictions along the way. I'm addicted to checking my email, constantly surfing the net for the latest news (I look at basically the same 8 to 10 sites each day) and checking my cell phone throughout my day. For the record, if I text you, I want you to text me back within twenty minutes or so … or else I get

The Dance Of Imperfection

impatient and even annoyed. You got that? LOL. One of Robocop's archenemies only gave his enemies "twenty seconds to comply." Heck, I'm being much more generous. I'm giving you twenty minutes to comply!

It's as if I latched onto the idea that texting is like the express checkout line at the supermarket. What's the point of having an "express line" if it isn't quick and convenient? Similarly, what's the point of texting if you're not going to get right back to me? Why can't you get right back to me when I text you? It's fast, easy and super-convenient, like the express checkout line, is it not? Granted, I know that I can never know if you got my text as soon as I sent it, and I can't know if your phone is even on your person or within earshot. I can't know if you're actually busy doing something more pressing, but even though I am aware of these things, it doesn't always seem to register. Come on, what's the delay? Are you avoiding me on purpose just to mess with me? Is my text unimportant to you? Do I humor you?

While I also realize it's my expectations and not the slow reply that causes my annoyance, it doesn't always help. At any rate, these preoccupations don't really impact the quality of my life or my degree of happiness, so for the moment, I am okay with them. Who knows what tomorrow brings? Hold on for a second, I must go check my email – be right back. Just kidding.

Living In Perfect Harmony With Life

To be human is to be addicted. Most humans are pretty intelligent with the ability to discern, evaluate, compare and distinguish. Unlike any other species we know of, humans have the capacity to not only be self-aware, but to reflect on their present experience – and alter their future course if they so choose. Despite the ability to discern, evaluate and judge, humanity is challenged when it comes to fully recognizing the difference between truth and illusion. We can say all along it's been our Achilles heel, coded in our DNA. In our wholehearted willingness to admit this, we surrender to our situation and become more aware of the many instances where we're addicted.

Readily admitting that we have a tendency to be easily seduced by the senses, we give ourselves a greater degree of vigilance and discernment. Like Jesus, Socrates was put to death for attempting to teach the importance and value of discernment saying things like, *"Obscurity is dispelled by augmenting the light of discernment, not by attacking the darkness."* In this world of duality, we are fortunate to possess the awareness to immediately detect what doesn't serve us by noticing how our bodies react to the presence of certain sensation and stimuli. Truth is simple and our bodies are not to be ignored if we want harmony. Being aware of and avoiding these types of sensation

The Dance Of Imperfection

and stimuli is all that's really required for us to ultimately transcend these destructive forces.

Addiction attaches desire and imprisons the energy of desire to certain behaviors, things or people. Consequently, these objects of attachment become obsessions and preoccupations, stealing our capacity to be present in our own lives and in the lives of those we most love and care about. This attachment nails our desires (in a laser-like fashion) to people, specific behaviors or ways of thinking – and creates addiction. The very same forces responsible for addiction to substances like alcohol and drugs are also responsible for our addiction to ideas, beliefs, moods and patterns of thinking. We find ourselves in bondage, in a hypnotic entrancement of our own making, and yet, paradoxically, our addictions are virtually beyond our control. Many people still think it's a matter of choice whether we drink too much, smoke too much or beat ourselves up too much.

But upon closer examination, it's not too difficult to see that we aren't pulling our own strings. Yes, it appears that way, but if we dig deeper, we see that we're not the Master puppeteer after all. It's as if our will has been hijacked, conditioned to engage in ways of thinking or behaving that isn't for our highest good. As I stated in my book, *"Born To Be Happy – How to Uncover Your Natural State of Happiness,"* "If happiness is really a choice, why would we ever choose to be unhappy?" Why would we intentionally engage in thoughts and behaviors that bring pain and suffering?

Like the man behind the curtain in The Wizard of Oz, there's more than meets the eye when we delve deeper. When we pull back the curtains, we see we aren't pulling the control levers. We notice forces and energies that are happening spontaneously and without our conscious intention. Addiction isn't something we can easily rid ourselves of with our intellectual capacity, or by applying some simple remedy or strategy, for it is in the very nature of addiction to prey on our attempts to control or master it! There isn't any cookie-cutter solution that will cure what ails us. There is a cunningly deceptive intelligence to addiction – and it has no boundaries or lengths it won't go to. Integrity and dignity are the last things it cares about. It will take over the person with the lowest IQ just as easily as the person with the highest IQ.

It's sitting on our shoulder, and its voice can be heard mostly in times when we seek to soothe ourselves, or run from something we'd rather not face. Our object of desire (whether a substance, a behavior or way of thinking or perceiving) whispers in our ear, convincing us to call upon it in our time of need. In our more conscious moments, we may think it all the way through, perhaps refraining from engagement *this* time, but as long as we think we're ultimately in control, it's only a matter of time before we heed its call and empty promises. In a zombie-like state, we find ourselves hopping on the familiar wheel of suffering, spinning around, experiencing the inevitable highs and lows that ensue. Until we really *see* this, we forever remain in its grips, allowing the addiction to remain in control.

Self-deception and denial, two of the most influential factors/symptoms of addiction, brings more darkness and ignorance. Surrendering and admitting defeat dispels darkness, and enlightens us. It's the difference between the attitudes of "I can do this all by myself" to "I cannot do this alone." It's the difference between will and pride to willingness and humility. Our orientation makes all the difference. Allowing our intellect to entertain its delusions of grandeur – along with its ability to "know" what's best, we forever remain in the dark to the causes of our afflictions. Our intellect dreams up, and then comfortably bathes in a wide variety of plausible excuses, justifications and minimizations. Simultaneously, it remains *uncomfortably* hypnotized by these very forces, leading us to further engage in these habitual behaviors.

When willpower is all that is present, desire ultimately wins. When willpower is busy at the wheel, we're in the backseat thinking we're driving. What's remarkable is that even if we intellectually recognize that our behavior is self-destructive and possessing a downward spiral effect, this recognition often has *no deterring impact whatsoever* – even though we often think it does. It is only when we humbly recognize that our way doesn't work that we begin to figure out that a kinder, gentler approach (based in reality) is needed. This approach includes faith in a brighter future, deep humility, and an unreserved acceptance of our present lot. Intellectual knowledge and honest admittance of our addiction(s) has never given us the power to control them or make them go away. It's only a good first step – and a critical one at that.

Wisdom clearly shows us that serving two masters never works, at least not in the long run. We can hear the words of Jesus when he said, *"A slave cannot serve two masters, otherwise that slave will honor the one and offend the other."* We hang on as long as we can, trading short-term pleasure for long-term pain. And we tell ourselves (and those concerned for us) we're choosing the behavior!

Since absolutely everything is energy, inherent in any thought, intention, belief, or behavior is a vibration – and that distinct vibration has a distinct and corollary vibration that determines our experience.

In other words, if I choose a behavior, I also choose the consequence. It's that duality working again. Wisdom clearly shows us that we can only serve one master, heaven or hell, but not both. We *can* serve both, but the wisdom of no escape demands we must suffer the consequences. Hell is the inevitable byproduct of choosing the behaviors that divide and fracture – and not something imposed on us by a punitive and judgmental God. Heaven is the inevitable consequence of the decisions and behaviors already in harmony with nature and the law of our experience – and dare I say, a life living in "perfect contentment" ... where nothing needs to be added or subtracted.

It's no secret that groups like AA, NA and OA (Overeaters Anonymous) all maintain that if there's any hope for the addict, one must hoist up the white flag and admit complete and absolute defeat. Step one of the 12-Step program, says, *"We admitted we are powerless over alcohol (or drugs, food or whatever) and that our lives had become unmanageable."* Unless we voluntarily take this crucial first step, nothing changes. Excuse the crass metaphor, but I really like the visual: until we take this step, and *mean* it, we're just pissing in the wind – often a gale force wind! Wisdom sees that the person who seeks support is acting from strength, not weakness. Ego sees the opposite – and yet we believe ego is on our side.

Wisdom blooms when that person thanks its ego for sharing, and then in humility, gets that support for as long as it takes. That's integrity, knowing what you need in the moment. No man is an island. There's something very attractive about real humility. Prideful people certainly don't

Living In Perfect Harmony With Life

understand the transcending power of paradox; they are too identified with thinking they know what's best, fearing what they imagine might happen if they don't know. Simply put, they're looking in the wrong direction. They unwittingly attempt to hide the ego's fragility, not only to themselves, but to others as well. Until they get honest, they won't ever stop running. They will continue to be chased by the very thing they want to be delivered from.

Allow me to interject something very important here: If there's only one thing that you take away from this book, I would wish for you to see how critical it is to understand the true nature of paradoxes – and how they operate in your life. Granted, this was the topic of chapter four, but the paradoxes in addiction are essential to understand. I would wish for you to see how your mind naturally resists paradoxes, and how to best orient yourself in such a way that you live in harmony with your own experience ... all with the mind's assistance. Your mind can be a wonderful servant, but only if you use it correctly. If you don't, you are its slave.

Once you truly understand paradoxes, and once you see how they operate in and through almost every aspect of your life, then you'll notice you're also in perfect harmony with Life, for they are one and the same. I can't possibly overstate the significance of this understanding. It can only be seen and realized when you examine for yourself. Look until you see. Don't just "get this" conceptually. Keep going.

The Dance Of Imperfection

Conceptual understanding is limited, and therefore, doesn't constitute real knowing. You "get this" when you experience the transformational power of understanding (and living from) the paradoxes, experientially. This is when you know. This is the knowing that transforms.

Enlightened beings have all conveyed the same thing: the vast majority of the human population is "trapped within a dream," driven by unseen forces and tendencies that creates division that must alienate and fracture. Being unaware of this phenomenon, humans typically continue to suffer for the greater portion of their lives. Like a sentimental handmade quilt or scarf we inherited from Grandma, we don't want to give up our ways, even though they hurt. We are creatures of habit; we like what's comfortable, even it it's not working. We pray to God to help us experience relief from the burden of our sins. We go to confession in the hopes of alleviating the guilt, shame and remorse we can't seem to shake.

We conclude that salvation seems to be for the lucky few, but not for us. What often takes a backseat is remembrance of the transformative power of positive thinking and detachment from negative thinking *as* a doorway to transcendence. We lose sight of the knowing sense that compassion, too, is the doorway to grace. We walk around in a trance-like state, mostly repeating the same thoughts, beliefs and behaviors. Somehow we find ourselves in a very tenuous situation, strapped with this limited and dissatisfied mind that continues to torture us – yet on some level, we seem to enjoy creating all the drama it provides.

We don't recall ever asking to come into this human form with all its challenges, sorrows and eventual demise; we don't recall asking for our particular set of parents, especially through the "my parents really annoy me stage." And we definitely don't remember the meaning of it all! Our main struggle in life then, appears to be a vain attempt to rise above this confounded and painful mystery we're seemingly enveloped in. Yet inwardly, we sense that mysteries aren't to be solved, but lived and surrendered to. In truth, the traditional resolutions of love and prayer are still validated scientifically in our experience. What we entertain and engage in, we must experience.

Until we see that we already possess within ourselves the power of our own salvation (through grace and our willingness to surrender) we remain stuck, just like Winnie the Pooh in the rabbit hole, without any honey in sight. Not only are we unable to fulfill our desires that we sense will bring us contentment, we often ignore those desires to do so. Like the unpopular schoolboy forced to the back of the bus, our truer desires are pushed back for "some time in the future" when we have our act together.

The Dance Of Imperfection

We live life on the layaway plan, acting as if it's a dress rehearsal. The longings in our hearts disappear from our conscious awareness and its energy usurped by forces that are not at all compassionate and loving. In fact, our desires are shackled and we give ourselves over to things, that in our moments of real honesty, we don't want. In our unconsciousness entrancement, we somehow become willing partners with our addiction – and *literally trade* the peace and happiness we really want for continued engagement in the very activities and consequences we *don't* want.

The adage, "we can never get enough of what we don't really want" rings true and becomes our living reality. We become numb to the fact that we can't ever separate the behaviors from the repercussions – and despite what Pink Floyd might claim, it isn't always comfortable. As the Apostle Paul said so succinctly, *"I do not understand my own behavior; I do not act as I mean to, but I do the things I hate. Though the will to do what is good is in me, the power to do is not; the good thing I want to do, I never do; the evil thing which I do not want – that is what I do."*

Even before the time of Jesus, we've intimately known of our limited human nature, and yet somehow, we haven't been able to connect the dots staring right at us. In its infinite "wisdom", the mind still thinks it knows best. It is this mistaken conclusion that overshadows the seeing that our *weaknesses,* as they are, are meant to be with us, and can lead us to a deeper appreciation of grace and surrender. In fact, they can render us powerless, bringing us to our knees. It is this letting go that renders us powerful. It is *this* very condition of being on our knees when grace reveals itself, and either eases our burden, or permanently removes our obsession to that which enslaved us.

This once-seen enemy to our human freedom (that breeds willfulness and attempts to control) is the very doorway to our salvation. Because it forces us to worship objects of attachment, addiction forces us to isolate and alienate ourselves from each other. This prevents us from freely loving others and ourselves. It eats away at our integrity and dignity. Personally, I know very good-hearted and intelligent people "in the know," possessing a lot of common sense, but don't yet see the essential paradoxes that would free them.

What often goes unnoticed is the glue that holds it together. Addictive negative patterns of thinking, lack of humility and self-deception is that glue. They don't yet see that the way to win is to give in, to hoist up the white flag once and for all. Willful pride is in the driver's seat and grace is in the backseat, patiently waiting to be called on. I suspect that shame and guilt play a large role, too. Fear of facing who they think they'd be if they surrendered can be a real barrier. It's not real, but it feels real.

The Dance Of Imperfection

Taking responsibility for other's challenges, even if it's your own grown children you love and adore, is a symptom of misunderstanding how it all really works. Most of all, identification with the contents of the mind plays the most significant role.

Since illusion is the second most powerful force (behind grace) in the world, this can be difficult to see. Being enmeshed with the contents of the mind is easy; noticing you aren't the mind and its contents is not so easy. Nonetheless, it's the difference that determines the quality of one's life. Even though we're conditioned biologically to seek pleasure and avoid pain (as a function of survival) ...having complex human brains, we get carried away into the psychological realm. Imaginary forces, mostly driven by irrational fears and misdirected desires take hold. Fortunately, it all crumbles when we clearly see through illusion.

The more we seek pleasure and avoid pain, the more painful it gets. It's like having poison sumac and thinking that scratching will make it better. The more we itch, the more it spreads. The temporary highs are followed by excruciating lows – and the compulsive cycle strengthens. Faced with painful stories about our so-called imperfections or real disabilities, our upbringing, uncomfortable feelings like pain, hurt, anxiety, numbness, apathy and withdrawal, the tendency to want to alleviate these feelings arises ... and we're back engaging in the very behaviors that keep us down.

So how do we invite grace into our lives in such a way as to actually feel it moving through us? How do we invite grace into our experience and let it know it's a welcome guest, free to stay as long as it wants? Grace comes in a variety of forms. It comes in the form of an insight, an understanding, an opening of our hearts and minds ... or the experience of being totally broken. We've all had very difficult times in our lives and when we look back, even though we remember feeling hopeless and confused, we see we somehow made it through. We also recognize that it was in those times where we transformed the most. We can say anything that helps us cope better is grace.

Any time we experience compassion and embracing something or someone, grace is operating in us – especially if we found it extremely difficult to open to that something or someone previously. Where we once had real difficulty trusting, now we can trust. That's grace. But first, we must be willing *to* trust. Sometimes grace is very subtle and difficult to sense. Sometimes it's fierce and comes in the form of a sledgehammer, and sometimes it is soft and tender. Grace blossoms when we see that we really aren't ultimately in control our lives, and that something far greater than our limited and finite minds can perceive or understand is essentially in

The Dance Of Imperfection

control. Anyone who ever drove home during a blackout knows this.

Most people who suffer from drug and/or alcohol addiction will tell you that fighting addiction is like fighting a grisly bear. What sane person would fight a grisly bear? What are the odds of survival? What are the odds of winning a battle with a grisly bear? I don't know about you, but if I suddenly encountered a grisly bear, I'd immediately get into a subservient position and play dead. I'd offer no resistance whatsoever. When the bear noticed there wouldn't be any opposition, or threat, there's a very good chance I'd be left alone. Addiction is like this. Anytime we go to battle with addiction, we lose. When we fight addiction, it sees your resistance as opposition, and therefore, a threat to its survival.

Like the bear, it won't back down. In fact, in order to continue to survive, it'll fight back even harder. But if we get down on our knees and give in to it, we take the fight right out of it. Don't be insane; don't ever fight a grisly bear – or your addiction. Never is it a fair fight. It's a losing battle, every time. Sane people know the reality of their situation. Sane people don't fight what ails them.

Thinking and believing that we are in control of our lives is perhaps the greatest obstacle to accepting the grace that's ever-present, all the time. When we turn our lives over to that which is greater than us, that which is cradling us all the time, only then can we feel its power and presence in our lives. Even though we can't fool grace, real prayer from the heart can be an effective way to invite grace into our life. Grace knows when we're being phony, and it knows when we're being self-serving. When we say to whoever we understand to be our higher power, "Your will, not mine," or "Give me whatever I need to get through this," we're inviting grace into our lives.

When we sincerely say something similar to what Francis of Assisi said, "Give me what I need to see, Lord, so that I may be an instrument for your peace and love on this earth; whatever it takes, Lord, I am willing to do" – and mean it, we're inviting grace to move within us. Is there any way out of being so attached to the way we view things, including ourselves? Is there a way to finally and fully embrace both our strengths *and* weaknesses? Can we just "opt out" like we can when we click the link at the bottom of an email, notifying the sender to unsubscribe us? Can we remove ourselves from the situation and unsubscribe from that thing, behavior, thought or belief that causes us stress?

In a very certain sense, yes, we most definitely can – but we must go about it in the way that works, using our good sense. "Removing ourselves" is just what we do – but perhaps not in the way you might think, and certainly not in the sense of running away or disassociating. As I like to remind, in order to

The Dance Of Imperfection

understand something, we must first be aware. So, we must first see the particular thing, pattern of thinking or behavior that causes our struggle. Can I ask you to think of something right now that causes you ongoing stress and strain? Do you have this specific thing in your mind? Okay, now that you do, doesn't it make sense that in order to transcend it, you must learn how to be with it in a very different way than before – and perhaps learn how to dance in sync with it so as not to step on its toes?

In other words, can you learn how to *be* or *dance with* this itch in your mind, without scratching it? In order to do this, you'd have to be more conscious, present and awake to its movements and tendencies within you, agreed? If so, that means you must toss out running, justifying, minimizing, judging, comparing, beating yourself up and resisting *as* a strategy to transcend, right? *Expecting* perfection goes right out the window, too, doesn't it?

Naturally, if we want to recover from a certain addiction, or as Whitman says, "dismiss what insults our soul" – then it stands to reason that coming out of our hypnotic, trance-like state (that invited our affliction) involves us being more aware than before. We must learn how to be with these uncomfortable, yet familiar sensations in a way where we don't run and hide, space out or numb out. As Jesus said in the Gospel of Thomas, "*Know what is in front of your face, and what is hidden from you will be disclosed to you.*"

Living In Perfect Harmony With Life

This dance involves us shifting our attention from control to surrender, from dis-ease to ease.

Without focusing on a particular result, we remove from the dance, all our conclusions and expectations, all our attachment to our painful stories – and we dance with what is. Putting on our new dancing shoes, we trust in being, knowing that our mind doesn't have the ultimate solution. If the mind steps in and asks how, we respond, "Simply by letting go of the struggle, right now, that's how." We notice that what we pay attention to expands. Therefore, if we pay attention to and resist only the "bad" side of our affliction (even though both sides arise together) we won't get to experience the "good" side that ultimately frees us from enslavement.

If addiction and grace do indeed arise together, you give up everything you *think* you know about how to go about it. You let go, right now, any and all effort to try to escape the condition you find yourself in. It is only when we allow ourselves NOT to know that a new potential can arise. But hey, don't believe me. The opposite of willfulness and pride is surrender and humility. The opposite of control is letting go. Without any intent to fix our selves, you openly and innocently meet your situation as it is, without wishing it would go away or be any different than it is. You simply notice how the mind still seeks to control the situation and tell you what's best. You

The Dance Of Imperfection

can just acknowledge the mind for its input, without identifying with it.

Silently you say, "Thanks for sharing, but let me try looking this way." Without any intent to "do" anything at all, you're just present and aware, making no conclusions at all. You may experience some confusion initially, but you aren't concerned with understanding what's happening or how it will happen; that's just more mind seeking control. Understanding will come in time, and it will be the kind from below the neck, where wisdom resides. What you *are* concerned with is dancing face-to-face, and eye-to-eye – an intimate look. If you're confused or trying to understand, you relax and see that the awareness *of* confusion isn't confused – and that the awareness *of* trying to understand isn't trying to understand.

We think our lives are so important, and everything comes to mean so much. In one sense they are, and in another they aren't at all. As a result, we tighten up. In doing so, we remove ourselves from the flow and simplicity of life. However, we can just rest – and trust that when life moves us to move in a certain way, we'll move. We rest in the knowing sense that absolutely everything is perfectly okay as it is; we know and trust that what's *presently arising* in our experience cannot be any other way. What already arose couldn't have been any different, either. We laugh at our mind when it tries to convince us

Living In Perfect Harmony With Life

otherwise – that we *could have* or *should have known better*, and therefore, *could have* or *should have done better*.

It's all fit and fury, leading to nothing but unnecessary pain and suffering. In another sense, the desire to recover is also perfect – and falling or relapsing *during* that recovery is also perfect – all to the point where nothing needs to be added to or subtracted from. We're moving in perfect harmony, because in both senses, we're in sync. It's only our mind that tells us different – and we believed it. It's easy to forget that we're essentially all the same, just disguised differently, animated by the same source.

It's easy to forget that, in reality, we're merely small specks in the grand scheme of things, just passing through. If you don't yet see it's happening quickly, look again. We are a parenthesis in Eternity, here today, gone tomorrow. Although we can never know exactly what another is going through, we can be assured one thing for sure – and that is this: though another's particulars struggle appears different than ours, they arise from the same source. That source doesn't believe in the labels and descriptions *we* place on people, places and things – but it allows it. And what one man sees as imperfection, another sees as perfection. In closing, enjoy this poignant story from the Jewish tradition:

For a whole year I felt the longing to go to my Rabbi Bunan and talk to him. But every time I entered the house

The Dance Of Imperfection

I felt I wasn't man enough. Once though, as I was walking across a field and weeping, I knew that I must run to the Rabbi without delay. He asked, "Why are you weeping?" I answered, "I am after all alive in this world, a being created with all its senses and limbs, but I do not know what it is that I was created for and what I am good for in this world." "Little fool," he replied, "that's the same question that I have carried around with me all my life. You will come and eat the evening meal with me today."

Chapter 7
Hey, It's Just a Ride

"The world is like a ride at an amusement park, and when you choose to go on it, you think it's real, because that's how powerful our minds are. And it's fun, for a while. Some people have been on the ride for a long time, and they begin to question: 'Is this real or is this just a ride?' And other people have remembered, and they come back to us and they say, 'Hey, don't worry, don't be afraid – ever – because this is just a ride!' AND WE KILL THOSE PEOPLE."

~ Bill Hicks (1961-1994)

The Dance Of Imperfection

I really get a kick out of the chapter illustration because it perfectly expresses a favorite metaphor of mine. Imagine that you've been tossed from an airplane flying at 38,000 feet – and you have no parachute. You didn't ask to be tossed; you were just tossed. There's nothing at all you can do about that. As you're falling towards the earth, you consider your options. Seeing that you *will* impact the ground – and most likely splat – you see that you really only have two options. What are those options?

They're essentially depicted by the two characters riding together on the roller coaster ride: You can either be absolutely frightened, worried, try to fix it, alter it to your liking, control it, improve upon it or try to make it end, OR ... seeing that it's just a ride, you can simply enjoy it! After all, you have 38,000 feet to let go and rest in the most amazing experience you've ever had. This basically sums up life. You're already here, right? Even though you didn't ask to be here, you're already here. Indeed, you were born, and for certain, you're going to die. With birth comes death. It's that duality thing again.

While we're constantly reminded of the fact of our own mortality, we somehow push this fact as far away on the periphery as we can, thinking since it's not a good thing, the further the better. The truth is, it's neither a good or bad thing; it just is. At some particular point in time, whether it's a few moments from now or years from now, we won't be here anymore. One day we'll be six feet under, dead as a doornail, deep fried, taking a dirt nap, or in this metaphor, a big splatter on the ground.

Keeping this in mind, wouldn't we have a better appreciation for each day we wake up? I get a friendly reminder each day I drive up my driveway. To the left is a very old cemetery. It's that close, and I love it. (My dog Molly loves it, too.) Go look at the picture again. Which rider are you? Are you the relaxed rider who realizes the inevitable moment can't be any different – and thus enjoys the ride, or are you the uptight, fearful rider who clings to the notion that something other should or could be happening – and thus resists – and doesn't really enjoy the ride?

Let's examine this from a different perspective. When it comes to how you live your life, can you say *how* you go about it and why? Where do your intentions come from and what are they based in? How seriously do you take your life? Are you being driven by some compelling need or desire? Are you perhaps spending your attention and energy towards living the most perfect life that you can imagine – one that *others* would surely respect and admire? Is your life a direct manifestation of trying to live in such a way that it conforms to some ideal of what you "think" it should be?

What might be different if you had the "mind over matter" attitude – that if you don't mind, it doesn't matter? What might be different if you had the attitude that "what you think of me is none of my business?" What's fortunate is that most of us have the ability to live our lives as we desire. If we want enlightenment, great wealth, notoriety, recognition or fame, we can have that. No one is stopping us from achieving all that – and those things are all fine. But in going after those things, we do well to remember that it's just a ride! It may or may not happen according to plan, but when we know it's just a ride, we can enjoy it, wherever it ends up!

Although it certainly *appears* as if we do, we really don't have control over most of it anyway. In the end, what will it all ultimately mean? In the end, we already know the eventual outcome, don't we? What will we really "have" as a result? Won't we be one big splatter on the ground as soon as the ride is over? Ashes to ashes and dust to dust, right? Can we do anything about what's naturally going to occur? Won't we join the billions that have passed on before us? And so, if there is anything really worth "accomplishing" in life, don't you think the most worthy endeavor would be to just enjoy the ride – whatever YOUR ride looks like?

What is the purpose of *your* life? Have you really broken it down to the bare essentials, according to what you most value? Do your actions actually reflect your values? Have you distilled it down and crystallized your purpose? Without a clear target, we have nothing to aim for, right? We'd be like archers, bow and arrow in hand, with no bulls-eye in sight, basically suffering the slings and arrows of outrageous misfortune, wouldn't we? We'd basically be a rudderless ship, without any ability to successfully navigate to our intended destination.

There are many ways to enjoy our lives; one person's idea of enjoyment may be another's idea of misery. However, there are certain facts in life that we'd ALL do well to acknowledge and enjoy – because there's absolutely nothing we can do about them. For example, basically each person lives according to their own desires and interpretations of how things are – and how they'd like things to be. Based on self-interest, most people are essentially dialed into the WIFM channel – the "what's in it for me" channel. Having close to 7 billion channels being simultaneously tuned into one big network, there's bound to be lots of static created from all the opposing frequencies working against each other.

Your channel may be tuned into being in service to others and my channel might be tuned into taking from others. Your channel may be tuned into helping organize the chaos in other people's lives and mine might be tuned into making sure your agenda gets messed up. Most channels are tuned into controlling other people's channels with the hope they'll adhere more to their channel! As a result of so

The Dance Of Imperfection

many agendas of self-interest, it's no wonder why competing frequencies don't match up.

If we can realize the intelligence and good sense of tuning our channels to the clearest and best signal called, "enjoy the ride no matter what" channel – and not take life so seriously, we won't experience all the static and confusion that most continue to experience. If we insist on taking our lives so seriously, we can still opt to enjoy taking our lives seriously! If we want to remain concerned about our lives and concerned about the lives of those we most love and care for, we can also enjoy being concerned about those we love and care for.

Whatever it is we decide to make our lives about – and whatever channel we tune into, whether it's considered "worthy" or "unworthy" by those around us, we enjoy it because we're doing what *we* want. Being given the freedom to live as we choose, we enjoy that freedom. In the end, if for whatever reason we can't seem to work out that simple formula for happiness, we can at least remember that hey, it's just a ride! You must watch this three-minute video clip of this very funny and irreverent late comic, Bill Hicks. You'll be glad you did. Simply google, "Bill Hicks It's Just a Ride."

Have you noticed that so many people find it very difficult to laugh at themselves? I mean, really laugh at themselves, the kind of hearty laugh that comes from the belly and not just the throat? And have you noticed the awkward moment when you're laughing at another's expense and you see that *they* aren't laughing? Why do we take ourselves so seriously? Why is it that we are quick to laugh at another's foibles but not our own? From my perspective, I'd have to say attachment to our ego prevents us really being comfortable and secure in our own skin. And since egos are generally fragile and need constant reinforcement, we don't like it when we're laughed at or have become the butt of a joke.

What's most unfortunate is our identification with ego as who we are. We have no problem expressing or playing to our strengths, but when it comes to our weaknesses, we'd rather not have them out on full display for all to see. If we liken ourselves to an art gallery having an exhibit, we're much more likely to pull out all our great works and leave all of our "embarrassing" or "messed up" works in the back room. It is in denial and ignorance of our dual nature (as finite human beings) that we get caught between the infinite and the limited, the light and the dark, the good and the bad, the grandeur and the misery.

In our ignorance and tendency to engage in self-deception, we deny our *both and* nature, and place ourselves in a disordered state of being. In order to be a Saint, one must first be a sinner. In order to be happy, one must first be sad. In order to be awake,

The Dance Of Imperfection

one must first be asleep. In order to transcend the limits of our interpretations, one must first be mired *in* those limits. Those struggling with feeling good about who they are – warts and all – are operating under the illusion that they *should* be different than they are.

Granted, *you can* be different than you are, but not in this moment. You can only be as you already are in this moment. In another moment, you can be different, but not now. Wisdom sees the good sense of accepting who you are, right now – because if you don't, you only further entrench what you don't want. A preacher put this question to a class of children: *"If all the good people in the world were red and all the bad people were green, what color would you be?"* Little Jessica thought intensely for a moment and then her face lit up and she replied: *"Reverend, I'd be streaky!"* That's real wisdom from a child.

To think in terms of either or, teetering on the extremes of self-love and self-hate, aiming for perfection (because we have difficulty accepting our weaknesses) is paramount to keeping any real kind of contentment at bay. Splitting our selves in two, we find ourselves in a constant daily battle. In an ongoing struggle to be something we're not, and to achieve something we think will make us "happy", we face the opposite direction of where peace and fulfillment is found. Attempting to arrive at some place other than where we are guarantees discontent. Spending our attention and energy on trying to be the person others expect of us guarantees discontent.

It seldom occurs to us to just stop and rest, and look at where we are, and consider that just maybe everything is okay as it is. Maybe it's perfectly fine as it is, and that balance is found by relaxing into our dual nature – tuning into the channel that brings contentment. Seeing the reality of our situation – that we can only live from our dual nature, and that we already are living *from* our dual nature, we can relax in that knowing and notice what arises.

Only when we voluntarily recognize the nature of our situation are we able to respond in an intelligent and responsible way. Believing we are a victim of external forces and circumstances, carrying around a "woe is me" attitude will never induce the life we truly want. It's not rocket science. I don't want to speak for you, but I'd guess you're not different than most. All we really want is to be happy and enjoy life, right? By accepting and embracing BOTH halves of all of our characteristics – and knowing they arise together, we empower ourselves to allow happiness and enjoyment to arise in our experience.

If we chase after or strive for happiness, while suppressing our unhappiness, happiness will elude us. The paradox of happiness dictates that when we align ourselves with truth and not falsehood – and

The Dance Of Imperfection

stop arguing with reality – our natural state of happiness can't help *but* arise. It's a deconstruction project, where we look and see what covers over our natural state of happiness. After all, we were born to be happy!

To be wholly unconcerned, yet intimately engaged, it is requisite that we live our lives engaged in whatever life is moving us to do, without concern whether we're doing it right or performing to our best ability. Since there are no mistakes, our peace and security lies in knowing we can't do it "wrong". In fact, there's no such thing as "doing it wrong." To be wholly unconcerned and intimately engaged means that we aren't preoccupied with how we're being perceived, what it looks like, and how it will turn out.

Being detached from our interpretations and meanings of things, we transfer all that energy towards just showing up fully, without insisting our agenda be met. Where we once erected all kinds of walls and barriers between our selves and the moment, we meet what's happening innocently and fresh, knowing any other way is pure insanity. Wisdom sees that unhappiness arises when we don't want what we have, and happiness arises when we want what we have.

Wholly unconcerned and intimately engaged, no longer do we lie to ourselves about our finitude and mortality. With life comes death and nothing will ever change this fact; we enjoy the relatively short time we have in this human form. In our moments of clarity, we see that the only appropriate response to life is gratitude, giving thanks for the act of seeing, hearing, tasting, feeling and breathing – and the experiences of pain and joy, sadness and happiness. As no two snowflakes are the same, we express and enjoy our dual nature that only we uniquely possess. When we were made, the mold was destroyed!

No longer do we misplace our responsibility for our own experience; we know we're responsible for all of it. No longer do we lie to ourselves about the richness and beauty of life. No longer do we project ourselves backward in guilt and forward in anxiety – and we let our fictions end. In place of our stories and fictions *about* existence, we live authentically in a state of open discovery, noticing when we attempt to delude ourselves. We face our fundamental obligation to find out what's true and real, without relying on any outside source to tell us what's true.

When we look at the beauty of say, a waterfall cascading down a lush gorge, or a majestic mountain peak covered in snow with the setting sun just beyond it, our breath is taken away. At first sight of this scenery, we have a tendency to gasp in awe. All other activity is suspended and we're simply aware, noticing our desire to simply take in what we see. In this seeing, we find ourselves resting in the beauty of

The Dance Of Imperfection

the scene. We don't want anything *from* our object of affection; we find ourselves in deep gratitude just for the ability to see it. In this seeing, all grasping and egoic tendencies spontaneously dissolve and we are left relaxing into our basic and fundamental awareness.

Resting with the world, without any desire to change or fix it, all is perfect as it is. Much like grace, nature has a way of grabbing us against our will, thus suspending our will. We are ushered into a quiet clear space, free of desire, agitation and self-contraction. And in this space, where time is no longer sensed, we sense oneness with everything, without any boundary between our selves and what we see. The two are one – and there's not a snowballs chance in hell anyone could convince us otherwise.

In this quiet, open space where time is suspended, we find ourselves aware and totally present. In that moment, subtle revelations, deeper insights and flashes of higher truths may be revealed to us, stoking a fire inside that burns away anything unlike it. Temporarily transported from our daily lives, we revel in the magnificence of the scenery that removes any desire or need to have it any other way than it is. In fact, we are given a glimpse into what it's like to live in the timeless now, where no problems exist – where everything simply arises perfectly and completely.

It is in this calm moment of being in the eye of the storm where we realize that it is our mind that erects barriers, and judges what arises as good or bad, right or wrong. Without referring to thought to tell us about a thing, we see absolutely everything as already perfect the way it is. Nature reminds us, not so much by its scenery, but what it does *to* us and what it does *in* us: it steals our desire to be elsewhere.

This isn't merely an exercise in imagination. This is the real thing – the actual structure of the cosmos. This beauty pervades everything in the cosmos and it is only the mind that tells us a different story, a story based on what the five, limited sensory tools perceive. And then we believe perception is reality. It's like expecting an unawake man to explain the awakened perspective, or expecting a severely drunken man not to slur. No matter what explanation is given, it will never match reality. But what might happen if we could see the entire universe (and everything in it) as being immensely beautiful, like the exquisite scene in nature that suspends our will? What if we saw that every single arising, as it is, without exception, *as* an object of absolute beauty?

Just as the extraordinarily beautiful object in nature suspends our will, so too, would the contemplation of everything ordinary in the universe *as* an object of beauty, would open our awareness to the truth that whatever arises *is* as it should be. All of

The Dance Of Imperfection

our running towards pleasure and away from pain would immediately come to rest – and through grace, our self-contraction lifted. When this happens, we discover that we naturally embrace *all* that we are.

Nature is the best teacher. Henry David Thoreau said nature never apologizes, and apparently it's because nature doesn't have any concept of right and wrong, ugly and beautiful and this and that. It's evident that some of the things we call "opposites" do appear to exist in nature. For example, there are big fish and small fish, large rocks and small rocks, mature trees and immature trees – with sickly leaves and healthy leaves. But it isn't problematic for them. It doesn't toss them into fits of rage or attacks of panic. Perhaps there are dumb hippos and smart hippos, but it doesn't seem to bother them much. You just don't find inferiority complexes in hippos.

Similarly, there is both life and death in nature, but it doesn't seem to terrify nature like it does humans. An old cat isn't caught up in fear and anxiety over its impending death. When its time has come, it gracefully moves to a secluded corner, curls up and goes to sleep one last time. An ill sparrow that knows its time is near, perches quietly on a branch and stares off into the distance at its last sunset. When it sees the light no more, it closes its eyes one final time, and without any drama or fanfare, falls gently to the ground below. It's all so natural.

Living In Perfect Harmony With Life

What a stark contrast from the way most humans resist going into that good night, raging against the dying of the light! While pain and pleasure most certainly appear in nature, they never become problems to be concerned with. Dogs wag their tails in excitement when asked to go for a ride or a walk. When it experiences pain, it yelps. When not in any pain, it doesn't fret about it, nor is it concerned that it may come back later. It doesn't dread future pain and doesn't lament past pain. It's all a very natural and simple affair. We may say nature is just ignorant and doesn't know any better, but nature is far more intelligent than we'll ever be. Nature is not only smarter than we think – nature is smarter than we *can* think.

While many humans puff out their chests proclaiming to be the most intelligent species in the entire universe, nature humbly sits back and laughs knowing it produced the mind that claims that. Nature is label-free, forever lacking any desire to classify and discern all the numerous forms it displays. It doesn't need to say, "These animals look different from those animals, so let's call these animals *tigers* and these animals *giraffes*." Or, "Hurricanes are bad and do so much damage, but light rain showers are good for the growth of vegetables and flowers, so embracing light showers while resisting hurricanes is wise." No labels, no

The Dance Of Imperfection

problems. No boundaries, no problems. No story, no suffering. Absolutely everything arises from the same source and is independent of any story or feeling about it.

Like nature, wanting absolutely nothing other than what actually arises, and wanting nothing other than what you are – as you are – you are timelessly frozen in paralysis by the sheer beauty and perfection that shows up all around you. Being released from past clinging to misguided notions that you couldn't seem to shake, you are freshly undone as one who made distinctions, however small. As Eckhart said, *"To have that consciousness where distinction never gazed"* is what you're operating from. Being in the world, but not of it. And nothing is left out. Not a single particle of dust is excluded from this beauty, no matter how "unsightly," "scary" or "awkward."

You see it radiating from every object of your affection, and simultaneously, that same beauty radiates from within you, out to the world. No longer believing in the existence of boundaries, separation and division fall away. Free of pride and full of gratitude and authentic humility, you can't help *but* see perfection all around you. In that seeing, you know you *never* had imperfections – you just believed you did because you were taught to believe you did.

Embracing who you are *as* you are, you watch guilt, shame and remorse drop away. And with it, hope and fear, too. Who needs hope for a better tomorrow when it's always right now? Who needs to seek when what you're looking for is doing the looking? Who needs hope when you accept what is, as is? Since fear is born of separation, who invites fear when there is no separation? Who invites fear when it's seen that nothing external *can* cause our experience of fear? The source of our angst and anxiety was our habitual inclination to view the opposites as never coming together, never arising in unison.

We believed they were divorced from each other, like two good people from a bad marriage. Most of our problems came from believing that the opposites can and should be separated from one another. Most of our shame and insecurity came from resisting or running from the "bad" half, the side we deemed "imperfect" and "flawed." Realizing that all opposites are actually aspects of one underlying reality, we see through the illusion of *imperfection and perfection,* and free ourselves from the pairs of opposites. Consequently, we are liberated from the nonsensical challenges involved in the war of opposites.

No longer do we waste energy trying to hide from (or compensate for) what we may still perceive as the "less than ideal" side of our abilities and characteristics. Dropping that heavy burden we carried for so long, we can't help but notice how much lighter our load is. Recognizing that the point was never to pit one side against the other in search of peace, *we unify and harmonize the polarities by discovering the ground that encompasses both.* Resting in this ground that includes both the "positive and negative" aspects, we transcend both. But, we may ask, if we see the moment as it is without any need to alter or fix it – and if we see all of ourselves as we ARE, without any need to hide or compensate for, will we lose our motivation and drive in the name of progress?

What will happen to us if we see our opposites as one? What will happen if we become actually grateful for our so-called imperfections and see them in an entirely new light?

What if we finally recognize, that without our "less than ideal" half, we couldn't experience who we are, let alone experience anything at all? What might happen if we see the conditions of existence as mutually interdependent upon each other, as the quantum physicists have already proven? With any luck, we'll lose our misperception that our happiness depends on accepting our strengths and resisting our weaknesses. When the opposites of all of our characteristics and traits are seen as one – and *already* in harmony – already and always a beautiful melody of comfort and discomfort, pleasure and pain, insecure and secure, then our old battles and enemies become dances and lovers.

When we empty ourselves of all our notions and opinions, we are left with the fullness and completeness of life – all in perfect harmony. Then, and only, then, are we in a position to make friends with ALL of it, not just half of it.

Then, and only, then, are we in a position to just ENJOY THE RIDE.

www.ingramcontent.com/pod-product-compliance
Lightning Source LLC
Chambersburg PA
CBHW070525090426
42735CB00013B/2862